M000197032

SAVIOR OF THE WORLD

Savior of the World

A Theology of the Universal Gospel

CARLOS RAÚL SOSA SILIEZAR

BAYLOR UNIVERSITY PRESS

Translations of Scripture are by the author.

Cover Design by Savanah N. Landerholm
Book Design by Savanah N. Landerholm

The Library of Congress has cataloged this book under ISBN 978-1-4813-0995-0.

Printed in the United States of America on acid-free paper with a minimum of thirty percent recycled content.

Dedicado a Gabriela

"Las muchas aguas no podrán apagar el amor
ni lo ahogarán los ríos"
Cantar de los Cantares 8:7

CONTENTS

ACKNOWLEDGMENTS

Prof. Larry Hurtado deserves a place of honor in these paragraphs designed to acknowledge people's contributions to this project specifically and to my academic life generally. I am deeply grateful for the many significant ways he has invested in me. I take it as a high privilege to have had the opportunity to study under the supervision of one of the most accomplished scholars of early Christianity during the last fifty years. My admiration for his work is only surpassed by my respect for him as a person and as a friend.

For the specific opportunity to test initial ideas that are offered here in a developed form, I am indebted to the Studiorum Novi Testamenti Societas. The unexpected invitation, and financial award, to take part in their seventy-first meeting in Montreal in 2016 forced me to craft a paper that was engaged by senior Johannine scholars such as Johannes Beutler, who went beyond kindness when he later read and interacted with an earlier version of the whole book. My participation in that conference also gave me the opportunity to enjoy the encouragement of Paul Anderson, Santiago Guijarro Oporto, Armand Puij i Tàrrech, and Bernardo Estrada.

However, the time and resources necessary to write this book were generously provided by Wheaton College. This second-to-none institution provides an ideal environment to pursue rigorous scholarship. Especially, I express my sincere gratitude to Jill Peláez Baungaertner, who was highly influential in my decision to accept a permanent post at Wheaton College and secured resources from the G. W. Aldeen Memorial Fund for me to take a research trip to Rome, Italy, and to have a course release that allowed me to complete the last stages of this project. Also, Provost Margaret Diddams continues to support my academic development through her brilliant leadership.

The initial drafts of the manuscript were improved by my assistant, Ellen Howard, who read several versions of each chapter. Furthermore, Carey Newman and his team at Baylor University Press provided timely support and advice during the editing and production phases of the book.

My praise here for all these people cannot compare with the gratitude I owe to my wife, Gabriela, to whom this book is solely dedicated. After almost a decade together, the text we used in our wedding has become a reality every day in our marriage.

Antigua Guatemala
MAY 2018

INTRODUCTION

The Gospel of John has been regarded as "the greatest of the books of Scripture."[1] Early church fathers considered it the "first fruit of all Scripture."[2] Christians throughout the centuries have treasured it as an inexhaustible source of spiritual insight and theological complexity. This first-century text has helped followers of Jesus around the world in innumerable ways.

However, oftentimes major Johannine themes have given rise to conflicting interpretations. This is the case with competing readings of the Gospel as either a sectarian or a universal text. The absence of the noun "gentile" or the threefold reference to excommunication from the synagogue (John 9:34; 12:42; 16:22) can be interpreted as indications that the Gospel of John lacks interest in the world beyond Judaism and can lead to the conclusion that the group behind this text was a discrete community markedly distinct from the types of Christianity that were developing at the end of the first century. This interpretation conceives of the people behind the Gospel as an alienated group of Christians, understands the text's intention as an attempt to reinforce the sectarian mentality of its readers, and portrays Jesus as a stranger

---

[1] Maurice F. Wiles, *The Spiritual Gospel: The Interpretation of the Fourth Gospel in the Early Church* (Cambridge: Cambridge University Press, 1960), 158.

[2] Origen, *The Commentary of Origen on St. John's Gospel: The Text Revised with a Critical Introduction*, ed. A. E. Brooke, 2 vols. (Cambridge: Cambridge University Press, 1896), 1:6.

from heaven who entered foreign territory in his incarnation. Even to this day, this is an important component of the dominant scholarly interpretation of the Gospel of John. The contemporary implications of such a reading are paramount. What are the challenges associated with developing a distinctive Christian worldview today using as authority a text that was written to deter Jesus' followers from engaging the world? Christians living in a global community today may find that the Gospel of John, read along those lines, offers little if any help as they strive to understand their mission.

The reading strategy of the interpretation of the Gospel of John as a sectarian text is based on, among other things, the exclusion of important sections of the text (e.g., John 21) as later additions and considerations that the text has undergone several stages of composition. A change in the reading strategy has the potential of offering an alternative interpretation of the Gospel of John, a different portrayal of its Christology, a distinct characterization of its early readers, and eventually a new set of questions and answers about the place and significance of Christianity in the global world today.

Embarking in a new reading of a major Johannine theme is quite an adventure. It demands attention to the whole text in its final form, consideration of a wider range of instances of universal language, detailed discussions of passages that reflect the comprehensive scope of Jesus' significance in the order in which they occur, and examination of the broader literary contexts of John's Old Testament quotations. The journey is worth taking because it may challenge the dominant scholarly perception of the Gospel of John as a sectarian text. More positively, the completion of the journey has the potential to enhance the interpretation of John's use of instances of universal language, to uncover the full import of Jewish tradition in Johannine universalism, and to clarify the perception of the Gospel of John as a universal text.

The reading proposed here begins with attention to the Johannine presentation of Jesus in the prologue (John 1:1-18) and in the first encounters with people in Jerusalem, Judea, Samaria, and Galilee (John 1–4). John begins his account with the preexistence of the Word, with a description of his involvement in the creation of the world, and with the testimony of John the Baptist. The story then moves to Jerusalem, where Jesus challenges the centrality of the temple in religious life. It immediately zooms in on three individuals who have conversations with Jesus in different geographical areas. Collectively, these episodes highlight the comprehensive scope of Jesus' significance as the owner of creation, who came to what has been his since the beginning.

The sequential reading of the Gospel then takes us to a set of discourses and controversies that show that Jesus engaged humanity with his light (John 5–12). A man unable to walk, crowds in Judea and Galilee, a man born blind, and even some Greeks are all exposed to Jesus' insights about his Father. Those who embrace Jesus and his message are enlightened, but those who reject the light are judged.

The owner of creation came to this world to publicly offer light to humanity. However, Jesus' light also shone in private. John includes a set of private conversations between Jesus and his disciples before the arrest that conclude with Jesus' personal prayer to his Father (John 13–17). The disciples are charged with actualizing a new community framed by love and shaped by mutual service and sacrifice. The Spirit not only witnesses to that new reality; as the Helper whom Jesus will send from the Father, he is himself the one who makes such a reality possible. The universal mission of the Son should be embraced by the disciples in the power of the Spirit. They should engage the world with the same light and life that they have received from Jesus.

The narrative concludes with the dramatic irony of Jesus' passion and resurrection (John 18–21). The one who was involved in the creation of everything that exists is arrested, prosecuted, and crucified by his own creation. The giver of life is put to death. The light of the world remains in a tomb the night before the first day of the week. However, the reader is invited to interpret those events from a different perspective. Jesus brings glory to the Father through his passion. He is abandoned, rejected, falsely accused, and finally executed. However, he has overcome the world. His obedience to the Father demonstrated in his passion brings honor to God and salvation to humanity. He is not alone, because the Father is in him. He will be embraced by his disciples as Lord and God. His interrogation is an opportunity for him to give testimony about the truth for the benefit of the representative of the world in Jerusalem. His death means the gathering of the children of God. Therefore, Jesus' passion and resurrection are, from a Johannine perspective, a cosmic conquest. The ruler of this world is cast out, and Jesus takes his rightful place as the owner of his creation.

A sequential reading of the Gospel leads to a consideration of literary components and rhetorical devices that he has used to create a narrative with universal significance. The analysis of point of view, narrative time, plot, Old Testament quotations, cosmography, and irony yields answers to the important questions about why and how John accomplishes a narrative that portrays the universal significance of Jesus and the message about him.

Before addressing the Gospel of John from this perspective, it is important to say a word about "Johannine universalism." An initial reading of the Gospel of John shows that Jesus has authority over the created order, he interacts with people beyond those traditionally associated with Judaism, and his message is intended for the whole world. These initial observations function as a heuristic guide toward a working definition that should include all relevant data for a full-scale study of universalism in this Gospel. Yet the noun "universalism" remains a modern, loaded term with a number of different meanings.[3] Although the Gospel of John does not use the word "universalism," it has explicit and implicit ideas that point to the extension of God's authority to the whole world and to the multiethnic nature of Jesus' ministry.[4] This Gospel reflects a positive attitude toward the world, because, in one way or another, through Jesus the world has access to the God of Israel, and those who believe in his name can become children of God without having to convert to Judaism.[5] John portrays the significance of Jesus as comprehensive in scope because this significance stems from the unlimited claim that God makes on his whole creation.

---

[3] On the problematic and somewhat slippery nature of the term "universalism," see A. Sherwood, *Paul and the Restoration of Humanity in Light of Ancient Jewish Traditions*, Ancient Judaism and Early Christianity 82 (Leiden: Brill, 2013), 1–2.

[4] N. Q. King, "The 'Universalism' of the Third Gospel," in *Studia Evangelica*, ed. Kurt Aland et al., TUGAL 73 (Berlin: Akademie-Verlag, 1959), 199–205, here 199.

[5] T. L. Donaldson, *Judaism and the Gentiles: Jewish Patterns of Universalism (to 135 CE)* (Waco, Tex.: Baylor University Press, 2007), 4.

I

1

THE OWNER OF CREATION

The first major section of the Gospel of John[1] introduces the comprehensive significance of Jesus in relationship to the world.[2] The standpoint of the narrator is *sub specie aeternitatis*, universal.[3] Notably, his perspective is up front and exclusively shared with the reader.[4] The

---

[1] It comprises its first four chapters, according to Rudolf Schnackenburg, *The Gospel according to St. John*, 3 vols. (New York: Seabury, 1980), 1:477; and Johannes Beutler, *Das Johannesevangelium: Kommentar* (Freiburg: Herder, 2013), 172. The designation "book of signs" (*le livre des signes*) for this section is found in Henri Van den Bussche, *Jean: Commentaire de l'Évangile spirituel*, Bible et vie chrétienne (Bruges: Desclée De Brouwer, 1967), 63.

[2] The density of Jesus' presentation in John 1–4 is complex. He is the Word, Son of God, Lamb of God, Messiah, King of Israel, the one promised in Scriptures, prophet, the one who baptizes with the Spirit, the bridegroom, the Son of Man, the one who does signs to demonstrate glory, and the one who accomplishes the Father's work. See Marianne Meye Thompson, *John: A Commentary*, NTL (Louisville: Westminster John Knox, 2015), 115–16.

[3] Wayne A. Meeks, "The Man from Heaven in Johannine Sectarianism," *JBL* 91 (1972): 50; H. Clavier, "L'ironie dans le quatrième Évangile," in *Studia Evangelica*, ed. K. Aland, F. L. Cross, J. Daniélou, H. Riesenfeld, and W. C. van Unnik, TU 73 (Berlin: Akademie-Verlag, 1959), 261–76, here 276.

[4] Christos Karakolis, "The Logos-Concept and Dramatic Irony in the Johannine Prologue and Narrative," in *The Prologue of the Gospel of John: Its Literary, Theological, and Philosophical Contexts; Papers Read at the Colloquium Ioanneum 2013*, ed. Jan G.

initial prologue[5] is quickly followed by a set of narratives about Jesus' interactions with three individuals in Jerusalem, Samaria, and Galilee. The universal language found in this section is used to highlight the Word's involvement in the creation of the whole world, to secure his unique role as the one who offers to humanity a proper relationship with God, to portray Jesus' universal authority during his earthly ministry, and to demonstrate Jesus' right to offer life to diverse people in different geographical locations. The overall impression the reader gets is that Jesus is the owner of creation who moves in territory that has been his since the beginning and whose mission concerns people from different ethnic and social backgrounds.

PRESENTATIONS OF JESUS TO THE WORLD

The reader encounters three opening presentations about the universal significance of Jesus and the message about him. First, the narrator introduces the Word as taking an active role in the creation of everything that exists. Second, John the Baptist gives testimony to Israel about the comprehensive scope of Jesus' mission on earth. These two presentations of the universal significance of Jesus are explicit since it is clearly said that the Word created the world and that Jesus is the Lamb of God who takes away the sin of the world. The third presentation is implicit. Since it is likely that the cleansing of the temple took place in the court of the gentiles, a case can be made that Jesus introduces himself publicly in Jerusalem for the benefit of people not traditionally associated with Judaism.

---

van der Watt, R. Alan Culpepper, and Udo Schnelle, WUNT 359 (Tübingen: Mohr Siebeck, 2016), 139–56, here 140–41.

[5] The unique relationship between the Word and God in 1:1 and between Jesus and the Father in 1:18 can be taken as signaling a literary unit that scholars have traditionally called "prologue." For an argument about the self-evident delimitation of John 1:1-18, see Franz Prosinger, "Vorschlag einer dynamisch-konzentrischen Struktur des Johannesprologs," *Bib* 97 (2016): 244–63. For a challenge to this perspective, see J. Ramsey Michaels, *The Gospel of John*, NICNT (Grand Rapids: Eerdmans, 2010), 45; P. J. Williams, "Not the Prologue of John," *JSNT* 33 (2011): 375–86; and Martinus C. De Boer, "The Original Prologue to the Gospel of John," *NTS* 61 (2015): 448–67.

The Word in Creation

The Gospel of John begins with a prologue that sets the tone for the reading of the rest of the narrative.[6] It begins with ἐν ἀρχῇ (1:1) and, therefore, by setting the Word before creation. The story does not begin in a particular geographical setting but with the Word who was with God before everything was created. The placing of ὁ λόγος before creation gives the story that follows "cosmic significance."[7] The strategy of beginning the narrative with ἐν ἀρχῇ is also meaningful because the story does not begin with a hero such as Jacob, Moses, or Caesar who can be claimed by a particular group such as the Samaritans (4:12), Jews (5:45), or Romans (19:12). There is no initial indication that a particular group can claim ownership of the Word because he existed with God in the beginning, before the existence of any human being. Those who encounter Jesus meet someone who is beyond this world and beyond this time.[8]

The story immediately moves to creation in 1:3. This verse begins with two parallel phrases, "all things (πάντα) were made through him" and "without him was not anything (οὐδὲ ἓν) made that was made."[9]

---

[6] R. Alan Culpepper, "The Prologue as Theological Prolegomenon to the Gospel of John," in van der Watt, Culpepper, and Schnelle, *The Prologue of the Gospel of John*, 3–26. For the view that the prologue belongs to the Gospel, see Ulrich Busse, "Theologie oder Christologie im Johannesprolog?" in *Studies in the Gospel of John and Its Christology: Festschrift Gilbert van Belle*, ed. Joseph Verheyden, Geert van Oyen, Michael Labahn, and Reimund Bieringer, BETL 265 (Leuven: Peeters, 2014), 1–36.

[7] Andrew T. Lincoln, *The Gospel according to Saint John*, BNTC 4 (New York: Hendrickson, 2005), 93. Cf. C. K. Barrett, *The Gospel according to St. John: An Introduction with Commentary and Notes on the Greek Text* (Philadelphia: Westminster, 1978), 151–52: "The soteriological work and position of Jesus, being universal in scope, are represented against a cosmological background." See also Adele Reinhartz, *The Word in the World: The Cosmological Tale in the Fourth Gospel*, SBLMS 45 (Atlanta: Scholars Press, 1992), 17–18.

[8] Barrett, *John*, 152.

[9] The idea that God is the creator of "all" was current in ancient Judaism (Isa 44:24; Sir 18:11; 2 Macc 1:24-25; Philo, *Somn.* 1.67; Josephus, *Ag. Ap.* 2.190; *Ant.* 1.225; 12.22) and in other pagan (Diogenes Laertius, *Lives* 7:147; Aelius Aristides, *Or.* 43:7) and religious sources (see Jean Zumstein, *Das Johannesevangelium*, ed. Dietrich-Alex Koch, KEKNT [Göttingen: Vandenhoeck & Ruprecht, 2016], 76; Thompson, *John*, 28; Craig S. Keener, *The Gospel of John: A Commentary* [Peabody, Mass.: Hendrickson, 2003], 1:375–81; Udo

By repeating his point using a positive and a negative statement,[10] John emphasizes the comprehensive nature of Christ's claim on creation.[11] Therefore, when the Word "becomes incarnate and comes to his own, he comes into a sphere of existence that already truly belongs to him and is not simply alien territory."[12]

This vision of creation signals that there is no original division in humanity.[13] The introductory verses of the Gospel portray a unified humanity and, indeed, a unified cosmos created through the same Word in the beginning.[14] Therefore, nothing is outside the scope of the Word's creation.[15] The narrator indicates that life was in the Word and that life was the light of humanity (1:4).[16] Since ἀνδρός is used to express "man" in 1:13, τῶν ἀνθρώπων in 1:4 should be taken as referring to humanity as a whole; and since the previous context in 1:3 is about creation, the plural noun ἀνθρώπων should be understood in

---

Schnelle, *Das Evangelium nach Johannes*, THKNT 4 [Leipzig: Evangelische Verlagsanstalt, 2016], 49).

[10] Zumstein, *Johannesevangelium*, 76. Edwyn Clement Hoskyns (*The Fourth Gospel*, ed. Francis Noel Davey [London: Faber and Faber, 1967], 142) finds this "antithetical parallelism" to be a Hebraic characteristic found elsewhere in the Gospel of John (3:16, 36; 6:50). See also Beutler, *Johannesevangelium*, 84.

[11] Ernst Haenchen, *John 1: A Commentary on the Gospel of John, Chapters 1–6*, ed. Robert W. Funk with Ulrich Busse, trans. Robert W. Funk, Hermeneia (Philadelphia: Fortress, 1984), 113. Schnackenburg, *John*, 1:238, indicates that the "distich undoubtedly intends to bring out the universal significance of the Logos."

[12] Lincoln, *John*, 99.

[13] Hoskyns, *Fourth Gospel*, 142.

[14] Schnackenburg, *John*, 1:239, suggested that the universal role of the Word in creation "would be defending indirectly the goodness of all created things." The world, then, does not own its origin to an evil principle, according to Schnackenburg, *John*, 1:258; Raymond Edward Brown, *The Gospel according to John*, 2 vols., The Anchor Bible 29 (Garden City, N.Y.: Doubleday, 2000), 1:26.

[15] Rudolf Bultmann, *The Gospel of John: A Commentary*, trans. G. R. Beasley-Murray, R. W. N. Hoare, and J. K. Riches, The Johannine Monograph Series 1 (Eugene, Ore.: Wipf & Stock, 2014), 37. See also Hoskyns, *Fourth Gospel*, 137.

[16] The original reading preserved in Codex Vaticanus (s. IV) omits τῶν ἀνθρώπων. This codex has ⁒ between the end of v. 4 (ἦν τὸ φῶς) and the beginning of v. 5 (καὶ τὸ φῶς) (ΦΩC⁒ΚΑΙ). The margin includes ⁒τῶν ἀνθρώπων. The reading followed here is the one that includes this phrase and that is found in the earliest manuscripts.

the broadest possible sense.[17] All humanity was a unity because they all had the same life that gives light,[18] and all humanity is a unity because they all have their origins in the Word who was with God in the beginning. The narrative then concerns all humanity.

Throughout the narrative thus far, John uses several terms that find resonances in multiple ancient backgrounds. The nouns λόγος and θεός are used three times each in 1:1-2 and are widely known from several cultural milieus in the first century. They find resonances in a diversity of readers coming from different cultural backgrounds.[19] At least the first phrases of the Gospel are not overtly hostile to a particular religious group.[20] The careful selection of these two nouns seems to encourage readers from different cultural backgrounds to keep

[17] Michaels, *John*, 55.

[18] Barnabas Lindars (*The Gospel of John: Based on the Revised Standard Version*, NCB [Grand Rapids: Eerdmans, 1981], 77) rightly observes that "the characteristics of man as the apex of Creation are ascribed to the Word: life . . . and light." He continues, "John's use of the themes of light and life depends . . . on the universal employment of them in the religious language of his time" (86). For Schnackenburg (*John*, 1:241–42) the Word being the life that was the light of men indicates a life that distinguishes people from the rest of creation (see also Michaels, *John*, 55–56).

[19] Scholars often find links between the Johannine Word and instances of λόγος in Stoicism ("the rational principle of the universe," according to Lindars, *John*, 83; Thompson, *John*, 28; Troels Engberg-Pedersen, *John and Philosophy: A New Reading of the Fourth Gospel* [Oxford: Oxford University Press, 2017], 56–60), Philo, the Targums (מימרא), Jewish wisdom traditions (Wis 9:1-2; 1 En. 42:2), Old Testament creation accounts (Gen 1:1; Ps 33:6), torah traditions (Prov 6:23), or even early oriental gnostic thought (Bultmann, *John*, 24, 28–30). A list of uses of λόγος in ancient sources is found in Peter M. Phillips, *The Prologue of the Fourth Gospel: A Sequential Reading*, LNTS 294 (London: T&T Clark, 2006), 80–138. The idea that the Gospel of John gave free play to ideas beyond Palestinain Judaism has been in the market for many years now. See Johann Gottfried von Herder, *Von Gottes Sohn, der Welt Heiland: Nach Johannes Evangelium; Nebst einer Regel der Zusammenstimmung unsrer Evangelien aus ihrer Entstehung und Ordnung* (Riga: Hartknoch, 1797).

[20] Jörg Frey, "Between Torah and Stoa: How Could Readers Have Understood the Johannine Logos?" in van der Watt, Culpepper, and Schnelle, *The Prologue of the Gospel of John*, 189–234, here 201: "The text of the prologue, with its utilization of the term ὁ λόγος, addresses a universal dimension that could easily be connected with the wider discourse about the world and creation that goes far beyond the biblical discourse about God's word in revelation and Torah."

engaging the narrative.[21] Like λόγος and θεός, terms such as "life,"
"light," and "humanity" are familiar from many ancient backgrounds,
thus maintaining the inclusivity of the text.[22] Thus, these verses are
also, in a sense, universal.

The noun "light," in particular, takes prominence in 1:4-9. It
encounters darkness but it is not overcome by it (1:5). This light is a
true light that enters creation in order to enlighten every human being
(πάντα ἄνθρωπον, 1:9).[23] This implies that the light invites "a salvific
response of faith to all—whether they know the outward story of Jesus
or not."[24] This is one of the most universal statements in the Gospel of
John. It is not, however, a support for theological universalism, that is,
the idea that all human beings will be saved.[25] Instead, it seems to be a
challenge to *all* religious soteriological claims. "The incarnate expression of God's love is much fuller than a code, a text, a rite, a regulation,
or even the finest of religious systems."[26] The prologue, then, provides
a "revelational answer" instead of a "religious answer" to the issue of
salvation.[27] This idea might not be grasped in the first reading of the
prologue. However, as the Gospel's story unfolds, the noun "light" is
clearly identified with the exclusive revelation that Jesus brings to his
creation. The Word who became flesh and dwelled among us is the
light of the world (8:12; 9:5; 11:9). Although readers acquainted with
the traditions that shaped the Gospel of Matthew and the Gospel
of Luke might have understood that Jesus was born in Judea, John
chooses the general term "world" (κόσμος, 1:9) to indicate the sphere

[21] See Phillips, *Prologue*, 150.
[22] Barrett, *John*, 157–58; Donatien Mollat, *Études Johanniques*, Parole de Dieu
(Paris: Éditions du Seuil, 1979), 24.
[23] Schnackenburg, *John*, 1:253, "The power of the Logos to give light and life is
universal."
[24] Paul N. Anderson, *The Riddles of the Fourth Gospel: An Introduction to John*
(Minneapolis: Fortress, 2011), 34.
[25] Anderson (*Riddles*, 184) observes a "common misconception about the Light
and its universality. Despite being accessible to all, this does not mean that all will
recognize the Light as such."
[26] Anderson, *Riddles*, 184.
[27] Anderson, *Riddles*, 184.

Jesus entered with his incarnation.[28] The Word who was in the beginning with God before creation now enters his own territory in order to
provide universal illumination.[29]
The unity of humanity based on the universal illumination of the
true light is soon broken. Although the light was in the world and the
world was created through him (1:10),[30] creation refused to embrace
its origin in God and, therefore, rejected the Word.[31] Ironically, the
world failed to acknowledge its source of life and light.[32] The division between light and darkness anticipated in 1:5 takes the form in
1:10 of an active separation from the Word. Yet the world is offered
the opportunity to recognize its plight, because the Word came to his
own territory and to his own people to offer an appropriate relationship with God (1:11-12).[33] The use of the neuter plural τὰ ἴδια in 1:11
has no restriction in the previous context and, actually, can be linked
to the neuter plural πάντα used in 1:3 to indicate the creation of all
things.[34] Since the previous context is clearly universal (e.g., "all," v. 7;

[28] Hoskyns, *Fourth Gospel*, 67, "[There is] no final distinction between Israel and
the world, between Jew and Greek. As the creation of God, all men are his property . . . and Jesus was in the world, not merely in Israel." Although the incarnation is
fully expressed in 1:14, John 1:9 can be taken as an anticipation of this event.

[29] Lincoln, *John*, 101. Michaels (*John*, 61) calls this light the "supreme and universal 'Light of the world.'" Jewish tradition, in particular, understood that the light
of the law was for all humanity. Thus Peder Borgen, "Logos Was the True Light:
Contributions to the Interpretation of the Prologue of John," *NovT* 14 (1972): 115–30,
here 125. For example, Wis 18:4 indicates that the "light of the law" (νόμου φῶς) was
to be given to the world (τῷ αἰῶνι δίδοσθαι). Similarly, T. Levi 14:4 has "you want to
destroy the light of the Law which was granted to you [sons of Israel] for the enlightenment of every man." Sverre Aalen, *Die Begriffe 'Licht' und 'Finsternis' im Alten Testament, im Spätjudentum und im Rabbinismus* (Oslo: J. Dybward, 1951), 289, observed
that this universalism is based on the particularism of the law.

[30] The first pronoun in v. 10 could be translated "it" or "he." Although "light" in
v. 9 is neuter, the translation "he" is preferred because the pronoun in the phrase "knew
him not" is masculine.

[31] Bultmann, *John*, 55.

[32] Karakolis, "Prologue," 146; Michaels, *John*, 65. Schnackenburg (*John*, 1:255)
thinks that the irony is actually a "brutal and shattering fact."

[33] Karakolis, "Prologue," 143, 145–46.

[34] Bultmann (*John*, 56) finds that εἰς τὰ ἴδια ἦλθεν (v. 11) corresponds to ἐν τῷ
κόσμῳ ἦν (v. 10) and the phrase οἱ ἴδιοι αὐτὸν οὐ παρέλαβον (v. 11) corresponds to

"everyone," v. 9; "the world," v. 10),[35] there is room to posit that verse 11 addresses a wide audience. Similarly, the masculine plural οἱ ἴδιοι may refer to humanity as a whole, since τῶν ἀνθρώπων in 1:4 is also masculine plural. Therefore, the Word issues an open invitation to all (ὅσοι, 1:12) who want to receive him, to believe in his name.[36] All who have been created through the Word have the possibility of realizing their true origin, of establishing a proper relationship with God, and, therefore, of becoming his family.[37]

The people of God that the Word authorizes are united by the same belief in the name of the one through whom everything was created (1:12).[38] Instead of providing an ethnic definition for God's family, the Gospel of John proposes a theological understanding of God's community. In fact, the possibility of any human definition of the children of God is strongly denied in 1:13. Ethnic descent is not the most important factor for establishing a family relationship with God. The striking claim that as many as did receive the Word became children of God "is the first hint that John reshapes the identity of the 'children of God,' neither linking that identity to ethnic heritage nor denying it to any on that basis."[39] The creation of the world through the Word was emphasized in 1:3 using two statements, one positive and the other negative. The idea of birth, similarly, is highlighted in 1:13 using three negative statements and one positive phrase: "not of blood

---

ὁ κόσμος αὐτὸν οὐκ ἔγνω (v. 10). Schnackenburg (*John*, 1:259) also thinks that the reference in v. 11 is to the world as the domain or property of the Word (thus Michaels, *John*, 65; Zumstein, *Johannesevangelium*, 82). Other scholars, however, prefer a more restricted sense for "his own," i.e., "the chosen people of Israel" (Brown, *John*, 1:10; Barrett, *John*, 163; Lindars, *John*, 78, 90; Lincoln, *John*, 102; Keener, *John*, 1:395; Thompson, *John*, 31).

[35] Beutler, *Johannesevangelium*, 91.

[36] Hoskyns, *Fourth Gospel*, 146. Walter Bauer (*Das Johannesevangelium*, HNT 6 [Tübingen: Mohr Siebeck, 1933], 21) interpreted ὅσοι to imply a small number of people: "one can count them." This is rejected by Haenchen (*John 1*, 118), who thinks that the "notion of a small number is not implied" in ὅσοι because it usually precedes πάντες, πάντα elsewhere in the Gospel of John (e.g., 16:15; 17:7).

[37] Bultmann, *John*, 56, "If they refuse, then in so doing they assign to themselves another origin."

[38] Lincoln, *John*, 102–3.

[39] Thompson, *John*, 32.

lines," "nor of fleshly desire," "nor a husband's desire," but "of God."[40] It is not ordinary human birth (blood and flesh) that provides a right relationship with God. The relationship roles described as Creator and creation earlier is now depicted explicitly as children and implicitly as Father.

The Word has a place of prominence in the family of the Father, and his unique relationship with God existed even before creation. While every human being was created through the Word (1:3, 10) and can establish a proper relationship with God through the Word (1:13), only the Word is said to have become flesh (1:14). The idea anticipated in 1:9 that the true light was coming into the world is fully expressed in 1:14, "the Word became flesh."[41] The Word not only enters his own territory but also becomes part of his own creation.[42] The selection of the noun σάρξ instead of a word that expresses a particular ethnicity is striking.[43] Although the unity of humanity expressed earlier in the prologue is by now replaced by a division between those who believe and those who do not receive the Word (1:11-12), the Word is said to have become flesh, which is something general but at the same time concrete.[44] Even at this point readers would find that the Word shares with them his own human condition. Since ὁ λόγος is fully committed to his creation, he cannot ignore it or even reject it. He did the opposite of what the world did to him. The Word became flesh in order to share his fullness with all those who want to believe in him (1:16). He became one of his own so that his own may become one with God.

---

[40] Hoskyns, *Fourth Gospel*, 146–47.

[41] The contrast between v. 1 (θεὸς ἦν ὁ λόγος) and v. 14 (ὁ λόγος σὰρξ ἐγένετο) makes the incarnation a dramatic event.

[42] Bultmann (*John*, 66n6) takes the phrase "among us" (ἐν ἡμῖν) as a reference to "mankind in general" (thus Schnackenburg, *John*, 1:270; Brown, *John*, 1:13). The justification for such an interpretation is the parallelism between "among us" and "flesh" (σάρξ). Barrett (*John*, 166), however, believes the plural refers to the "apostolic church."

[43] It is even striking that the noun chosen is not "man" (Lindars, *John*, 93). For Schnackenburg (*John*, 1:267), larger Johannine thought indicates that "flesh" refers to that which is "earth-bound" (3:6) and "transient and perishable" (6:63). For the Gospel of John, Christ in the flesh is "the leader who brings earth-bound [humanity] home to the heavenly world of life and glory" (268).

[44] Brown, *John*, 1:13.

The uniqueness of the Word is also constructed through the use of universal language in 1:18, "no one (οὐδείς) has seen God, ever (πώποτε)."[45] The position of the adverb, at the end of the sentence in Greek, is emphatic.[46] The Son alone was with God before creation, and he alone reveals God.[47] The previous reference to Moses indicates that not even this important figure can claim a vision of God.[48] Thus, John uses universal language in negative terms to express the dramatic condition of humanity. They cannot claim they have seen God. The world has failed to recognize its Creator. Humanity has even rejected its source of life and light.

The several instances of universal language highlighted so far are clearly linked to Jewish tradition: for example, "glory," "encamped," "name."[49] There is also a clear mention of Moses in 1:17 and a reference to John the Baptist in 1:6, situating the story that follows within the larger context of Judaism.[50] The story the narrator is about to tell took place in a particular geographical area where a specific ethnic group witnessed Jesus' miracles. At the same time, the correct interpretation of this story should be framed by the larger universal outlook emphasized in the introductory section of the Gospel.

---

[45] This phrase is "not directed against the Jews' claim to possess the revelation . . . but against any claim to enjoy the vision of God," according to Bultmann, *John*, 79.

[46] Michaels, *John*, 91.

[47] Schnelle, *Johannes*, 63.

[48] Lincoln, *John*, 108. Although several figures in the Old Testament and Jewish tradition are said to have seen God, such encounters are usually qualified to prevent the conclusion that they actually saw God's face (Thompson, *John*, 35–36). According to Exod 33:20-23, it is impossible to see God and live.

[49] Actually, the prologue can be regarded as an exegetical narrative of Genesis and Exodus, according to Ruth Sheridan, "John's Prologue as Exegetical Narrative," in *The Gospel of John and Genre Mosaic*, ed. Kasper Bro Larsen, Studia Aarhusiana Neotestamentica 3 (Göttingen: Vandenhoeck & Ruprecht, 2015), 171–90.

[50] The lack of conjunction between ὁ νόμος διὰ Μωϋσέως ἐδόθη and ἡ χάρις καὶ ἡ ἀλήθεια διὰ Ἰησοῦ Χριστοῦ ἐγένετο in 1:17, however, indicates that there is no explicit polemic between Moses and Jesus Christ (1:17). Cf. Catrin H. Williams, "(Not) Seeing God in the Prologue and Body of John's Gospel," in van der Watt, Culpepper, and Schnelle, *The Prologue of the Gospel of John*, 79–98, here 88, who sees a comparison and a contrast between Jesus and Moses even in 1:14-16, 18.

The Testimony of John

Soon after the portrayal of the Word's role in the creation of everything that exists and his presentation as the life and light of humanity (1:1-5), the reader encounters a reference to John the Baptist in 1:6.[51] The lack of an explicit geographical location and audience for his testimony in 1:6 gives the impression that his message is open to all who read about him.[52] This interpretation is immediately confirmed in 1:7, "so that all (πάντες) might believe through him."[53] There is no restriction in the context for πάντες since the only previous use of this word is found in 1:3 in reference to creation.[54] His mission here is not limited to Israel but is "given a more universal audience."[55]

Although John's testimony can be taken as universal in scope, he later testifies before religious leaders from Jerusalem (1:19) using Israel's Scriptures (1:23; Isa 40:3).[56] The inclusion of the phrase "as the prophet Isaiah said" at the end of 1:23 is an invitation to the reader to relate John's testimony to Isaiah's prophecy. In fact, the larger context of this Old Testament text finds resonances with the introductory section of the Gospel of John. The most obvious one is Isaiah's prediction

---

[51] The function of John is clearly mentioned in 1:28, but the appellation "the Baptist" is not Johannine. I use it here for clarity, so as not to confuse him with "John" the author of the Gospel according to church tradition (Irenaeus, *Haer.* 3.1.1).

[52] Since he is sent from God in 1:6, the Baptist is presented as coming from the side of the light. At the same time, John is part of the created order because he is a human being (ἄνθρωπος) that is part of "all things" that were made through the Word.

[53] The purpose of John's witness (not the result) is that all may believe (Barrett, *John*, 159). Thus πάντες shows the "universal salvific" purpose of God, according to Schnackenburg, *John*, 1:252.

[54] Zumstein, *Johannesevangelium*, 80.

[55] Lincoln, *John*, 100.

[56] The form of the text resembles the LXX. See Brown, *John*, 1:43; Barrett, *John*, 173; Lindars, *John*, 104. The presentation of Jesus as the Lamb of God who takes away the sin of the world is idiosyncratic to this Gospel. The Gospels of Mark and Luke portray John as proclaiming a baptism of repentance "for the forgiveness of sins" (Mark 1:4; Luke 3:3). Luke also quotes Isa 40:3-5 in reference to John, a passage that indicates that "all flesh (πᾶσα σάρξ) shall see the salvation of God" (v. 5). The Gospel of Matthew has an angel ordering Joseph to call his son Jesus, because "he will save his people from their sins" (1:21).

that "the glory of the Lord will be seen" (ὀφθήσεται ἡ δόξα κυρίου, 40:5). This phrase is strikingly similar to John 1:14, "we have seen his glory" (ἐθεασάμεθα τὴν δόξαν αὐτοῦ). The prophecy of Isaiah is intended for the people of Israel (40:2, Ιερουσαλημ). Similarly, the Baptist's testimony is given to religious leaders from Jerusalem (ἐξ Ἱεροσολύμων, 1:19). Specifically, both texts refer to priests using the same noun: ἱερεῖς (Isa 40:2; John 1:19).

Isaiah's prophecy is intended for Israel but, at the same time, is universal in scope: "All flesh (πᾶσα σάρξ) shall see the salvation of God" (40:5). This universalism is grounded on the all-encompassing authority of God. The Lord holds the circle of the earth and stretched the heaven out like a tent (σκηνήν) to live in (40:22). He created all things (πάντα ταῦτα, 40:26)[57] and prepared the ends of the earth (40:28). Isaiah's portrayal of God resonates with the Johannine description of the Word as actively involved in the creation of all things (πάντα, 1:3) and dwelling (ἐσκήνωσεν) among us (1:14). The Johannine innovation in relation to Isaiah's prophecy is that the Word is said to have taken an active role in the creation of everything that exists, and the identification of the Word with Jesus.

The message of the prophet Isaiah is about salvation for Israel but judgment for the nations. The sin of Israel "has been done away with," and "she has received from the Lord's hand double that of her sins" (40:2). For the nations, however, there is judgment. The prophet indicates that "all flesh (πᾶσα σάρξ) is grass" because it withers (40:6-7). The Lord measures "all the earth by the handful" (40:12), and accounts nations (πάντα τὰ ἔθνη) "as the sinking of a balance" (40:15). However, the judgment of the Lord is specially directed against the rulers (ἄρχοντας): "He blew upon them, and they withered, and a tempest will carry them off like brushwood" (40:23-24).

Readers of the Gospel who knew this prophecy might expect that in using Isa 40:3 to introduce his ministry, John shares the view that

---

[57] This same text (Isa 40:26) portrays God as the one who "produces his universe by number." Natalio Fernández Marcos and María Spottorno Díaz-Caro, *La Biblia griega: Septuaginta*, 4 vols., Biblioteca de Estudios Bíblicos 128 (Salamanca: Sígueme, 2015), 4:189, observe that τὸν κόσμον is not found in the Hebrew text and that its inclusion here might reflect the Greek influence from Alexandria.

Jesus Christ came to save Israel but to judge the nations. This expectation is soon adjusted. The narrator has already anticipated that "we all received . . . grace upon grace" through Jesus Christ (1:16-17), and John the Baptist now identifies Jesus as "the Lamb of God who takes away the sin of the world (τὴν ἁμαρτίαν τοῦ κόσμου)" (1:29).[58] Since the whole world is under sin (see 8:34), the lowly Lamb of God takes away the sin of the whole world.[59] John shares with Isaiah the perspective that Israel is in sin (40:2, ἡ ἁμαρτία)[60] but expands his message to include the whole world as the beneficiary of the work of the Lamb of God.[61] The world not only "shall see the salvation of God" (40:5), it

---

[58] The second time John looked at Jesus, he identified him only as "the Lamb of God" (1:36). This time, however, John is not giving testimony to people about Jesus, he was standing with only two of his disciples (1:35). An early papyrus adds ο αιρων την αμαρτιαν του κοσμου after τοῦ θεοῦ in 1:36 (the original reading of 𝔓⁶⁶). This, however, might be an attempt to harmonize 1:36 with 1:29.

[59] Schnelle, *Johannes*, 76.

[60] For Johannine readers shaped by Jewish Scriptures, the "Lamb of God who takes away the sin of the world" might find resonances with the Servant of God in Isa 52–53. The Servant "bears our sins (τὰς ἁμαρτίας) and suffers pain for us" (53:4). He has been weakened "because of our sins (τὰς ἁμαρτίας)" (53:5). The Lord gave "him over to our sins (ταῖς ἁμαρτίαις)" (53:6). He himself "shall bear their sins (τὰς ἁμαρτίας)" (53:11). He "bore the sins (ἁμαρτίας) of many" and because of "their sins (τὰς ἁμαρτίας) he was given over" (53:12). The Servant shall be exalted and glorified exceedingly (52:13), but his appearance is without glory from men (52:14). The Servant has no deceit in his mouth (53:9). Similarly, Jesus tells the truth which he heard from his Father (John 8:40), does not receive glory from men (5:41), but will be glorified by the Father with the glory which he had before the foundation of the world (17:5). Another striking feature of the Isaianic Servant is his universal significance. Isaiah prophesizes that "many nations (ἔθνη πολλά)" shall be astonished at him (Isa 52:15). Even those who were not "informed about him shall see" and those who "did not hear shall understand" (Isa 52:15). Furthermore, Isa 53:15 can be translated "he shall inherit many" (αὐτὸς κληρονομήσει πολλούς). This translation can be interpreted in a universal sense: the Servant will inherent many people after he has borne their sins. The Servant is compared to a silent lamb (ἀμνός) who does not open his mouth before the one shearing him (Isa 53:7). Haenchen (*John 1*, 153), however, rejects an allusion to Isaiah in John 1:29.

[61] Jesper Tang Nielsen, "The Lamb of God: The Cognitive Structure of a Johannine Metaphor," in *Imagery in the Gospel of John: Terms, Forms, Themes, and Theology of Johannine Figurative Language*, ed. Jörg Frey, Jan G. van der Watt, and Ruben Zimmermann, WUNT 200 (Tübingen: Mohr Siebeck, 2006), 217–56, here 242–43. Apart

will also experience a removal of sin.⁶² John explicitly indicates that his work of baptizing with water was intended that Jesus might be revealed to Israel (1:31), but his witness is intended so that all might believe through him (1:7).⁶³

The first interaction between John and his disciples evokes the universal role of the Word in creation. His disciples tell him that all (πάντες) are going to Jesus (3:26), and he replies indicating that people cannot receive "even one thing (οὐδὲ ἕν) unless it is given him from heaven" (3:27). The phrasing of this brief conversation recalls 1:3, "all things (πάντα) were made through him" and "without him was not anything (οὐδὲ ἕν) made that was made." Surely, the use of πάντες has a restricted sense in 3:26, since it refers to some people from the Judean countryside coming to Jesus (3:22), but it prepares the reader for the other part of John's testimony about Jesus' universal authority in 3:31, 34.

John testifies about Jesus that he "comes from above" and is "above all" (3:31). He repeats this idea twice to signal the importance of recognizing that Jesus' authority is absolute.⁶⁴ The neuter plural here (πάντων) can refer to creation as a whole, as in 1:3.⁶⁵ Jesus, in his unique

---

from Isa 53:4-12, the imagery associated with the "Lamb of God" might also be influenced by Exod 12:1-11 (e.g., Brown, *John*, 1:63; Lindars, *John*, 109; Lincoln, *John*, 113).

⁶² Hoskyns (*Fourth Gospel*, 176) finds that "the sacrifices in the Temple caused the Jews to consider them as possessing universal significance." Hoskyns refers to Josephus, *War* 4.324, where priests are regarded as presiding "over the universal worship"; and Philo, *Legat.* 306, where the prayer on the day of atonement is for the peace and prosperity "of all men." Since the phrase "universal worship" (τῆς κοσμικῆς θρησκείας) in *War* 4.324 is followed by references to visitors in Jerusalem from "every quarter of the earth" (τῆς οἰκουμένης), it may mean not that sacrifices were for the benefit of the world but that their ceremonies were significant to temple visitors from all over the ancient world. Similarly, *Legat.* 306 does not refer to sacrifices offered for the benefit of the world. It describes prayers offered by the high priest in the inmost part of the temple for the peace of all mankind (ἅπασιν ἀνθρώποις).

⁶³ Just as Jesus' message to Israel would touch all humanity, John's testimony to Israel is for the benefit of "all," according to Brown, *John*, 1:8–9.

⁶⁴ If the reading preserved in 𝔓⁷⁵ is followed (also Sinaiticus), the idea is repeated twice. If that was not the original reading, the repetition was likely an early unintentional change.

⁶⁵ It can also be taken as masculine plural (Schnackenburg, *John*, 1:381) in which case the meaning would be "above the whole realm of man" (Brown, *John*, 1:157).

relationship with God,[66] is superior to all human beings, because they all are from the earth.[67] An important component of John the Baptist's testimony is providing privileged information that the reader already encountered in the prologue: Jesus is on the side of God and, therefore, has universal authority (1:1-3, 10).

The all-encompassing authority of Jesus is not restricted to his preexistence, nor is it exclusively manifested in his work of creation. The testimony of the Baptist serves the important purpose of demonstrating that the universal significance of Jesus extends to his earthly ministry. The Father gave the Son all things (πάντα) into his hand because he loves him (3:35).[68] Presumably this took place during Jesus' preexistence. However, the limitless endowment he has received is made manifest during his earthly ministry. There are two specific capacities that Jesus receives from God: the ability to speak the words of God and the Spirit (3:34).[69] The "fullness" of Jesus (1:16) stems from him having received all things from the Father in his hand.[70] The threefold repetition of Jesus' universal authority creates a deep impact upon the reader.

3:31	ὁ ἄνωθεν ἐρχόμενος	ἐπάνω πάντων ἐστίν
	ὁ ἐκ τοῦ οὐρανοῦ ἐρχόμενος	ἐπάνω πάντων ἐστίν
3:35	ὁ πατὴρ ἀγαπᾷ τὸν υἱὸν καὶ	πάντα δέδωκεν ἐν τῇ χειρὶ αὐτοῦ

Although John is introduced for the first time in the story as the one who gives testimony about the light so "that all might believe through

---

[66] Zumstein, *Johannesevangelium*, 159; Schnelle, *Johannes*, 116–17. Bultmann (*John*, 162) found that ἐπάνω πάντων portrays Jesus as "equal to God in his relation to the world."

[67] Lincoln, *John*, 161. Jesus "is in a class by himself" (Lindars, *John*, 169).

[68] The sequence the Father loves the Son and, consequently, has given all things into his hand contrasts with the previous assertion that God loved the world and, consequently, gave his only Son (Lincoln, *John*, 154).

[69] Thompson, *John*, 94. Lindars (*John*, 171) and Schnackenburg (*John*, 1:388) suggest that Jesus also received authority to give eternal life.

[70] Schnackenburg, *John*, 1:388.

him" (1:7), at the narrative level, he gives testimony only to people associated with Judaism.[71] Notwithstanding this restricted testimony, John's message has been preserved in the Gospel of John, and through the text it reaches the Johannine reader, either Jew or gentile.[72] John's testimony "persists as a clarion call . . . for all time, for the whole world."[73] Those who read the testimony of John about Jesus as the Lamb of God who takes away the sin of the world (1:29)[74] and about his absolute authority (3:31, 35) have the possibility of believing and, therefore, of receiving eternal life (3:16; see also 1:12).

The Incident in the Temple

Jesus is also presented in the temple in Jerusalem, the center of religious life (2:13-22). The explicit commentary about the meaning of Jesus' words and actions is found in 2:21: "He was speaking about the

---

[71] The Baptist gives testimony to priests and Levites in Bethany across the Jordan (1:28), to Jewish people close to the Jordan river (1:31), and to his disciples and at least one Jew in Aenon near Salim (3:23-25). Jesus even reminds Jews in Jerusalem that John gave testimony to them about him (5:1, 18, 33). Across the Jordan at the place where John had been baptizing, many Jews confirmed that John's testimony about Jesus was true, and many believed in him (10:40-41). Furthermore, the first followers of Jesus are previous disciples of John (1:37) and people from Galilee (1:43-46), including "an Israelite in whom there is no deceit" (1:47). Jesus also shows his glory for the first time in Cana in Galilee (2:1, 11). Peter J. Judge suggests that the former disciples of the Baptist that now follow Jesus reflect "the universal quest of humans in the view of the evangelist." However, it is difficult to assert whether this somewhat existential way of looking at 1:35-38 is actually the "view of the evangelist." See his "Come and See: The First Disciples and Christology in the Fourth Gospel," in Verheyden, van Oyen, Labahn, and Bieringer, *Studies in the Gospel of John and Its Christology*, 61–69, here 62.

[72] For Haenchen (*John 1*, 152), the lack of an explicit audience in John 1:29-34 gives the impression that John is addressing the reader with the presentation of Jesus as the Lamb of God who takes away the sin of the world. Similarly, Bultmann, *John*, 51, 95; Michaels, *John*, 108.

[73] Schnackenburg, *John*, 1:252.

[74] Hoskyns, *Fourth Gospel*, 138; Michaels, *John*, 60. Haenchen (*John 1*, 153) suggests that the identification of Jesus as the Lamb of God who takes away the sin of the world is "not really appropriate to the christology [*sic*] of the Evangelist" because elsewhere the Gospel indicates that Jesus came only for those whom the Father has given to him (6:39; 17:12). This perspective, however, diminishes the prominent place of instances of universal language in 1:3, 7, 10.

temple of his body."[75] A case can be made to suggest that the cleansing of the temple points to the comprehensive scope of Jesus' significance by paying attention to the place where these events likely took place, Jesus' relationship to the temple as highlighted by the quotation from Psalm 69:10 (John 2:17),[76] and the use of this episode in the Synoptic tradition.[77] The reading offered here presupposes a reader with knowledge of the larger context of the Old Testament quotation and, at least, some knowledge of the traditions that shaped the Synoptic Gospels.[78]

The first observation is the location where Jesus performs the cleansing of the temple. Although John indicates only that the events took place in the temple (τῷ ἱερῷ, τοῦ ἱεροῦ, 2:14-15; cf. ὁ ναός, 2:20), it is likely that this incident happened in the court of the gentiles.[79] Early readers of the Gospel of John familiar with traditions about the

---

[75] Zumstein, *Johannesevangelium*, 129.

[76] Brown, *John*, 1:124: "the context of the verse [Ps 69:9] may have been intended as well."

[77] C. H. Dodd, *The Interpretation of the Fourth Gospel* (Cambridge: Cambridge University Press, 1953), 302–3, also suggested that readers located in Ephesus (a possible place of composition for the final form of the Gospel of John) would read John 2:13-22 in connection with texts such as 1 Corinthians (written from Ephesus). There, temple imagery is applied to the body of believers, Jews and gentiles (1 Cor 3:16; 12:27; cf. Col 1:18). Dodd went as far as to suggest that readers in Ephesus would interpret John 2:12-22 as the inauguration of the church. However, he cautiously commented that Hellenistic readers of the Gospel of John would not find this reading spontaneously in the text.

[78] The Johannine dependence on the Synoptic account is presupposed in Jacob Chanikuzhy, *Jesus, the Eschatological Temple: An Exegetical Study of Jn 2,13-22 in the Light of the Pre-70 CE Eschatological Temple Hopes and the Synoptic Temple Action*, CBET 58 (Leuven: Peeters, 2012), 97n1. Resonances of Ps 69 can be detected in several places in the Gospel of John. For examples, see Margaret Daly-Denton, *David in the Fourth Gospel: The Johannine Reception of the Psalms*, AGJU 47 (Leiden: Brill, 2000), 129.

[79] Bultmann, *John*, 123n6; Brown, *John*, 1:115, Schnackenburg, *John*, 1:346; Michaels, *John*, 158; Zumstein, *Johannesevangelium*, 125–26; Colin G. Kruse, *The Gospel according to John: An Introduction and Commentary*, TNTC 4 (Downers Grove, Ill.: InterVarsity, 2008), 100; Jey J. Kanagaraj, *John: A New Covenant Commentary*, New Covenant Commentary Series (Cambridge: Lutterworth, 2013), 24. Haenchen (*John 1*, 182) rejects this possibility because by the time of the writing of the Gospel the temple was destroyed and the author did not have "the latest archaeological data" about the temple at his disposal. On this last point, Haenchen might be right. However, traditions about the temple were vividly remembered after its destruction. A summary of various Jewish

Jewish temple would understand that the selling of animals for sacrifice would have taken place either in the first (outer) or second (inner) enclosure of the temple. Josephus, for example, indicates that the inner enclosure was encompassed by a stone wall, and it had an inscription that forbade any foreigner to enter under pain of death (*Ant.* 15.11.5).[80] There is evidence that Jerusalem was an "interesting place for educated Greeks, pagans and adventurers" and held "international significance in the Roman empire."[81] If merchants were conducting business in the court of the gentiles, their financial activities might have negatively affected the worship of gentiles.[82] Since Jesus' actions and words are directed against the sellers, not the buyers,[83] he is not directly opposing gentile visitors sympathetic with the temple.

The second observation is found in John 2:17. The phrase "will consume (καταφάγεται) me" in the disciples' reminiscence of Psalm 69:10 is an interpretative key to Jesus' actions in the temple. The context of Psalm 69:10 is that of a person who is suffering to the point of death: "waters came as far as my soul" (v. 1); "I was stuck in deep mire, and there is no foothold" (v. 2); "my enemies who persecuted me unjustly became strong" (v. 4).[84] The commitment of this person to the Lord and his temple was the cause of his sufferings: "for your sake I bore reproach" (v. 7); "the zeal for your house consumed me" (v. 9); "the reproaches of those who reproach you fell on me" (v. 9).[85]

---

responses to the destruction of the temple in 70 CE is found in Chanikuzhy, *Temple*, 44–96.

[80] The famous warning inscription at the temple written in Greek is found in Jean Baptiste Frey, *Corpus Inscriptionum Judaicarum: Recueil des inscriptions juives qui vont du IIIe siècle avant Jésus-Christ au VIIe siècle de notre ère* (Rome: Pontificio Istituto di Archaeologia Cristiana, 1936), 2:1400.

[81] Martin Hengel, *The "Hellenization" of Judaea in the First Century after Christ* (London: SCM; Philadelphia: Trinity Press International, 1989), 11, 13.

[82] Kanagaraj, *John*, 24. Keener (*John*, 1:524) allows this possibility but stresses that the Gospel of John does not emphasize it. Lindars (*John*, 137) finds this interpretation unlikely because gentiles already had the right to worship in the court of the gentiles.

[83] Schnackenburg, *John*, 1:346; Michaels, *John*, 158.

[84] The sufferer in Ps 69:8 regards himself as "estranged" (ἀπηλλοτριωμένος) and a "visitor" (ξένος) because of his zeal for God's house.

[85] This psalm is used elsewhere in the Gospel of John in relation to Jesus' sufferings. Jesus quotes Ps 69:5 ("[they] hated me without a cause") in John 15:25 in reference

Jesus' zeal for the temple will bring suffering to him, even to the point of death:[86] "Destroy this temple. . . . [H]e was speaking about the temple of his body" (John 2:21). Jesus, however, will be raised from the dead (2:22).[87] Since the temple is "the temple of his body," the implication is that the encounter between God and humanity will take place in Jesus (1:14, 18),[88] both for Jews and for gentiles. Before the incident in the temple in Jerusalem, the traditional place of God's glory on earth, John narrated an episode in Galilee where Jesus "manifested his glory" (2:11), anticipating the conclusion that a proper encounter with God takes place through Jesus.[89]

---

to those who have rejected him. There is also an allusion to Ps 69:22 ("they gave gall as my food") when Jesus is hanging on a cross in John 19:28-29. Other early Christian texts consistently use Ps 69 in reference to Jesus' passion: Rom 15:3; Matt 27:48; Acts 1:20. Furthermore, almost every phrase of Ps 69 is quoted or alluded to in the New Testament, according to Barnabas Lindars, *New Testament Apologetic: The Doctrinal Significance of the Old Testament Quotations* (London: SCM, 1961), 105; Daly-Denton, *David*, 42.

[86] Maarten J. J. Menken, *Old Testament Quotations in the Fourth Gospel: Studies in Textual Form*, CBET 15 (Kampen: Kok Pharos, 1996), 40–41.

[87] Some scholars have found an allusion to Zech 14:21 in John 2:16 (e.g., Beutler, *Johannesevangelium*, 130). Michaels (*John*, 160), however, rejects it. The LXX has "the Chananite (Χαναναῖος) shall no longer be in the house (τῷ οἴκῳ) of the Lord Almighty on that day" (Zech 14:21). The MT has כנעני, which can be translated either "Canaanite" or "tradesman" (e.g., Job 40:30). The translation could be "there shall no longer be a *trader* in the house of the Lord." Although Zech 14 expects judgment against sinful nations, the prophecy also anticipates that "the Lord will become king over all the earth" (14:9) and announces that people from nations that came against Jerusalem will "go up year after year to do obeisance to the King, the Lord Almighty, and to keep the feast of tent pitching" (14:16; cf. John 1:49). Under God's eschatological authority "all aspects of life" will be sacred, and, therefore, there will be no need of traders in the temple who provide appropriate currency. Lincoln (*John*, 138) and Lindars (*John*, 139) interpret the quotation as pointing to "universal holiness." One observation that militates against this suggested allusion is that Zech 14:21 seems to refer to the eschatological Feast of Tabernacles (σκηνοπηγίας; cf. 7:2), while John clearly indicates that the incident in the temple took place when the "Passover of the Jews was at hand" (2:13).

[88] Schnackenburg, *John*, 1:352; Zumstein, *Johannesevangelium*, 129. See also Uta Poplutz, "'. . . und hat unter uns gezeltet' (Joh 1,14b): Die Fleischwerdung des Logos im Licht der *Schechina*-Theologie," *SacScript* 13 (2015): 101–14.

[89] Chanikuzhy, *Temple*, 2, 404. Temple imagery is also applied to Jesus in 1:14, according to Daly-Denton, *David*, 122.

With his actions in Jerusalem, Jesus disrupts, at least momentarily, current worship in the temple through the sacrifice of animals.[90] The narrator indicates in John 2:14 that Jesus found those who were selling oxen, sheep, and pigeons and that he drove the sheep and oxen out of the temple (2:15).[91] Those were typical animals used in the sacrificial system of the temple (e.g., Lev 1:2, 14). Implicitly, Jesus' action "is to symbolize that Jesus removes the need for animal sacrifices to obtain forgiveness of sins and deliverance" because "Jesus himself is the sacrifice to remove human sin."[92] Jesus was already introduced as the Lamb of God who takes away the sin of the world (1:29).[93] At the same time, Jesus' actions in the temple are intended to purify this sacred place.[94] He refers to it positively as "my Father's house" (2:16), and he risks his

[90] Chanikuzhy (*Temple*, 404), however, interprets that the pericope "shows that the time of the Jewish temple cult is *now* ended" (my emphasis). However, Jesus' death as the Lamb who takes away the sin of the world still lies ahead in the narrative. For Daly-Denton (*David*, 116), Jesus' actions in the temple portend "the events of the 'hour' which are to result in the replacement of the Jewish cultic system."

[91] The Gospel of John is the only canonical Gospel that mentions the oxen and sheep (Lindars, *John*, 138).

[92] Haenchen, *John 1*, 187. See also Lincoln, *John*, 137; and Kanagaraj, *John*, 25. Haenchen (*John 1*, 184) interprets that Jesus attacks the "delusion that man can buy God's favor," not the sanctity of the temple precincts. His opinion might be strengthened by looking at 1:16: "from his fullness we have all *received*, grace upon grace." A different opinion, i.e., Jesus does not put a stop to the sacrificial system, is expressed by Thompson, *John*, 72. Hoskyns (*Fourth Gospel*, 194) suggests that Jesus' actions are a sign that the end of the sacrificial system is at hand.

[93] Barrett, *John*, 198, referring to J. C. Fenton, *The Gospel according to John*, New Clarendon Bible (Oxford: Clarendon, 1970), 49–50. Daly-Denton (*David*, 126–27) proposes that the citation from Ps 69:10 has a figurative level of meaning since it points to the Father's acceptance of Jesus' death as perfect sacrifice. She bases this interpretation on Old Testament imagery about sacrifices where the verb "to consume" may refer to sacrifices (e.g., 2 Chr 7:1).

[94] Beutler, *Johannesevangelium*, 129–31; J. H. Ulrichsen, "Jesus—der neue Tempel? Ein kritischer Blick auf die Auslegung von Joh 2,13-22," in *Neotestamentica et Philonica*, ed. D. E. Aune, T. Seland, and J. H. Ulrichsen; NovTSup 106 (Leiden: Brill, 2003), 202–14; Kåre Sigvald Fuglseth, *Johannine Sectarianism in Perspective: A Sociological, Historical, and Comparative Analysis of Temple and Social Relationships in the Gospel of John, Philo, and Qumran*, NovTSup 119 (Leiden: Brill, 2005), 157.

life for his commitment to the restoration of its holiness.[95] Therefore, the reader is left with questions about the appropriate place to worship God and the relationship between the temple and the destruction and raising of Jesus' body. Those questions will find a fuller answer in Jesus' dialogues with the Samaritan woman in 4:20-24 and the Jews in 5:23.[96]

The third observation that may direct some readers to understand the cleansing of the temple as an implicit instance of the comprehensive scope of Jesus' significance is the use of this narrative in the Synoptic tradition (Matt 21:12-17; Mark 11:15-19; Luke 19:45-48). This incident occurs in contexts that highlight the rejection of Israel: for example, the fig tree (Matt 21:18-22; Mark 13:28-31) and the laborers in the vineyard (Matt 20:1-16; Luke 20:9-18).[97] At the same time, the rejection of Israel implies that the kingdom of God is given to others (Matt 21:31, 43; 22:9-10). In Mark 11:17, the specific episode of the cleansing of the temple highlights that this is "a house (οἶκος) of prayer for all the nations (πᾶσιν τοῖς ἔθνεσιν)" (cf. Isa 56:7). If readers of the Gospel of John knew the traditions that shaped the Synoptic Gospels, they might be aware that the temple incident is closely related to the failure of Israel and the inclusion of others in the kingdom of God.

Overall, the temple incident shows that Jesus claims indirect ownership of the temple by referring to it as his Father's house. Jesus took an active role in creation and is the rightful owner of the whole world, including the conventional place where people encountered God according to Jewish tradition. At the same time, his challenge to the temple points to him as the point where humanity can find God. That these claims and challenges likely took place in the court of the gentiles shows the universal significance of Jesus and the message about him.

---

[95] Jesus will even make the temple his preferred place for teaching (18:20). Cf. Beutler, *Johannesevangelium*, 127.

[96] Barrett (*John*, 195) interprets the incident at the temple as pointing to Jesus' body as "the house of prayer for all the nations" but clarifies that "John does not in the present section work out the implications of this claim."

[97] Dodd, *Interpretation*, 302; Brown, *John*, 1:121; Chanikuzhy, *Temple*, 124–49.

ENCOUNTERS WITH REPRESENTATIVE INDIVIDUALS

The following personal encounters narrated in the Gospel take place in three different locations. Nicodemus' conversation with Jesus might have taken place in Jerusalem around the time of the Passover since there is no geographical transition from 2:23 to 3:1.[98] Jesus' knowledge of "all people (πάντας)" (2:24) and of "what was in man (ἀνθρώπῳ)" (2:24-25) takes place in Jerusalem (2:23). His knowledge is illustrated in the following story about "a man (ἄνθρωπος) from the Pharisees" (3:1). Next, Jesus' conversation with a woman takes place in a Samaritan town called Sychar (4:4-5), when he left Judea and departed for Galilee (4:3). After staying two days in Samaria (4:40), Jesus departed for Galilee (4:43), where many Galileans welcomed him (4:45). There Jesus encountered a man who was located in Capernaum (4:46). At the end of the story, the reader is again reminded of a geographical location: "Jesus did [this sign] when he had come from Judea to Galilee" (4:54).

These three individuals seem to represent larger groups.[99] Nicodemus is a member of the Pharisees, a ruler of the Jews (3:1). The second "you" in 3:7 is plural (ὑμᾶς), indicating that Jesus' words apply to religious leaders in general.[100] The woman is "from Samaria" (4:7) and testifies to her fellow Samaritans (4:28). The man in Capernaum is an official in Galilee (4:46). The indefinite τις βασιλικός ("a certain royal official," 4:46) facilitates his identification as a representative character

---

[98] There seems to be a geographical distinction between Jerusalem (2:13–3:21; 5:1-47; 7:10–10:39; 11:55-57; 12:12–20:31) and Judea (3:22-36; 11:1-54; 12:1-11) in the Gospel of John (Teresa Okure, *The Johannine Approach to Mission: A Contextual Study of John 4:1-42*, WUNT 2/31 [Tübingen: Mohr, 1988], 198). Beutler (*Johannesevangelium*, 177–78) distinguishes four phases in John 2–4, i.e., Jerusalem, Judea, Samaria, and Galilee (cf. Acts 1:8). See also Johannes Beutler, "Jesus in Judäa," *In die Skriflig* 49 (2015): 1–6.

[99] Thus Craig R. Koester, *Symbolism in the Fourth Gospel: Meaning, Mystery, Community*, 2nd ed. (Minneapolis: Fortress, 2003), 45.

[100] Lincoln, *John*, 151. Meeks ("Man from Heaven," 55) finds that Nicodemus represents those Jews mentioned in 2:23-24. Hoskyns (*Fourth Gospel*, 215), however, interprets that the plural "you" indicates that "the demand of God is universal" (also Keener, *John*, 1:570). Koester (*Symbolism*, 45) also observes that the plural "we" in 3:2 suggests that Nicodemus speaks for a group of people.

(4:47).[101] He is taken as a member of a larger group in Jesus' saying: "unless you (pl. ἴδητε) see signs" (4:48).

Although all three narratives depict personal encounters with Jesus, the stories include instances of universal language. This is particularly clear in the dialogues with Nicodemus and the Samaritan woman. Scholars customarily highlight differences between these two characters. The obvious observation that one is male while the other one is female naturally invites further contrasts.[102] However, there are also similarities between the two dialogues.[103] One of them is the often-overlooked fact that there are clear instances of universal language at the end of each story (3:16-17; 4:42).[104]

A Religious Leader in Judea

The personal conversation in 3:1-21 encourages the reader to interpret the first part of this dialogue (3:1-15) in a restricted sense. The invitations to be born of the Spirit (3:8) and to believe in order to obtain eternal life (3:15) are offered specifically to Nicodemus and, more broadly, to the group he represents. Since Nicodemus identifies Jesus as a Jewish rabbi who comes from God (3:2), since the narrator introduces Nicodemus as a man from the Pharisees (3:1), and since Jesus refers to this ruler of the Jews as the teacher of Israel (3:10), the offer of eternal life can be understood as applicable to those traditionally associated with Judaism. This impression is further highlighted by the prominence of topics found in Jewish tradition such as the kingdom of God (3:5) and

---

[101] The "positive and consistent portrayal" of anonymous characters in the Gospel of John "facilitate[s] the reader's entry into and involvement with the narrative world," according to David R. Beck, *The Discipleship Paradigm: Readers and Anonymous Characters in the Fourth Gospel*, BibInt 27 (Leiden: Brill, 1997), 33.

[102] Lists of differences between both characters are found in Colleen M. Conway, *Men and Women in the Fourth Gospel: Gender and Johannine Characterization*, SBLDS 167 (Atlanta: Society of Biblical Literature, 1999), 104–5; and Margaret M. Beirne, *Women and Men in the Fourth Gospel: A Genuine Discipleship of Equals*, JSNTSup 242 (London: Sheffield Academic Press, 2003), 67–104.

[103] For example, both misunderstand Jesus' words (3:4; 4:11).

[104] Ironically, Nicodemus does not understand Jesus' message about him being sent into the world so that the world might be saved (3:17), but the Samaritans confess he is the savior of the world (Brown, *John*, 1:185).

Moses and the serpent in the wilderness (3:14; see Num 21:8-9). The Greek version of this Old Testament story includes the phrase "everyone who is bitten, when he looks at it, shall live" (πᾶς ὁ δεδηγμένος ἰδὼν αὐτὸν ζήσεται, Num 21:8). The adjective πᾶς refers, in context, to those Israelites who were about to die because of the serpents. Once they look at the serpent they will live (ζήσεται).

The second part of this personal encounter, however, has explicit instances of universal language (3:16-21) that are enhanced by reading them in light of the previous testimony of John the Baptist (1:29) and the prologue (1:1-18). The assertion "God loved the world (τὸν κόσμον)" (3:16)[105] immediately reminds the reader of the three previous instances of the noun "world": the true light was coming into the world (1:9), the world was created through the Word (1:10), and Jesus is the Lamb of God who takes away the sin of the world (1:29).[106] The universal scope of God's soteriological initiative is emphasized by repeating the noun "world" four times in 3:16-17.[107] The same world that was created through the Word is now the object of God's love and Jesus' salvation. This observation further enhances the irony found in 1:11. The world not only rejects its Creator (1:11), it refuses to embrace God's love showed through his only Son (3:16-18).[108] Jesus' presentation of God as the one who loves the whole world and of himself as

---

[105] Lindars (*John*, 159) observes that in the Old Testament (e.g., Deut 7:8) God loves "his people" but here in John 3:16 God's love has universal application and "is not confined to the Chosen People." Similarly, Keener (*John*, 1:567) compares the giving of the "law" to Israel in the Old Testament with the giving of the Son to the world.

[106] Barrett, *John*, 216; Michaels, *John*, 201, 204n117.

[107] Schnackenburg (*John*, 401) uses the phrase "universal salvific will of God." Thompson (*John*, 85) has noticed a parallelism between John 3:16 and 3:17: God gave his Son / whoever [believes] / not perish / but have everlasting life (3:16), and God sent the Son / (to) the world / not to condemn / but to save (3:17). The adjective πᾶς in 3:16 is paralleled to the noun κόσμον in 3:17. This same kind of parallelism was already found in the opening section of the Gospel: πάντα δι᾽ αὐτοῦ ἐγένετο (1:3) // ὁ κόσμος δι᾽ αὐτοῦ ἐγένετο (1:10).

[108] For the use of irony in the Gospel of John, see R. Alan Culpepper, "Reading Johannine Irony," in *Exploring the Gospel of John: In Honor of D. Moody Smith*, ed. C. Clifton Black and R. Alan Culpepper (Louisville: Westminster John Knox, 1996), 193–207; and the pioneer study by David W. Wead, *The Literary Devices in John's Gospel*, Theologische Dissertationen 4 (Basel: Friedrich Reinhardt Kommissionsverlag, 1970), 47–68.

bringing salvation to humanity (3:16)[109] highlights the truly universal sense of God's love, "without precondition and without exclusion."[110] The world is the sphere that Jesus enters with his incarnation in order to provide salvation for humanity (3:17).[111] His exaltation will bring life not only to Israel but to the whole world because all humanity is under the influence of sin.

Resonances between 3:16-17 and the previous literary context are not restricted to 1:29. Language found in 3:16-17 recalls the prologue's assertion that God sent his Son into the world (εἰς τὸν κόσμον, 3:17).[112] The opening section of the Gospel indicates that the true light "was coming into the world" he created (εἰς τὸν κόσμον, 1:9). The link between the creation of the world and the offer of salvation for that same world can be seen as follows:

1:3		πάντα	δι' αὐτοῦ ἐγένετο
1:10		ὁ κόσμος	δι' αὐτοῦ ἐγένετο
1:17		ἡ χάρις καὶ ἡ ἀλήθεια	διὰ Ἰησοῦ Χριστοῦ ἐγένετο
3:17	ἵνα σωθῇ	ὁ κόσμος	δι' αὐτοῦ

The same agent of creation is the current agent of salvation. The universal significance of the Word in creation is similar to the comprehensive

---

[109] Some scholars have taken some sections as the narrator's own theological reflection (3:16-21, 31-36). For example, see Schnackenburg, *John*, 1:383; Keener, *John*, 1:581; and D. Moody Smith, *John*, ANTC (Nashville: Abingdon, 1999), 106. The lack of any clear transition between Jesus' words and the putative narrator's comment makes it difficult to distinguish between the two. Since it is not unusual to have long discourses in this Gospel (e.g., 6:26-70; 15:1–16:33), it is entirely possible that Jesus' discourse extends until 3:36.

[110] Zumstein, *Johannesevangelium*, 147. See also Beutler, *Johannesevangelium*, 140.

[111] Lincoln (*John*, 154–55) sees here the larger Johannine motif of a trial. God's salvation is described as a process of judgment, because salvation comes through the establishment of justice and the restoration of life "in place of exploitation and death." Jesus puts the world on trial not to condemn it but to save it.

[112] Notice also the reference to Jesus as "his only Son (τὸν υἱὸν τὸν μονογενῆ)" in 3:16 and as μονογενοῦς παρὰ πατρός and μονογενὴς θεός in 1:14, 18 (Schnackenburg, *John*, 1:400). Also, the reference to "the name of the only Son of God" recalls 1:12, "all who . . . believed in his name" (Lindars, *John*, 160).

scope of God's soteriological initiative through Jesus Christ. These observations indicate that God offers to the world the life that was intended for it since the beginning.[113] God's love is universal, and so is his offer of salvation, and those who believe in Jesus can enjoy eternal life (1:12; 3:16).[114] The literary relation between the opening section of the Gospel and Jesus' message to Nicodemus is further supported by the assertion that "the light has come into the world (τὸ φῶς ἐλήλυθεν εἰς τὸν κόσμον)" but "people (οἱ ἄνθρωποι) loved the darkness (τὸ σκότος) rather than the light (τὸ φῶς)" (3:19). This shows the world's estrangement from God.[115] The reader has already encountered the contrast between light and darkness in 1:5, has learned that the light that was in the Word was the light of men in 1:4, and has read that the true light was coming into the world (1:9).[116] Although the Word was the light of men (τῶν ἀνθρώπων), people (οἱ ἄνθρωποι) loved darkness (3:19).

The universal outlook found in 3:16-21 invites the reader to reinterpret the first part of Jesus' dialogue with Nicodemus (3:1-15). Initially, Nicodemus identifies Jesus as a traditional Jewish rabbi capable of performing signs (3:2)[117] and the narrator portrays Nicodemus as a representative of religious leaders (3:1). At the end of the story, however, Jesus can be seen as the representation of God's love for humanity and Nicodemus as the representation of the world's ambiguous relationship to the light.[118] This conclusion is supported by the description of Nicodemus as a "man" in 3:1 and as someone who has experienced only a worldly birth (3:4). The use of ἄνθρωπος in 3:1 recalls humanity as a whole in 1:4 and anticipates humanity's puzzling preference for the darkness over the light.[119] Furthermore, the seemingly restricted

---

[113] Thompson, *John*, 85; Schnelle, *Johannes*, 108.

[114] Michaels, *John*, 203.

[115] Koester, *Symbolism*, 45.

[116] Schnackenburg, *John*, 1:405; Zumstein, *Johannesevangelium*, 149.

[117] Michael R. Whitenton ("The Dissembler of John 3: A Cognitive and Rhetorical Approach to the Characterization of Nicodemus," *JBL* 135 [2016]: 141–58) offers evidence that leads one to conclude that Nicodemus misunderstood Jesus' identity even before interacting with him.

[118] Koester, *Symbolism*, 45–46.

[119] Additionally, the verb "to accept" and the noun "testimony" are found in John 1:7, 12; 3:11.

meaning of the phrase "whoever believes in him (πᾶς ὁ πιστεύων ἐν αὐτῷ)" in 3:15 is amplified by the use of the same phrase in 3:16 (πᾶς ὁ πιστεύων εἰς αὐτόν). The prominence of God's universal love in 3:16 indicates that πᾶς ὁ πιστεύων ἐν αὐτῷ in 3:15 also has universal application.[120] Similarly, the salvation of Israel in the wilderness illustrated with the lifted up serpent (3:14; see Num 21:8-9) is made available in Jesus to the whole world.[121] John appropriates the words "life" and "all" from Num 21:8-9 and sets them in a context that points to God's universal concern for humanity.[122]

The condition of humanity is dramatic. They are not living in darkness because they ignore its true nature as darkness. They love darkness (3:19). Humanity in general (οἱ ἄνθρωποι)[123] rejected the light (see 1:11).[124] God, however, loves his world, and he shows that love by approaching humanity through his Son to offer eternal life (3:16). God's love then is creative (schöpferisch) in the sense that it seeks the transformation of the world by bringing judgment to the power of death and by giving eternal life to those who believe.[125] Humans, however, alienate themselves from God by loving darkness instead of the one who loves them, and by rejecting the Word who created them

---

[120] John 3:15 offers the first of many instances of "eternal life" in this Gospel (Michaels, *John*, 199). The initial link between the Word and life in John 1:4 is here explained as eternal life in the Son.

[121] Beutler (*Johannesevangelium*, 140) uses the expression the "human family" (*Menschheitsfamilie*) to identify the "world." The phrase "the savior of all (τὸν πάντων σωτῆρα)" in the retelling of Num 21:8 in Wis 16:7 may refer to those Israelites who saw the serpent in the wilderness. For the idea that Isa 52:13 LXX is the source of this image, see Dominic Obielosi, "Καὶ καθὼς Μωϋσῆς ὕψωσεν τὸν ὄφιν . . . (John 3,14-15) and the Influence of Isaiah 52,13 LXX," *EstBíb* 72 (2014): 217-35.

[122] John 3:14-15 lacks enough clues to enable a clear link between Jesus' crucifixion and his being lifted up. The reader needs to wait for 8:28 and 12:32 to make this link explicit. See Catrin H. Williams, "Another Look at 'Lifting Up' in the Gospel of John," in *Conception, Reception, and the Spirit: Essays in Honor of Andrew T. Lincoln*, ed. J. Gordon McConville and Lloyd K. Pietersen (Eugene, Ore.: Cascade, 2015), 58–70, here 66.

[123] Bultmann, *John*, 157; Schnackenburg, *John*, 1:404; Zumstein, *Johannesevangelium*, 149.

[124] Beutler, *Johannesevangelium*, 141.

[125] Zumstein, *Johannesevangelium*, 147.

(1:11). The whole 3:1-21 includes the world without denying that the possibility of being born of the Spirit and the possibility of belief are available to the specific group Nicodemus represents (3:16).[126]

A Woman in Samaria

While John the Baptist's testimony about the universal significance of Jesus is still resonating ("the Father loves the Son and has given all things into his hand," 3:35), the narrative immediately continues with Jesus' encounter with a woman from Samaria. The geographical and cultural locations of Jesus are clearly marked by the narrator's comment that it was necessary for Jesus to pass through Samaria (4:4) and by the multiple references in the story to Samaria, Samaritans, and the Samaritan woman (4:5, 7, 9, 39, 40). Although Sychar, the place where Jesus talks to the woman, belongs historically to Joseph and its well belongs to Jacob (4:5-6), the reader knows that all things are in Jesus' hand because they were given to him by the Father who loves him (3:35). This context makes one of the Samaritan woman's questions sound ironic: "Are you greater than our father Jacob?" (4:12).[127] She indicates that their father (τοῦ πατρός) Jacob gave (ἔδωκεν) them a well (4:12). The reader knows that the Father (ὁ πατήρ) loves the Son and has given (δέδωκεν) not only a well but all things (πάντα) into his hand (3:35).[128] Indeed, Jesus is greater than Jacob because he is "above all" (3:31).

The description of the conversation makes clear the differences between two ethnic groups.[129] The narrator indicates that "Jews have

---

[126] Brown (*John*, 1:147) suggests that John 3:16-17 is an "implicit reference" to the Akedah because even the mention of "the world" fits with the idea that "Abraham's generosity in sacrificing his only son was to be beneficial to all the nations of the world" (Gen 22:18; Sir 44:21; Jub. 18:15). Others also embrace this connection, e.g., Michaels, *John*, 202–3. However, the passages used by Brown point to God blessing the nations through his seed, not because of the (unfulfilled) sacrifice of his son.

[127] Okure, *Mission*, 129.

[128] Carlos Sosa Siliezar, "Tres rostros de Dios en el Cuarto Evangelio," *Greg* 94 (2013): 727–37, here 729.

[129] Josephus rejected the Samaritans' claim to belong to Israel (*Ant.* 11.291, 341; 12.257). Nevertheless, J. Bourgel ("Bretheren or Strangers? Samaritans in the Eyes of Second-Century BCE Jews," *Bib* 98 [2017]: 382–408) claims that in the late first and

nothing to do with Samaritans" (4:9).[130] The Samaritan woman also distinguishes between two places for worship, "on this mountain," according to "our fathers," and Jerusalem, according to "you" (4:20). Even Jesus makes clear this ethnic distinction: "you (ὑμεῖς) worship what you do not know; we (ἡμεῖς) worship what we know" and "salvation is from the Jews" (4:22).[131] These geographical and ethnic contexts shape four instances of universal language in the story: the offer of living water, the discussion about worship, the theme of mission, and the reference to Jesus as the savior of the world.

Jesus says to the woman that whoever (ὃς . . . ἂν) drinks of the water he gives will enjoy eternal life (ζωὴν αἰώνιον, 4:14). Jesus' offer is not restricted to people from Judea but is here extended to a woman in the town of Sychar. The phrasing of the invitation is indicative of a wide offer. Instead of saying "if you drink" and thus limiting his invitation to the Samaritan woman, Jesus says "whoever drinks" and thus suggests that the woman's own people can be included in this invitation.[132] The use of "whoever" might even be a call to the reader of the

---

early second century CE "the question of the Samaritans' status in relation to that of the Jews was still hotly debated and controversial."

[130] This clarification seems to presuppose a gentile readership (Lindars, *John*, 181; Lincoln, *John*, 172). The assertion that Jews have nothing to do with Samaritans might indicate that they were considered in between the gentile and the Jewish worlds (Lincoln, *John*, 172) or that they were regarded as gentiles by the Jews (Lindars, *John*, 181). However, it is likely that the Samaritans saw themselves as descendants of the house of Joseph and as part of the people of Israel. For this reading, see Hans Förster, "Die Begegnung am Brunnen (Joh 4.4-42) im Licht der 'Schrift': Überlegungen zu den Samaritanern im Johannesevangelium," *NTS* 61 (2015): 201–18.

[131] In distinction from Jesus' dialogue with Nicodemus, which lacks an emphasis on Jesus' relationship to Judaism, the dialogue with the Samaritan woman highlights this dimension of Jesus' identity. The statement found in 4:22 is not surprising for the reader because the official presentation of Jesus was made through Israel's Scriptures: "Make straight the way of the Lord" (1:23; Isa 40:3). Jesus has also been identified as the king of Israel (1:49) and has been consistently linked to Jewish tradition (1:17; 2:6, 16; 3:14). Jesus addresses the Samaritan woman as a Jew would address a gentile (Michaels, *John*, 251).

[132] This observation does not oppose the correctly remarked individualism of this episode specifically and of the Gospel of John generally. C. F. D. Moule, "The Individualism of the Fourth Gospel," in *Essays in New Testament Interpretation* (Cambridge: Cambridge University Press, 1982), 91–109, here 101–4; Okure, *Mission*, 130.

text.[133] In light of the previous context (3:1-35), Jesus not only offers life to the Samaritan woman, he gives her the opportunity of an effective entrance into the kingdom of God. Since Jesus gives the Spirit without measure (3:35), and since the Spirit is closely related to water in 3:5, Jesus' words to Nicodemus about entering the kingdom through a new birth of water and Spirit are actualized in his invitation to the Samaritan woman to drink of the water he gives for eternal life.

The conversation about water soon changes to a discussion about worship. The link between the two topics is the Spirit. As we observed in the previous paragraph, the noun πνεῦμα has already been associated with water in 3:5, and, therefore, "living water" in the story of the Samaritan woman may be a reference to the Spirit that Jesus gives without measure (3:34).[134] Jesus now says that God is πνεῦμα (4:24), and true worshipers worship in πνεῦμα and truth (4:23-24). Although Jesus clearly states that salvation is from the Jews (4:22), he does not ask the Samaritan woman to become a member of those who worship in Jerusalem but to drink from the water he offers.[135] Notwithstanding the clear distinctions between the two ethnic groups, Jesus does not identify true worshipers with those traditionally associated with Judaism and false worshipers with Samaritans. There is no division here between Israel worshiping in the north and Judeans worshiping

---

[133] Michaels, *John*, 245; Anne Fortin, "Jésus et les gens de Samarie," *SémiotBib* 157 (2015): 15–33. A wider meaning for "whoever" is supported by looking at 3:16 in comparison with 4:14. Since τὸ ὕδωρ . . . γενήσεται ἐν αὐτῷ πηγή . . . εἰς ζωὴν αἰώνιον (4:14) corresponds to ἔχῃ ζωὴν αἰώνιον (3:16), οὐ μὴ διψήσει εἰς τὸν αἰῶνα ἀλλά (4:14) to μὴ ἀπόληται ἀλλ᾽ (3:16), and πίῃ ἐκ τοῦ ὕδατος οὗ ἐγὼ δώσω αὐτῷ (4:14) to ἵνα πᾶς ὁ πιστεύων εἰς αὐτόν (3:16), the phrase ὃς δ᾽ ἄν (4:14) should be equivalent to ἠγάπησεν ὁ θεὸς τὸν κόσμον (3:16).

[134] This reading is later confirmed by 6:63; 7:38-39; 14:26; 16:13. Larry Paul Jones, *The Symbol of Water in the Gospel of John*, JSNTSup 145 (Sheffield: Sheffield Academic, 1997), 113; Ruben Zimmermann, "From a Jewish Man to the Savior of the World: Narrative and Symbols Forming a Step by Step Christology in John 4,1-42," in Verheyden, van Oyen, Labahn, and Bieringer, *Studies in the Gospel of John and Its Christology*, 99–118, here 115.

[135] Michaels, *John*, 252.

in the south.[136] Through Jesus true worshipers will worship the Father in πνεῦμα and truth wherever they are.[137]

Jesus' denial of the importance of a particular place for proper worship extends even to the future. Those who will worship the Father are not going to be tied to a specific sacred place (4:20-21).[138] The initial reading of the cleansing of the temple in 2:13-22 was somehow ambiguous. On the one hand, if Jesus is purifying the temple, he is supporting proper worship there not only for Jews but also for those who only had access to the court of the gentiles. On the other hand, if Jesus asks to destroy the temple (2:19), one may well imagine that he was challenging the centrality of this religious symbol as a place of proper worship. This ambiguity is partially resolved in this dialogue. Jerusalem will not be the proper place to offer worship to the Father (4:21).[139] Adequate worship does not stem from past religious traditions

[136] This "mountain" (ὄρει) is a reference to Mount Gerizim. The Greek version of Deut 11:29 has "you shall give the blessing on Mount Garizin (ὄρος Γαριζιν; MT הר גרזים)." Evidence for the association of Samaritans with this mountain is found in a stele from Delos dating between 150 and 50 BCE, Οἱ ἐν Δήλος Ἰσραελεῖται οἱ ἀπαρχόμενοι εἰς ἱερὸν Ἀργαριζείν. The word Ἀργαριζείν comes from the Hebrew *Har Garizim* and should be translated "Mount Gerizim." This is suggested by P. Bruneau, "Les Israélites de Délos et la juiverie délienne," *BCH* 106 (1982): 465–504, here 471 (*sacré Gerizim*). This suggestion is followed in S. R. Llewelyn, ed., *A Review of the Greek Inscriptions and Papyri Published 1984–85*, NewDocs 8 (Grand Rapids: Eerdmans, 1998), 148. A. T. Kraabel ("New Evidence of the Samaritan Diaspora Has Been Found on Delos," *BA* 47 [1984]: 44–46, here 45) observes that the Samaritans behind this inscription called themselves "Israelites" because they wanted to lay claim on their heritance as "those from (the Northern Kingdom) of Israel."

[137] Beutler, *Johannesevangelium*, 168.

[138] Schnackenburg, *John*, 1:434. The absolute "the Father" should "not be taken to mean worship of the universal Father in a non-sectarian . . . way" (Lindars, *John*, 188), since the Gospel of John has already stressed the need of believing in Jesus (3:16-19).

[139] However, this will happen in the future. This is indicated by the double repetition of the phrase "the hour is coming" (ἔρχεται ὥρα, 4:21, 23) and the future tense προσκυνήσουσιν in 4:23. At the same time, the indication that the "hour is now here" (4:23) points to a present dimension of such a worship. The previous subtle reference to Jesus' hour as indicative of the manifestation of his glory (2:4, 11) and the conceptual association between the raising up (ἐγερῶ) of the temple (2:19) and the Son of Man being lifted up (ὑψωθῆναι, 3:14) support this double dimension. Jesus' hour has not yet come (2:4), the temple will be raised up in three days (2:19), the Son of Man will be lifted up (3:14), and true worshipers will no longer worship in Jerusalem (4:21).

but from the future:[140] "The hour is coming, and is now here, when the true worshipers will worship the Father in spirit and truth" (4:23). Far from encouraging the woman to travel to Jerusalem or to the Samaritan mountain to worship the Father, he points to himself as the proper place to encounter God.

The woman embraced Jesus' message[141] about living water, which represents the Spirit that he gives without measure. The Samaritans believed in Jesus' words and accepted her testimony, fulfilling the earlier statement: "Whoever receives Jesus' testimony certifies that God is true" (3:33). They are true worshipers (4:20). Since they can be counted among those who are "born of the Spirit," the enigmatic saying found in 3:8 is fulfilled in them: "The wind blows where it wishes, and you hear its sound, but you do not know where it comes from or where it goes."[142] It is not possible to find a particular location where worship offered by true worshipers takes place. They worship in πνεῦμα. Those who do not believe ("you do not know," 3:8) are unable to guess the true origin and destiny of those who worship in such a way. The woman and her fellow Samaritans are actually those who worship the Father in πνεῦμα and truth in Samaria.[143] The identity of such worshipers goes beyond ethnicity.

The dialogue between Jesus and the Samaritan woman is interrupted by the arrival of the disciples. Their offering of food to Jesus

---

Yet Jesus manifested his glory in Galilee (2:11), and the hour for true worshipers to worship the Father in πνεῦμα and truth "is now here," available through him (4:23).

[140] Zumstein, *Johannesevangelium*, 181. Schnelle (*Johannes*, 126) calls this a "universal worship" that does not allow discrimination in terms of religion, nationality, or gender.

[141] It remains a possible reading of her leaving her water jar in 4:28 as indicative of her reception of the true water that Jesus offers. Cf. Zimmermann, "Savior of the World," in Verheyden, van Oyen, Labah, and Bieringer, *Studies in the Gospel of John and Its Christology*, 116: "Her jar is too small to hold this universal meaning of the living water." See also Janeth Norfleete Day, *The Woman at the Well: Interpretation of John 4:1–42 in Retrospect and Prospect*, BibInt 61 (Leiden: Brill, 2002), 173.

[142] Thompson, *John*, 105.

[143] The plural "you" in 4:21 refers in context to the Samaritan people, according to Lindars, *John*, 188.

prompts a teaching about mission (4:31-38).[144] Jesus initially hinted at this topic in 4:23, where he portrayed the Father in a mission: "for such [worshipers] the Father seeks (ζητεῖ) to worship him" (4:23).[145] Similarly, Jesus fulfills his mission in his encounter with the woman from Samaria. Since Jesus' mission concerns the whole world,[146] his encounter in Samaria is an illustration of the comprehensive scope of his earthly ministry. Jesus' existence, his "food," is to do the will of him who sent him (τοῦ πέμψαντος) and to accomplish his work (4:34).[147] This is precisely what he has been doing in Sychar, since he offered a woman living water for eternal life (ζωὴν αἰώνιον, 4:14).[148] In turn, the Samaritan woman brings to Jesus his "true food" because through her testimony many Samaritans believed in and came to Jesus (4:39).[149] Jesus invites his disciples to be part of this mission to the world that he has started to accomplish.[150] Jesus encourages them to lift up their eyes and see that the fields are white for harvest (4:35), sends (ἀπέστειλα) them to reap that for which they did not labor, and indicates that they have entered the labor of others (4:38).[151] Since the

---

[144] The whole section (4:1-42) offers a "deliberate, sustained and consistent effort on the part of the Evangelist to emphasize Jesus' unique and exclusive role in the missionary enterprise" (Okure, *Mission*, 286).

[145] Benny Thettayil, *In Spirit and Truth: An Exegetical Study of John 4:19-26 and a Theological Investigation of the Replacement Theme in the Fourth Gospel*, CBET 46 (Leuven: Peeters, 2007), 119: "In the Scriptural tradition, we do not hear of God seeking worshipers and a movement from God in which [he] seeks the worshiper is a new notion."

[146] The true light gives light to everyone (1:9). Jesus is the Lamb of God who takes away the sin of the world (1:29). The Father sent (ἀπέστειλεν) his Son into the world so that the world might have eternal life (3:16-17).

[147] Okure (*Mission*, 104) takes Jesus' thirst in 4:7 to mean Jesus' "longing to accomplish the Father's work" because "Jesus lives for his mission" (105).

[148] Thompson, *John*, 108.

[149] Lincoln, *John*, 180.

[150] Schnackenburg (*John*, 1:449) identifies the "white fields" with "the approaching Samaritans" in "their white garments." Michaels (*John*, 263) prefers to take "white" as indicative of maturity, as in "white hair of old age," or redemption (purity).

[151] The suggestion that the "only mission hitherto mentioned in the Gospel" is that of John and his followers is found in John A. T. Robinson, "The 'Others' of John 4, 38: A Test of Exegetical Method," in *Studia Evangelica* 1 (1959): 510–15, here 512. This, however, ignores that Jesus' dialogue with the Samaritan woman is part of Jesus'

mission of the Father through the Son has concerned the whole world (3:16-17), the labor the disciples are entering should also be comprehensive in scope.[152]

The immediate fruit that they will gather is the many Samaritans that believed in Jesus (4:39, 41)[153] through the testimony of the woman.[154] At the end of the story (4:28-30, 39-42), her actions resemble the mission that the Baptist fulfilled earlier, that is, giving testimony so that others may believe. Since the story of the Samaritan woman is immediately preceded by a reference to John (3:22-36), the reader is inclined to compare both testimonies. The universal significance of John the Baptist's testimony was introduced early in the Gospel. He is said to have come as a witness (μαρτυρίαν) to bear witness (μαρτυρήσῃ) about the light, that all might believe through him (ἵνα πάντες πιστεύσωσιν δι᾽ αὐτοῦ, 1:7). Similarly, the Samaritan woman testifies to the people of her town about Jesus (4:29). As a result, they went out of their town and came to him (4:30). The narrator clarifies that "many Samaritans believed (πολλοὶ ἐπίστευσαν) in him because of her testimony (διὰ τὸν λόγον τῆς γυναικὸς μαρτυρούσης)" (4:39). The prologue has promised that all (ὅσοι) who receive Jesus and believe (τοῖς πιστεύουσιν) in his name receive the right to become children of God (1:12). This familial relationship with God is not acquired by ethnic affiliation ("not by blood or by the will of the flesh nor the will of man, but of God," 1:13). Many Samaritans received Jesus and the testimony about him (4:40) and believed (ἐπίστευσαν) in him. The idea of "believing" is repeated three times in 4:39-42 to encourage the conclusion that the Samaritans became children of God.[155]

---

mission of completing the works of his Father (4:34). Cf. Schnackenburg (*John*, 1:453), who rejects the possibility that the Father has been working. For the opposite interpretation, which I find more likely, see Okure, *Mission*, 286.

[152] Schnelle, *Johannes*, 131. The phrase "I sent you" (4:38) resembles the sending of the Son in 3:17, God sent his Son into the world so that the world might be saved.

[153] Lincoln, *John*, 180.

[154] Okure (*Mission*, 168) even suggests that the disciples in mission are represented by the Samaritan woman.

[155] Esther Kobel, *Dining with John: Communal Meals and Identity Formation in the Fourth Gospel and Its Historical and Cultural Context*, BibInt 109 (Leiden: Brill, 2011), 74; Conway, *Men and Women*, 125. For the possibility that the phrase "children

The identification of the Samaritans as part of the "world" is made explicit in their acclamation of Jesus as the savior of the world in 4:42. The Samaritans asked Jesus to stay with them, and he stayed two days in Samaria before leaving for Galilee (4:40, 43). This recalls the opening section of the Gospel: "The Word became flesh and dwelt among us" (1:14). Jesus' further interactions with the Samaritans during these two days led them to conclude that he is "indeed the savior of the world" (4:42).[156] The "universal scope of the worship mediated" by Jesus corresponds to the "universal salvation embodied in Jesus."[157] The Samaritans are portrayed giving testimony to something that is truth in the narrative world of the Evangelist because Jesus has been introduced as taking an active role in the creation of the world (1:3, 10), entering the world for its salvation (3:17),[158] and having authority over all things (3:31).[159] The Samaritans also function as witnesses for the reader about the universal significance of Jesus and the message about him. Just as John witnessed that Jesus is the Lamb of God who takes away the sin of the world (1:29), the Samaritans confess that he is the savior of the world (4:42).[160] The initial (and correct) judgment of the

---

of God" echoes the Stoic conception of God as the father of humankind, see Dietrich Rusam, "Die Samen- und Vererbungslehre der Stoa als religionsgeschichtlicher Hintergrund für die Bezeichnung der Glaubenden im Johanneischen Schrifttum," *BZ* 59 (2015): 279–87.

[156] Although the text does not indicate what Jesus taught to the Samaritans during his stay with them (4:40), their conclusion that he is the savior of the world might reflect part of Jesus' teaching to them (Michaels, *John*, 270).

[157] Lincoln, *John*, 181. See also Keener, *John*, 1:627.

[158] The formula "savior of the world" should be taken as more than short for "the one coming into the world," according to Reinhartz, *Word*, 30.

[159] At the same time, the confession found in 4:42 recalls 4:22, according to Marion Moser, *Schriftdiskurse im Johannesevangelium: Eine narrative-intertextuelle Analyse am Paradigma von Joh 4 und Joh 7*, WUNT 2/380 (Tübingen: Mohr Siebeck, 2014), 72.

[160] Some scholars have observed that the Assyrians imported five nations after the destruction of Samaria in 722 BCE (2 Kgs 17:24). More recently, Zimmermann, "Savior of the World," in Verheyden, van Oyen, Labah, and Bieringer, *Studies in the Gospel of John and Its Christology*, 110. Some even argue that the "five husbands" of the Samaritan woman in 4:18 point to those nations (e.g., Michaels, *John*, 247), but this interpretation has been opposed by others (e.g., Barrett, *John*, 235). If John intended to evoke those five nations, Jesus' universal significance in this narrative is even clearer. Dodd (*Interpretation*, 317) even claims that the Samaritans represent the gentile world in the Gospel of John.

Samaritan woman that Jesus was a Jew (4:9) is amplified at the end of
the story by the Samaritans' confession that Jesus' soteriological import
reaches the whole world.[161]
This acclamation is intentionally ambiguous in terms of its background. A case can be made to relate it to Christian tradition previous to the writing of the Gospel (e.g., Rom 1:8; Heb 7:25),[162] ancient
Judaism (e.g., Wis 16:7; Philo, *Fug.* 162; *Spec.* 2.198),[163] pagan religions
(e.g., Epictetus, *Diatr.* 1.22.6)[164] or imperial traditions,[165] or even public
benefactors.[166] A wide readership might find connections between this
designation and its own peculiar experiences of saviors. The Samaritans, however, acknowledge that Jesus is truly (ἀληθῶς) the savior of
the world.[167] The selection of this phrase is then strategic since it resonates meaningfully in Jewish and Hellenistic contexts.[168]

An Official in Galilee

The third encounter focuses on a distinctive character. The official is a
man but he is not a religious leader. His identification is not shaped by

[161] Haenchen, *John 1*, 226; Zimmermann, "Savior of the World," in Verheyden,
van Oyen, Labah, and Bieringer, *Studies in the Gospel of John and Its Christology*, 111.

[162] Hoskyns, *Fourth Gospel*, 248.

[163] Barrett, *John*, 244; Thompson, *John*, 109.

[164] George Long, *The Discourses of Epictetus with the Encheiridion and Fragments*
(New York: A. L. Burt, 1900), 74: "Why then do we build temples, why set up statues
to Zeus . . . and how is Zeus the Savior?" Schnelle (*Johannes*, 130) suggests that the
identification of Jesus as savior of the world was the result of Hellenistic influence in
Christianity. See also Arthur Darby Nock, *Early Gentile Christianity and Its Hellenistic
Background* (New York: Harper & Row, 1964), 36–44.

[165] C. R. Koester, "'The Savior of the World' (John 4:42)," *JBL* 109 (1990): 665–80.
This title was associated with worldwide dominion and was applied to several imperial
figures, e.g., Julius Caesar, Claudius, Augustus, Nero, Vespasian, Trajan. See also Sjef
van Tilborg, *Reading John in Ephesus*, NovTSup 83 (Leiden: E. J. Brill, 1996), 47–48.

[166] An inscription from Cilicia (second century CE) states that Demas' work in
public office was "for the salvation of the people (ἐπὶ σωτηρίαι τοῦ δήμου)." The text
is found in J. R. Harrison's section of S. R. Llewelyn, ed., *A Review of the Greek Inscriptions and Papyri Published in 1986–87*, NewDocs 9 (Grand Rapids: Eerdmans, 2002), 4.

[167] Thompson, *John*, 110.

[168] The Hellenistic background of this phrase is investigated in M. Karrer, "Jesus,
der Retter (Sōtēr): Zur Aufnahme eines hellenistischen Prädikats in Neuen Testament," *ZNW* 93 (2002): 153–76.

his religious affiliation (3:1) or his marital status (4:17). He is a father (ὁ πατήρ, 4:53), with a household and servants, whose son is ill. Since this father was in Capernaum (4:46),[169] his story demonstrates that the offer of living water is extended to people in Galilee.[170] The story then illustrates the claim made earlier by the Samaritans: Jesus is indeed the savior of the world.[171] Although there is a previous miracle that took place in Cana (2:1-12), this is the first time that the narrator describes Jesus' reception in Galilee apart from his family and disciples.[172]

The story is introduced by Jesus' warm reception in Galilee (4:45), which contrasts with Jesus' negative judgment that a prophet has no honor in his own hometown (4:44). The impression so far is that the more Jesus leaves Jerusalem, the warmer his reception is (4:40, 45).[173] This positive reception in that northern region stems from what he did in Jerusalem "at the feast" (4:45). So far in the narrative, the only visit to Jerusalem for a festival is found in 2:13 (Passover), where Jesus performed many signs (2:23). The mention of such a visit recalls the incident in the temple where Jesus cleansed his Father's house, most likely the court of the gentiles. Jesus demonstrated his zeal by echoing

[169] The identification of this man as "gentile" (thus Barrett, *John*, 196) is not explicit in the narrative. The similarities between this story and Matt 8:5-13 and Luke 7:1-10 might support the idea that he was a gentile. However, Jesus seems to include him among the Galilean Jews in his rebuke: "Unless *you* see signs and wonders you will not believe" (4:48). Furthermore, the noun βασιλικός is used in other texts to refer to someone who works for a king (e.g., Josephus, *J.W.* 1.45; *Life* 400–401). Since Herod Antipas (4 BCE–38 CE), a Jew, is ironically called king in Mark 6:14, it is expected that his servants may be called "officials." In any case, the possibility that this man was a gentile cannot be ruled out (Lindars, *John*, 202). See also A. H. Mead, "The βασιλικός in John 4.46-53," *JSNT* 23 (1985): 69–72. I submit that the point of the lack of clarity about the ethnic background of this official is that readers, both Jews and gentiles, can identify with him. Michaels (*John*, 281), similarly, suggests that readers can identify with the faith journey of this man.

[170] Lindars, *John*, 198; Schnelle, *Johannes*, 133.

[171] Thompson, *John*, 110.

[172] Schnackenburg, *John*, 1:464. Philip, from Bethsaida, became a follower of Jesus. Nathanael identified Jesus as king of Israel (1:43-49). Although Andrew and Peter are also from Bethsaida, the description of their calling to discipleship lacks an explicit interest in their geographical location (1:35-42, 44).

[173] This does not mean, however, that those who welcomed Jesus had an appropriate faith in him (2:23-25; 4:48), according to Bultmann, *John*, 204; Lincoln, *John*, 185.

Zechariah 14:21, a text embedded in a larger context that predicts that "the Lord will become king (βασιλέα) over all the earth" (14:9) and that peoples from many nations will do obeisance to the King (14:16, τῷ βασιλεῖ). Nathanael has also identified Jesus as the King (βασιλεύς) of Israel in Galilee (1:43, 49).

This larger context makes the portrayal of the βασιλικός from Capernaum indicative of Jesus' authority even over those who were thought to have political power on earth.[174] He approaches Jesus (4:47), refers to him with respect (κύριε, 4:49), and believes (ἐπίστευσεν) Jesus' words (4:50). Even his household believes (ἐπίστευσεν) in him (4:53).[175] The object of his initial faith is Jesus' words about the healing of his son. The second instance, however, lacks an explicit object. The reader is invited to supply "in him," as an indication that this official, just as the many Samaritans from the previous story (4:39)[176] also believed in Jesus.[177] A further link between this story and the dialogue with the Samaritan woman is the verb ζάω ("to live," 4:50, 51, 53).[178] The verb might have two meanings. It initially refers to the physical restoration of the official's son, but, upon further consideration, it might also refer to the larger idea of salvation or eternal life.[179] This further

---

[174] Michaels, *John*, 275; Fuglseth, *Sectarianism*, 296–97.

[175] Several commentators (e.g., Barrett, *John*, 248; Lindars, *John*, 205; Bultmann, *John*, 208–9; Keener, *John*, 1:633; Schnelle, *Johannes*, 135) find that "household" is used in early Christian missionary tradition (Acts 10:12; 11:14; 16:15, 31-34; 18:8; Rom 16:5; 1 Cor 1:16; Phil 2). Therefore, they find a missionary motif here.

[176] The phrase "in him" is lacking in 4:39 according to Sinaiticus.

[177] Schnelle (*Johannes*, 132) sees a progression in terms of people believing in Jesus: the disciples (2:11), people in Jerusalem (2:23), Samaritans (4:39), and the official and his household (4:53). For Beutler, *Johannesevangelium*, 172, this section shows that those "in the margins" embrace Jesus while those associated with the center of religious life in Jerusalem (e.g., religious authorities in 1:19 and Nicodemus in 3:1) are not said to have believed in Jesus

[178] This threefold repetition has been noted in Schnelle, *Johannes*, 132; and Beutler, *Johannesevangelium*, 178. For Thompson (*John*, 114), the faith of the official leading to all his household believing in Jesus also resembles the Samaritan woman leading her fellow Samaritans to Jesus (4:29).

[179] Lindars, *John*, 204. See also, Hoskyns, *Fourth Gospel*, 262; Schnackenburg, *John*, 1:464; Haenchen, *John 1*, 235; and Thompson, *John*, 110–11.

meaning is supported by the previous use of the participle form in the phrase "living water (ζῶν)" in 4:10-11.

This healing also recalls Jesus' words to Nicodemus: "As Moses lifted up the serpent in the wilderness, so must the Son of Man be lifted up, that whoever (πᾶς) believes (ὁ πιστεύων) in him may have eternal life" (3:14-15). Since this βασιλικός serves the political powers, he can be taken as a representative of the world.[180] Therefore, he is a clear example that God loved the world and gave his Son that whoever believes in him may have eternal life (3:16). This healing also recalls the first introduction of Jesus as Word (ὁ λόγος, 1:1, 14) since we learn that life was in him (ζωή, 1:4).[181] The official believed the word (τῷ λόγῳ, 4:50) and his son received life (ζῇ, 4:51). Jesus has power over death because, as the Father has life in himself, the Father also gave authority to the Son to have life in himself.[182]

This story completes a geographical sequence that shows that Jesus is the owner of creation. He did not come to foreign territory. He entered the same world God loves in order to offer the possibility of its salvation (3:16-17). The Samaritans capture this sense by acclaiming him as the savior of the world. Furthermore, the official in Galilee, as a representative of the world, obtains life for him and his family through believing in Jesus.[183]

SYNTHESIS

Jesus is introduced to the reader in the prologue, to religious leaders through the testimony of the Baptist, and to pilgrims in Jerusalem through the temple incident. All three presentations have in common several instances of universal language. The portrayal of the Word as taking an active role in the whole act of creation serves the important purpose of securing his unique role as the one who comes from the

---

[180] The noun βασιλικός can mean "a person of royal blood" or "a royal official" (BDAG, 170; Barrett, *John*, 247).

[181] Beutler, *Johannesevangelium*, 178; Dodd, *Interpretation*, 318.

[182] Schnelle, *Johannes*, 135. See also Zumstein, *Johannesevangelium*, 204.

[183] Lindars, *John*, 200; Fuglseth, *Sectarianism*, 300.

Father to offer a proper relationship with God.[184] The Word enters the world that belongs to him, but, ironically, the world did not know him and actively rejected him. Conversely, Jesus does not reject his creation but gives believers the right to become children of God. The narrator uses several strategies to convey the import of Jesus' universal significance in his *preexistence*. First, he begins the story of the Word before creation to clarify that his story is set within a cosmic setting. Second, he shapes the identity of the Word in his unique relationship with God. There is no particular group that can claim exclusive ownership of the Word because he alone was with God in the beginning. Third, the narrator uses commonplace words that find resonances with a variety of readers. The use of nouns such as "life," "light," or "humanity" might be intended to appeal to a wide readership. Even his selection of the noun "flesh" to indicate the incarnation of the Word may be intended to show solidarity with humanity as a whole. Fourth, the narrator depicts an original unified world where humanity has no division. They were all created by the Word and enjoyed life and light in him.

The Baptist's presentation of Jesus resonates with that of the narrator. There is no dissonance in their testimony about the universal significance of Jesus. This dimension of Jesus' significance is actually at the core of John the Baptist's testimony. He uses Jewish tradition to assert the *present* universal significance of Jesus in his testimony to Israel. At the same time, his testimony is intended to reach all people. The preservation of his testimony in the Gospel warrants the fulfillment of his universal mission. The Baptist uses several strategies to convey universal language. First, he quotes Isa 40:3 to shape his own mission on earth. The larger context of this text emphasizes the universal significance of God in his eschatological role as judge of the nations. Second, he uses the Jewish imagery of a Lamb to depict Jesus as taking away the sin of the world. The whole world is the beneficiary

---

[184] Andreas Lindemann ("*Orbis Romanus* und OIKOΥMENH: Römischer und urchristlicher Universalismus," in *Christ and the Emperor: The Gospel Evidence*, ed. Gilbert Van Belle and Joseph Verheyden, BTS 20 [Leuven: Peeters, 2014], 51–100, here 91), writes about "eine 'universale' christologische Perspektive" in the Johannine prologue (1:1-18) that stems from the Word's role in creation.

of Jesus' salvific action. Third, the Baptist says that Jesus is above all and all things are in his hands.

Jesus introduces himself in Jerusalem through a dramatic act in the temple. A case can be made to read this episode as indicative of the comprehensive scope of Jesus' significance. The use of universal language, however, is implicit in the narrative and might be detected only by a competent reader acquainted with the traditions that also shaped the Synoptic Gospels. Two observations support this possible reading. First, the episode likely took place in the court of the gentiles. Jesus at least shows concern for people who came to Jerusalem and had access only to this area in the temple. Second, the use of Psalm 69:10, Jesus' zeal directed toward those who sold animals, and the explicit comment that Jesus was talking about the temple of his body at least leave the reader wondering about the proper place and form to worship God. Although this issue is not fully resolved in this episode, the reader at least ponders whether a proper encounter between God and humanity (worshipers in Jerusalem and visitors to the temple) can take place only through Jesus.

Jesus is then depicted in three different regions talking to specific individuals. Collectively, the main episodes in John 3:1–4:54 show three dimensions of Jesus' universal significance.[185] First, Jesus teaches in territory that has been his since the beginning, because the Father has given him all things into his hand. Second, the love of God extends to the whole world, and it is manifested in his offering of salvation through his only Son. Third, Jesus is the savior of the world, who interacts with people from diverse geographical, cultural, and religious backgrounds. The narrator uses several strategies to deploy instances of universal language in this section. First, there is a clear progression from Jerusalem and Judea to Samaria and, from there, to Galilee where Jesus interacts with individuals who represent religious leaders (Nicodemus), the Samaritans (a woman), and the political powers (an official). Jesus' use of universal language in these three episodes coheres

---

[185] The dialogues also show the narrator's concern for dialoguing with several religious traditions represented in the first century, according to Christian Grappe, "Le debut du quatrième évangile (*Jean* 2 à 5), témoin d'un dialogue avec d'autres traditions religieuses?" *RHPR* 96 (2016): 113–25.

with what the narrator introduced in the prologue.[186] Second, Jesus uses Jewish imagery with wider application. The serpent in the desert is used to teach about God's love for the whole world. Jesus also uses the topic of worship to advance the claim that a proper encounter between God and humanity does not depend on a particular geographical place such as Jerusalem or a particular group of people such as people from Jerusalem. The Father seeks worshipers who worship in πνεῦμα and truth.

---

[186] The reading of John 3:16-17 and 4:42 in the light of the Johannine prologue is not idiosyncratic. It is noteworthy that the earliest reception of this Gospel, i.e., 1 John, puts together language that resembles the introductory section of the Gospel, John 3:16, and John 4:42. The author behind 1 John indicates that "the love of God was made manifest among us" in God sending "his only Son into the world, so that we might live through him" (1 John 4:9) and that "the Father has sent his Son to be the savior of the world" (1 John 4:14) in a context where echoes of the Johannine prologue are prominent: "little children" (1 John 4:4; John 1:12-13), "being born of God" (1 John 4:7; John 1:12-13), "no one has ever seen God" (1 John 4:12; John 1:18).

2

THE ENLIGHTENMENT OF HUMANITY

The introduction of the Word as actively involved in the creation of the world and the portrayal of Jesus encountering representative individuals in Judea, Samaria, and Galilee—territory that has been his since the beginning—were intended to highlight the comprehensive scope of Jesus' significance. The following controversies and discourses[1] advance such a presentation in significant ways. Cumulatively, this Johannine section highlights that the unlimited measure of the Father's revelation to Jesus authorizes him to enlighten humanity with the light of life. Jesus reveals the dramatic condition of the world, exposing its estrangement from God. Those who embrace Jesus obtain eternal life. Some, however, reject the enlightenment Jesus provides, and the light therefore becomes judgment for them.

The first three sets of discussions and discourses in John 5–9 center on Jewish tradition. The healing of a man triggers an argument about Jesus' authority to work on the Sabbath. The provision of food for a multitude close to the time of Passover elicits a discourse about Jesus as the bread from heaven. His brothers' invitation to celebrate the Feast of Tabernacles in Jerusalem allows him to identify himself with the light of the world. The following two sets of dialogues and

---

[1] These are found in John 5–12, which is the second major section of the first half of the Gospel of John.

discourses in John 10–12 focus on him as the shepherd who has other sheep who will hear his voice and on the possibility for Greeks to be attracted to him.[2] Overall, the narrator situates Jesus' death as the epicenter of reconciliation between God and humanity, extends Jesus' judgment to the ruler of the world, and emphasizes that Jesus' universal significance transcends his earthly ministry since it will be effective even in the future.

DISCUSSIONS WITH RELIGIOUS LEADERS

The first miracle performed by Jesus that took place during the Sabbath gives rise to discussions with religious leaders (5:1-47). Although they are initially identified with the blanket label "the Jews" (5:10, 15, 16, 18), Jesus indicates that they are those who were "sent to John" asking about his identity (5:33). They were priests and Levites from Jerusalem (1:19). Jesus' audience in his discourse after the provision of food for a multitude in Galilee also includes religious leaders. Although the miracle in the Sea of Tiberias was for the benefit of many people, the reader learns—almost at the end of the ensuing discussion—that the debate took place in the synagogue in Capernaum (6:59). Jesus' audience is referred to as "the crowd" (6:22, 24) or "the Jews" (6:41, 52), but the synagogue setting indicates that religious leaders might have been behind the questioning of Jesus. Several people interact with Jesus in John 7–9. They include his brothers (7:3-4), the Jews (7:15, 35; 8:22, 48, 52), Jews who believed in him (8:30-31), the crowd (7:20, 31, 40, 43, 44), some of the people of Jerusalem (7:25), the Pharisees (7:32; 8:13; 9:40), officers (7:45), and his disciples (9:2). Religious leaders, however, hold a prominent place. They act after noticing that the crowd was muttering concerning Jesus' teaching and identity (7:32, 45-49).

Works on the Sabbath

The first healing in Jerusalem takes place on the Sabbath (5:9, 10, 16), by the pool of Bethesda (5:2). Jesus selects a man who has been sick

---

[2] These chapters (John 10–12) are also related to Jewish tradition since there are references to Jewish festivals in 10:22; 11:55; 12:12 and the Old Testament in 10:34; 12:13, 15, 34, 38-40.

for thirty-eight years and orders him to get up, take his bed, and walk (5:8, 11). The miracle story and Jesus' reply to those who questioned him move from particular to universal and back to particular. The story is particular because it takes place in Jerusalem during a feast of the Jews (5:1).[3] The issue has to do with a specific component of Jewish tradition, the Sabbath (5:9, 16). Jesus' reply to those who question him (5:17), however, highlights that he has received universal authority from his Father. At the end of his intervention, we are back to particular when Jesus refers to the Scriptures and Moses (5:39, 45-46).[4] His offer of salvation is extended to his Jewish audience ("I say these things so that *you* may be saved [σωθῆτε]," 5:34), but it is not restricted to them. The goal of his mission is broader in scope: "in order that the world might be saved (σωθῇ)" (3:17). The focus in the following paragraphs will be on the universal components of Jesus' discourse in John 5.

The universal significance of Jesus and the message about him in the discussion following the miracle stems from the unlimited measure of revelation that the Son has received from his Father.[5] On the one hand, the Father shows the Son all (πάντα) that he himself is doing because he loves (φιλεῖ) him (5:20). On the other hand, the Son does what he sees his Father doing; he can do nothing (οὐδέν) of his own accord (5:19). The first instance where πάντα and οὐδέν were used side by side was in the opening section of the Gospel. There, the universality of the Word in creation was expressed by referring

---

[3] There is no explicit identification of this feast. Commentators such as Raymond Brown (*The Gospel according to John*, 2 vols., AB 29 [Garden City, N.Y.: Doubleday, 2000], 1:206), C. K. Barrett (*The Gospel according to St. John: An Introduction with Commentary and Notes on the Greek Text* [Philadelphia: Westminster, 1978], 251), and Craig S. Keener (*The Gospel of John: A Commentary* [Peabody, Mass.: Hendrickson, 2003], 1:635) suggest Purim, Pentecost, Tabernacles, or Rosh Hashanah.

[4] Similar literary movements were noticed in the stories of Nicodemus and the Samaritan woman. Jesus initially addresses Nicodemus individually, encouraging him to be born again (3:3) and using the tradition of the serpent in the wilderness to teach about salvation (3:14). Soon, however, instances of universal language take a prominent place: whoever believes in him may have eternal life (3:15), God loved the world (3:16), God sent his Son in order that the world might be saved through him (3:17). Likewise, Jesus initially offers the Samaritan woman living water (4:10) but soon the Samaritans will embrace Jesus as the savior of the world (4:42).

[5] Keener, *John*, 1:648.

to his involvement in the whole act of creation: "All things (πάντα) were made through him, and without him was not anything (οὐδὲ ἕν) made that was made" (1:3).⁶ The one who was involved in the creation of everything during his preexistence displays his universal authority during his earthly ministry. The present tense of the verbs "to do" (ποιεῖ) and "to show" (δείκνυσιν) in 5:19-20 indicates that Jesus received full revelation from his Father during his earthly ministry.⁷ The present reality and universal scope of this revelation is further clarified when looking at 5:19-20 in light of 3:35. John the Baptist claimed that the Father loves (ἀγαπᾷ) the Son and has given all things (πάντα) into his hand (3:35). Similarly, the love (φιλεῖ) that the Father has for his Son is translated in the unlimited endowment of revelation (πάντα) he gives to Jesus (5:20).⁸

The authority Jesus had during his earthly ministry is a clear reflection of God's own universal authority over the whole world. Jewish tradition consistently portrays God as the only source of life

---

⁶ Johannes Beutler, *Das Johannesevangelium: Kommentar* (Freiburg: Herder, 2013), 193. This similarity is even more striking in 𝔓⁶⁶, ουδε εν. Although the lack of εν in other manuscripts can be explained as an unintentional omission by a scribe when encountering two consecutive words beginning with ε (εν and εαν), it is better to follow the shorter reading attested in the majority of manuscripts. Curiously, instead of ουδε εν in 1:3, 𝔓⁶⁶ has ουδεν. Cf. the reading of 𝔓⁶⁶ in 5:30, ουδε εν. Marianne Meye Thompson (*John: A Commentary*, NTL [Louisville: Westminster John Knox, 2015], 127) also notes the similarity between 5:20 and 1:3 and concludes that these passages "lay the groundwork for Jesus' universal mission to all people." Rudolf Bultmann (*The Gospel of John: A Commentary*, trans. G. R. Beasley-Murray, R. W. N. Hoare, and J. K. Riches, The Johannine Monograph Series 1 [Eugene, Ore.: Wipf & Stock, 2014], 254) finds in the past tense of the verb "has given" in 5:36 a reference to Jesus' preexistence.

⁷ The relationship between the texts can be displayed as follows:

5:19 οὐ δύναται ὁ υἱὸς ποιεῖν ἀφ᾽ ἑαυτοῦ οὐδέν
    5:20 πάντα δείκνυσιν αὐτῷ
    1:3a πάντα δι᾽ αὐτοῦ ἐγένετο
1:3b χωρὶς αὐτοῦ ἐγένετο οὐδὲ ἕν

⁸ The parallelisms between 5:20, 24 and 3:35-36 are striking:

5:20 ὁ γὰρ πατὴρ φιλεῖ τὸν υἱὸν καὶ πάντα δείκνυσιν αὐτῷ ἃ αὐτὸς ποιεῖ
    5:24 ὁ . . . πιστεύων τῷ πέμψαντί με ἔχει ζωὴν αἰώνιον
3:35 ὁ πατὴρ ἀγαπᾷ τὸν υἱὸν καὶ πάντα δέδωκεν ἐν τῇ χειρὶ αὐτοῦ
    3:36 ὁ πιστεύων εἰς τὸν υἱὸν ἔχει ζωὴν αἰώνιον

for humanity and the only rightful judge of Israel and the nations (e.g., Isa 65–66; Zech 14).[9] The Gospel of John follows this theological conviction by asserting that the Father has life in himself (5:26) and has the power to raise (ἐγείρει) the dead and give them life (5:21). However, the Gospel of John also indicates that Jesus has in his hands the authority to give life (5:24) and to execute judgment (5:27). The restoration of one man among a multitude demonstrates that Jesus can give life to whomever he wants (5:3, 8, 21). The man who has been an invalid for thirty-eight years was "raised up" (ἔγειρε) as a picture of Jesus' authority to raise (ἐγείρω) the dead. The use of the plural "to whom (οὓς) he will" (5:21) indicates that the life he provides may be extended to others. His complete reflection of the Father's authority allows him to have full freedom to give life to whom he will.[10]

This power to give life was not limited to his earthly ministry. The future dimensions of Jesus' universal authority to give life are explicitly asserted.[11] Jesus himself predicts that "the hour is coming" when the dead will be resurrected either for life or for judgment (5:25-29). Although the phrase "the hour is coming" is immediately followed by "it is now here," the use of future-tense verbs indicates that he is referring to a resurrection that lies in the future.[12] This is more evident in the second instance of "the hour is coming" in 5:28, where the phrase "it is now here" is lacking. This second instance clearly refers to a future resurrection.[13] Those who believe in Jesus already receive life and they

[9] See also Marianne Meye Thompson, *The God of the Gospel of John* (Grand Rapids: Eerdmans, 2001), 73–80.

[10] Barrett, *John*, 260. Rudolf Schnackenburg (*The Gospel according to St. John*, 3 vols. [New York: Seabury, 1980], 2:106) correctly observes that this does not imply arbitrariness but authority. Those who were healed during Jesus' earthly ministry "are selected examples of what is to be universal at the end of the age" (Barnabas Lindars, *The Gospel of John: Based on the Revised Standard Version*, NCB [Grand Rapids: Eerdmans, 1981], 222).

[11] For J. Ramsey Michaels (*The Gospel of John*, NICNT [Grand Rapids: Eerdmans, 2010], 321) Jesus is here "Lord of the future."

[12] Troels Engberg-Pedersen, *John and Philosophy: A New Reading of the Fourth Gospel* (Oxford: Oxford University Press, 2017), 359n19. Edwyn Clement Hoskyns (*The Fourth Gospel*, ed. Francis Noel Davey [London: Faber and Faber, 1967], 268) takes this phrase to indicate that in "Jesus the world is confronted by the End."

[13] Barrett, *John*, 263.

will avoid the future judgment (5:24). Life and resurrection are already present in Jesus but will have full effect in the future when *all* will hear (πάντες ἀκούσουσιν) his voice (5:25, 28),[14] will come out of their tombs (5:29), and those who hear his voice will live (ζήσουσιν, 5:25).[15] These statements indicate that no one is outside the life-giving power of the Word.

At the same time, no one is outside God's judgment, because the Father has given the Son the sovereign right to execute all (πᾶσαν) judgment (5:22).[16] This is an unrestricted power to bring light to the world.[17] Jesus will summon all people, without exception, to judgment.[18] This absolute power does not mean independence from God. On the contrary, it reflects that Jesus fully partakes of divine prerogatives because the Father shows the Son all (πάντα) that he himself is doing (5:20). All the dead will hear the voice of the Son and will come out of their tombs. However, those who believe in Jesus will not come into judgment (5:24), but those who have done evil, in other words, those who reject Jesus as the revelation of the Father, will experience the resurrection of judgment (5:29). Using the symbolism of light introduced earlier in the Gospel (1:4-5; 3:16-21), it is possible to suggest that Jesus brings the light of life to the whole world. The rejection of this illumination produces judgment while its reception means eternal life (5:24). Jesus' authority then is universal in scope either to give life or to judge.

Jesus interprets the restoration of a man on a Sabbath by indicating that he works the works of his Father, and he does what his Father does (5:17, 19-20). This language is used again in 5:36 in reference to

[14] This presupposes that all humanity is actually dead (Schnackenburg, *John*, 2:111). Bultmann (*John*, 259) takes "the dead" as referring to "the men of the κόσμος." This includes those who have done good and those who have done evil works (Barrett, *John*, 263).

[15] According to Beutler (*Johannesevangelium*, 196), in the Gospel of John "to do good" means believing in the one sent by the Father and "to do evil" is refusing to embrace him (5:29).

[16] The idea that God judges all the earth was expressive of his universal dominion in Jewish tradition, e.g., Gen 18:25; Ps 82:8; Joel 3:1-2 (Lindars, *John*, 222).

[17] Udo Schnelle, *Das Evangelium nach Johannes*, THKNT 4 (Leipzig: Evangelische Verlagsanstalt, 2016), 145.

[18] Jean Zumstein, *Das Johannesevangelium*, ed. Dietrich-Alex Koch, KEKNT (Göttingen: Vandenhoeck & Ruprecht, 2016), 229.

his wider life-giving and judgment activities, and it evokes Jesus' mission on earth, specifically his words to his disciples in Samaria: "My food is to do (ποιήσω) the will (θέλημα) of him who sent me (τοῦ πέμψαντός με) and to accomplish (τελειώσω) his work (ἔργον)" (4:34). Jesus repeats in John 5 his own understanding of his mission indicating that he seeks the will (θέλημα) of him who sent him (τοῦ πέμψαντός με, 5:30) and that the works (ἔργα) that the Father has given him to accomplish (τελειώσω) bear witness that the Father has sent him (ὁ πατήρ με ἀπέσταλκεν, 5:36). The reading of the dialogues between Jesus and Nicodemus and between Jesus and the Samaritan woman led us to conclude that Jesus' mission concerns the whole world (3:16; 4:42; see also 1:9). The work of the Father is seeking people to worship him appropriately (4:23), and his will is that people may have eternal life (3:16). Jesus came to the world to look for appropriate worshippers in Judea, Samaria, and Galilee by providing a proper encounter between God and humanity. He received from the Father authority to give life and to execute judgment so that all (πάντες) may honor the Father by honoring the Son (5:23).

The all-encompassing authority of Jesus to execute judgment and to grant life stems from the unlimited measure of revelation he has received from the Father and will result in the Father and the Son receiving universal honor from humanity. The Father has given Jesus all (πᾶσαν) judgment so that all (πάντες) may honor the Son in the same way as they honor the Father (5:22-23). The word "all" implies "that the judgment is universal in scope," and the linkage between "judgment" (5:22) and "honor" (5:23) highlights that the universal execution of judgment has the glory of the Son as its goal.[19] The astonishing claim that "whoever does not honor the Son does not honor the Father who sent him" (5:23) illuminates the meaning of the temple incident.[20] One of the earlier stories that implicitly introduced Jesus' universal significance was the events in the temple (2:13-22). The reader

[19] Michaels, *John*, 313.
[20] There is a wide range of meanings associated with the verb τιμάω (e.g., "to estimate, to value" or "to honor"; BDAG, 1004). Since the literary context points to Jesus' full authority from the Father, the verb "to honor" should be allowed to carry here its full meaning, i.e., "to attribute high status to someone by honoring"; L&N, 735).

was left wondering about the implications of that incident. Where is the appropriate place to worship God? What is the relationship between the temple and the "destruction" and "raising" of Jesus' body? An initial answer to those questions was found in the dialogue between Jesus and the Samaritan woman. Ethnic distinctions or social location are not significant when it comes to worshiping the Father, since true worshipers will worship the Father in πνεῦμα and truth (4:23).[21] The meaning of the temple incident is further clarified with Jesus' remarks after the healing of a man in Jerusalem:[22] a proper encounter between God and humanity takes place through Jesus. The immediate audience in John 5 is invited to honor the Son, but the use of *all* extends the invitation to others. Samaritans can also become true worshipers that worship in πνεῦμα and truth. The remote audience, the reader, is also invited to honor the Father through honoring the Son.

Bread from Heaven

After the miracle and discussion in Jerusalem in John 5, the narrator now moves to the Sea of Tiberias in John 6. There Jesus also performs a miracle and has a discussion with religious leaders. In distinction from the miracle in Jerusalem, where only one person was the beneficiary of Jesus' actions, in Galilee Jesus provides food for a large crowd (6:1, 5, 14). Both stories and discussions take place during a feast of the Jews (5:1; 6:4).

This discussion also moves from particular to universal. It is particular because it takes place between Jesus and his Jewish people in a synagogue in Capernaum (6:24, 59), they both quote Israel's Scriptures (6:31, 45), and they discuss Jewish tradition.[23] However, Jesus uses uni-

---

[21] By using the phrase "an hour is coming" (5:25, 28), the narrator is intentionally reminding the reader of Jesus' dialogue with the Samaritan woman (4:23). Thus, Bultmann, *John*, 259; Lindars, *John*, 224; Michaels, *John*, 316.

[22] After the healing of a man in Jerusalem, Jesus finds him "in the temple" (ἐν τῷ ἱερῷ, 5:14). There might be a connection between Jesus as the Lamb of God who takes away the "sin of the world" (1:29) and his interaction with this man: "sin no more" (5:14). It might be argued that Jesus forgave his sins instead of asking him to offer sacrifices in the temple. However, this is not explicitly stated in the narrative.

[23] The manna theme is employed at least eight times in ancient Jewish literature, according to Paul N. Anderson, "The *Sitz im Leben* of the Johannine Bread of Life

versal language to highlight his significance beyond his Jewish people. Although the discussion reveals some distance between Jesus and his dialogue partners, such as the phrases "*our* fathers ate the manna" (spoken by the Jews) in 6:31 and "*your* fathers ate the manna" (spoken by Jesus) in 6:49 (see 6:58), he claims to be the bread from heaven that gives life to the world (6:33). This perceived distance, however, is not indicative of rejection. Jesus offers his immediate audience (ὑμῖν) "the food that endures to eternal life" (6:27; see 6:53).

The miracle of providing food for a multitude is followed by the gathering of twelve baskets with fragments from the five barley loaves (6:13). The narrator informs the reader that when the people saw the sign they said, "This is indeed the prophet who is to come into the world" (6:14).[24] The identification of Jesus as prophet is not necessarily erroneous.[25] The Samaritan woman was the first character in the Gospel to refer to Jesus using this designation (4:19).[26] The narrator also has implied that Jesus referred to himself as a prophet who has no honor in his own hometown (4:44). Similarly, the idea that Jesus came *into the world* is in accordance with previous information the

---

Discourse and Its Evolving Context," in *Critical Readings of John 6*, BibInt 22 (Leiden: Brill, 1997), 1–59, here 11. Other scholars see Jewish wisdom tradition behind the discourse about the bread of life. For example, see Petrus Maritz and Gilbert Van Belle, "The Imagery of Eating and Drinking in John 6:35," in *Imagery in the Gospel of John: Terms, Themes, and Theology of Johannine Figurative Language*, ed. Jörg Frey, Jan G. van der Watt, and Ruben Zimmermann, WUNT 200 (Tübingen: Mohr Siebeck, 2006), 333–52, here 345–49. A thorough study of the potential allusions to the Old Testament in John 6 is found in Susan Hylen, *Allusion and Meaning in John 6*, BZNW 137 (Berlin: de Gruyter, 2005). The Jewish tradition associated with the manna story and its links to John 6 is addressed by Peder Borgen, *Bread from Heaven: An Exegetical Study of the Concept of Manna in the Gospel of John and the Writings of Philo*, NovTSup 10 (Leiden: Brill, 1965).

[24] Several scholars find in 6:14 echoes of the "prophet like me" of Deut 18:15, 18. For example, Schnackenburg, *John*, 2:18; Thompson, *John*, 141. Others have linked it with Elijah, who multiplied bread, according to 2 Kings 4:42-44. For example, Brown, *John*, 1:235. However, neither candidate (Moses and Elijah) is said to have a universal role in these texts.

[25] Schnackenburg, *John*, 2:19; Michaels, *John*, 351.

[26] The many parallels between John 6 and John 4 can be found in Brown, *John*, 1:267.

reader has gathered from the reading so far (1:9; 3:17, 19).[27] However, it is not immediately clear how the confession of Jesus as the prophet who comes *into the world* relates to the multiplication of bread and the gathering of fragments.[28] This issue will be clarified in subsequent episodes, where Jesus' gathering sheep is expressive of his universal significance.[29] For now, the only information the reader gets is Jesus' reaction to people's identification of him as the prophet who comes into the world. He perceived that they were about to make him king (6:15). Jesus interprets the acknowledgment of his status as prophet who came *into the world* as a recognition of his authority to rule. Although the Father has given the Son all things into his hand (3:35), Jesus' kingship will be fully disclosed in the passion narrative. The reader will have to wait until 18:36 to learn that Jesus came into the world but his kingdom is not of this world.[30] What the narrator does demonstrate immediately is that Jesus is not only "the prophet," but he is ultimately the bread from heaven sent from God to give life to the whole world (6:51).[31]

The miracle is followed by a discussion based on Jewish tradition.[32] Jesus' interlocutors quote Scripture to support their con-

---

[27] The reader, however, has learned to be cautious about the accuracy of people's opinions about Jesus' identity. Nicodemus (3:2) and the Samaritan woman (4:19) can be taken as examples (Andrew T. Lincoln, *The Gospel according to Saint John*, BNTC 4 [New York: Hendrickson, 2005], 214).

[28] Similarly, Francis J. Moloney, "The Function of Prolepsis in the Interpretation of John 6," in *Critical Readings*, 129–48, here 133.

[29] The reference to the "fragments" might also be read in light of 6:39, "I should lose nothing of all that he has given me" (Michaels, *John*, 379). This might explain the use of the neuter in 6:39, since "fragments" is a neuter noun.

[30] Bultmann, *John*, 214; Barrett, *John*, 278; Keener, *John*, 1:671; Thompson, *John*, 142.

[31] C. H. Dodd, *The Interpretation of the Fourth Gospel* (Cambridge: Cambridge University Press, 1953), 344–45; Bultmann, *John*, 214; Edwyn Clement Hoskyns, *The Fourth Gospel*, ed. Francis Noel Davey (London: Faber and Faber, 1967), 290.

[32] Jesus' statement that he is God's bread that came down from heaven to give life to the world finds opposition. However, his dialogue partners do not dispute, at least explicitly, his universal significance. According to Thompson (*John*, 148), they seem to lack a full understanding of the significance of Jesus' promise to give life to the world. They focus on his claim about his origins. This observation is clearer when comparing Jesus' statements in 6:31, 41 with the people's own quotation of Jesus' words in 6:42. The phrase ζωὴν διδοὺς τῷ κόσμῳ in Jesus' statement (6:33) is omitted in the quotation

tention that their fathers ate the manna in the wilderness (6:31; Ps 77:24). Jesus corrects their interpretation and expands upon this Jewish tradition (6:32-33). The giver of bread is not Moses but the Father. The bread from heaven was not given only to their fathers but also to Jesus' interlocutors: "My Father gives *you* the true bread from heaven." The bread from God is the one who comes down from heaven. This bread from heaven not only fed Jesus' audience, as the manna fed their fathers, but gives life to the world (τῷ κόσμῳ). This is the distinctiveness of the bread Jesus offers.[33] Jesus, as the bread of life, not only feeds the people but also offers them life; and while the bread from heaven that their fathers ate was only given to Israel, Jesus' authority to grant life is extended to the whole world (6:33, 35).[34]

The narrator also highlights the comprehensive scope of Jesus' significance by attributing to him a quotation from the Old Testament whose larger context has clear universal overtones (6:45). This is the first time in the Gospel that Jesus is portrayed quoting Scripture.[35] The quotation from Isaiah 54:13 follows Jesus' statement that no one (οὐδείς) can come to him unless the Father draws him (6:44).[36] Jesus refers to the prophets who wrote, "And they will all be taught by God (καὶ ἔσονται πάντες διδακτοὶ θεοῦ)" (6:45). The quotation resembles the Greek version of Isaiah 54:13, "All your children will be instructed by God (καὶ πάντας τοὺς υἱούς σου διδακτοὺς θεοῦ)."[37]

---

of Jesus' words by his dialogue partners (6:42). This is clearly seen by putting all three statements together:

6:33   ὁ γὰρ ἄρτος τοῦ θεοῦ ἐστιν ὁ καταβαίνων ἐκ τοῦ οὐρανοῦ καὶ ζωὴν διδοὺς τῷ κόσμῳ

6:41   ἐγώ εἰμι ὁ ἄρτος ὁ καταβὰς ἐκ τοῦ οὐρανοῦ

6:42   ἐκ τοῦ οὐρανοῦ καταβέβηκα

[33] Schnackenburg, *John*, 2:43.

[34] Lincoln, *John*, 228; Michaels, *John*, 372; Zumstein, *Johannesevangelium*, 260.

[35] Michaels, *John*, 386.

[36] Maarten J. J. Menken, *Old Testament Quotations in the Fourth Gospel: Studies in Textual Form*, CBET 15 (Kampen: Kok Pharos, 1996), 75.

[37] Menken, *Quotations*, 73–76. For a different opinion, see Stephen E. Witmer, *Divine Instruction in Early Christianity*, WUNT 2/246 (Tübingen: Mohr Siebeck, 2008), 83. Witmer thinks that it is not possible to be certain whether John follows

The most significant differences between the LXX and the Gospel of John are the inclusion of the future verb ἔσονται and the omission of "your children" in John 6:44. This omission is usually explained by means of the universal outlook of the Gospel of John: "The fourth evangelist, reading that the eschatological people of God will consist not only of the sons of Jerusalem but also of proselytes, apparently felt authorized to omit 'your sons' in the quotation."[38] This phrase is emphatic in Isaiah 54:13 since it is repeated twice: "All *your children* will be instructed by God and *your children* will have great peace." The Gospel of John, however, preserves "all" (πάντες) repeating it twice: "They will *all* (πάντες) be taught by God. *Everyone* (πᾶς) who has heard" (6:45).[39] This universal outlook expressed by "all" is supported by the larger context of Isaiah 54:13. Since this discussion took place in the synagogue, as he taught in Capernaum (6:59), it remains the possibility that the audience there had access to the larger context of Isaiah 54:13. The prophet has already expressed that "your offspring will inherit the nations (ἔθνη)" (54:3) and that the holy God of Israel shall be called upon in all the earth (πάσῃ τῇ γῇ κληθήσεται, 54:5). The prophet even predicts that proselytes (προσήλυτοι) shall approach Jerusalem through God (δι᾽ ἐμοῦ, 54:15).[40] The prophet also claims that David was given as a testimony among the nations (ἔθνεσιν) and as a ruler (ἄρχοντα) for the nations (ἔθνεσιν, 55:4) and predicts that

the Greek or the Hebrew text. The majority opinion, however, is that John follows the Greek text, because the Hebrew uses the tetragrammaton while the Greek has θεός.

[38] Menken, *Quotations*, 76. See also M. J. Lagrange, *Évangile selon saint Jean*, 5th ed., EBib (Paris: Gabalda, 1936), 181: "Dans Isaïe . . . tous les fils d'Israël; dans Jo. qui omet 'tes fils,' tous les hommes"; and G. Reim, *Studien zum alttestamentlichen Hintergrund des Johannesevangeliums*, SNTSMS 22 (Cambridge: Cambridge University Press, 1974), 17. Michaels (*John*, 386) also explains this omission by indicating that in the Gospel of John Jesus is the only Son.

[39] Witmer (*Instruction*, 125) interprets that the use of "all" in the quotation "suggests that both Jews and Gentiles are taught by God." Thus Schnackenburg, *John*, 2:51; Lindars, *John*, 264. Witmer also observes that the rabbis interpreted "all" from Isa 54:13 as a reference to "all Israel" (Pesiq. Rab Kah. 12.21.1; TanB Yitro, Exod 5:13).

[40] Menken (*Quotations*, 76) argues that in Isa 54:15 "the translator apparently derived גור יגור from the verb גור: 'to dwell as stranger,' in middle Hebrew and Jewish Aramaic in *piel/pael*: 'to make a proselyte,' and translated the verse as ἰδοὺ προσήλυτοι προσελεύσονταί."

nations (ἔθνη) and peoples (λαοί) will be attracted to Jerusalem "for the sake of your God, the Holy One of Israel (τοῦ θεοῦ σου τοῦ ἁγίου Ισραηλ), because he has glorified you" (55:5). Jesus' discourse about the bread of life, however, has several striking turns when read against this background. People are being taught not only by God (6:45) but also by Jesus (6:32-33, 35-40, 68). The Father will give people to Jesus, who will come to him (6:37, 44, 65).[41] Jesus gives testimony about God. Jesus perceives that people will make him king (6:15). Jesus is recognized as the "holy one of God (ὁ ἅγιος τοῦ θεοῦ)" (6:69).

The quotation from Isaiah put on the lips of Jesus contrasts with the quotation used by his dialogue partners. The only time they quote Scripture in this dialogue they refer to Psalm 78:24, a text that lacks instances of universal language, and, ironically, its larger context has a number of instances about judgment upon the disobedient people of God. Jesus' quotation, on the other hand, highlights that "God's universal grace becomes a historical event in Jesus."[42]

Jesus explains the quotation from Scripture by extending his invitation to eat the bread that comes down from heaven to anyone who wants to have life (6:50-51). He even remarks that his own flesh is the bread that he will give for the life of the world (τοῦ κόσμου, 6:51).[43] However, "the manner in which Jesus' experience of death will provide nourishment for the life of the world still remains incomprehensible."[44]

---

[41] Menken warns that the "universalism" expressed by the quotation is relative because it depends on the Father drawing people to Jesus (6:37, 39). However, he clarifies that "in the view of the evangelist those whom the Father draws come from both Israel and the Gentiles" (*Quotations*, 76). Notice also that Jesus' universal significance as giver of life is a present reality but extends also into the future. Jesus claims that "all (πᾶν) that the Father gives me will come (ἥξει) to me" (6:37). According to Schnackenburg (*John*, 2:46–47), "the neuter πᾶν instead of the masculine is quite frequent in such contexts, probably to emphasise [*sic*] the universality of the process." God's election is universally oriented (*einer universal ausgerichteten Erwählung*). The offer of salvation is universal, but some will reject it (Zumstein, *Johannesevangelium*, 265–66). "It is in this framework of sovereignty and election that Jesus holds out the universal-sounding declaration" (Michaels, *John*, 377).

[42] Zumstein, *Johannesevangelium*, 268.

[43] Lincoln (*John*, 231) interprets that through Jesus' death the world, which is at present alienated from God, will be enabled to experience eternal life.

[44] Moloney, "Prolepsis," 141.

It will be clarified in the passion narratives. The association between Jesus' death and salvation hinted at in 1:29 ("the Lamb of God who takes away the sin of the world") is here further clarified.[45] His incarnation (1:14) and his death are for the benefit of the whole world.[46] The universal significance of Jesus stems from his relationship to Jewish tradition. He uses the story of Israel in the wilderness to assert that he is the bread from heaven (6:35).

Further evocations in John 6 of previous episodes highlight Jesus' universal authority. Jesus expresses his mission in the world as fulfilling the will of the one who sent him (6:39-40). The will of the Father is explained in both a passive and an active way in relation to the believer. The passive way is that people (πᾶν) are given to the Son by the Father so that he can raise them up on the last day (6:39). This passive statement is reinforced by the claim that no one (οὐδείς) can come to Jesus unless the Father draws him (6:44). The active way is that everyone (πᾶς) who looks on the Son and believes in him should have eternal life (6:40). The neuter in the first instance (ὅ, αὐτό) is replaced by the masculine in the second instance (ὁ, αὐτόν). The masculine coheres with the all-encompassing pronouns and participles immediately before this πᾶς. Since in early Christian literature the neuter "is sometimes used with reference to persons if it is not the individuals but a general quality that is to be emphasized,"[47] the switch to the neuter in 6:39 can be explained by referring to the "fragments" in 6:12 because the noun κλάσμα is neuter. Jesus explains his mission to people in Galilee in 6:36 using terminology similar to what he used with Nicodemus in Jerusalem: "whoever (πᾶς) believes in him may have eternal life" (3:15),

---

[45] Barrett, *John*, 298; Lincoln, *John*, 231; Michaels, *John*, 392.

[46] Schnelle, *Johannes*, 178. The reading of the bread discourse in the light of Jesus' incarnation seems to be attested in P.Egerton 2, a third-century fragment of papyrus with quotations from John 1:14, 29; 6:55, and in Epiphanius, *Pan.* 2.252. See Lincoln H. Blumell and Thomas A. Wayment, eds. *Christian Oxyrhynchus: Texts, Documents, and Sources* (Waco, Tex.: Baylor University Press, 2015), 299; and R. Yuen-Collingridge, "Hunting for Origen in Unidentified Papyri: The Case of P.Egerton 2 (= *inv.* 3)," in *Early Christian Manuscripts: Examples of Applied Method and Approach*, ed. T. J. Kraus and T. Nicklas, TENTS 5 (Leiden: Brill, 2010), 39–57, here 57n76.

[47] BDF, § 138.1. See also Brown, *John*, 1:270; Schnackenburg, *John*, 2:450n127; Barrett, *John*, 294; Michaels, *John*, 376.

God gave his Son to the world so that "whoever (πᾶς) believes in him should have eternal life" (3:16), and God sent his Son into the world (κόσμον) that the world might be saved through him (3:17). Similarly, the expression of Jesus' mission in terms of giving life in John 6 is evocative of two previous instances of universal language.[48] Jesus claimed in Jerusalem that the Son gives life to whom he will (5:21, 24) and that those in the tombs who will hear his voice will live (5:25, 28-29). He also said to his disciples in Samaria that his mission is to do the will of him who sent him (4:34).

Light to the World

The narrator includes in John 7-9 another set of discussions Jesus had with his brothers, crowds, and religious leaders. This section is emphatically connected to the Jewish Feast of Tabernacles (7:2, 8, 10, 11, 14, 37), and some of Jesus' teachings take place in the temple (7:14, 28; 8:20, 59).[49] The synchronization of the temple dedication with the Feast of Tabernacles figures in 1 Kings 8:2.[50] This festival underwent development in Jewish tradition, and by the time of Jesus' earthly ministry its main features comprised "the dwelling in booths, the daily water and willow ceremonies and the nightly light ceremonies."[51] The water and light elements seem to stem from the eschatological Feast of Tabernacles portrayed in Zechariah 14. The prophet predicts a worldwide pilgrimage to Jerusalem to worship the God of Israel and to celebrate the feast of Tabernacles (Zech 15:16, 18, 19).[52] On that eschatological day, there shall be no light, and "at evening time there shall be light" (Zech 14:6-7),[53] and "the Lord will become king over all the earth,"

[48] Michaels, *John*, 381.

[49] The narrative setting of 7:1–8:59 is found in the Feast of Tabernacles, according to Francis J. Moloney, "Narrative and Discourse at the Feast of Tabernacles: John 7:1–8:59," in *Word, Theology, and Community in John*, ed. John Painter, R. Alan Culpepper, and Fernando Segovia (St. Louis: Chalice, 2002), 155–72, here 155.

[50] Gerry Wheaton, *The Role of Jewish Feasts in John's Gospel*, SNTSMS 162 (Cambridge: Cambridge University Press, 2015), 128. Earlier I highlighted that Zech 14 might be echoed in the incident in the temple in John 2:1–22.

[51] Wheaton, *Feasts*, 129n7. See also Moloney, "Tabernacles," 156–59.

[52] Wheaton, *Feasts*, 138–39.

[53] Barrett, *John*, 335.

and he "will be one and his name one" (14:9). The prominence of the theme of light in John 7–9 is found in the twofold statement "I am the light of the world" on Jesus' lips in 8:12; 9:5, and in the space devoted to narrating the restoration of a man born blind in 9:1-41.

The first discussion in this section arises when the brothers of Jesus encourage him to leave Galilee and to go to Jerusalem for the Feast of Tabernacles (7:3-4). They think that Jesus should show himself "to the world" (τῷ κόσμῳ) because they wrongly assume that he is striving for public recognition and success (7:4).[54] Judea was the appropriate place for Jesus to manifest himself to the world because many visitors would be close to the temple for this important festival.[55] After the feeding of five thousand people in Galilee, the recognition of Jesus by the world was linked to his kingship (6:15-16). The current interaction between Jesus and his disciples, however, goes beyond misunderstanding or ignorance. Their failure to grasp the nature and timing of the manifestation of his kingship has a deeper meaning provided by the narrator's interventions in the narrative. The narrator clarifies that people from Judea were seeking to kill Jesus (7:11) and that his own brothers did not believe in him (7:5). These observations demonstrate that Jesus' brothers do not side with the light. They still belong to the darkness that opposes Jesus' ministry in the world.[56] His brothers' request prompts Jesus to teach about his universal significance. Jesus' work comprises testifying against the world that its works are evil (7:7).[57]

Jesus then moves to Jerusalem to teach in the temple (7:14, 28), evoking a previous miracle he performed by the Sheep Gate (5:2; 7:23). If the reader got the universal overtones of the temple incident

[54] Schnackenburg, *John*, 2:139.

[55] Ernst Haenchen (*John 2: A Commentary on the Gospel of John, Chapters 7-21*, ed. Robert W. Funk with Ulrich Busse, trans. Robert W. Funk, Hermeneia [Philadelphia: Fortress, 1984], 6), however, thinks that for Jesus' brothers Jerusalem is the world. It might be the case that they thought that Jerusalem was *the center of the world*, but there is no indication in the narrative that they equated the world with Jerusalem.

[56] Bultmann (*John*, 290) and Barrett (*John*, 311) think that Jesus' brothers represent the world. Michaels (*John*, 425), however, believes there "is nothing wrong with asking him" to reveal himself to the world (18:20).

[57] This produces hate from the world. Jesus is hated not only by religious leaders (7:1) but also by the whole world (7:7) (Brown, *John*, 1:306).

in 2:13-22, the reference to the temple in 7:14 at least predisposes the reader to encounter instances of universal language in his discussions with people from Judea at the Feast of Tabernacles. If the reader missed the universal overtones of the temple incident, the reference in 7:23 to the healing of a sick man in 5:1-17 may evoke previous memorable statements about Jesus' all-encompassing authority: the Father shows the Son *all* that he himself is doing (5:20), the Father has given *all* judgment to the Son (5:22), *all* may honor the Son (5:23), *whoever* believes in Jesus has eternal life (5:24), and *all* who are in the tombs will hear Jesus' voice (5:28).

The expectation of universal language in Jesus' teaching in the temple is not frustrated. For the first time in the narrative so far, the reader encounters the word Ἕλλην (7:35). His dialogue partners are puzzled by Jesus' words regarding his origins and destiny (7:33-34). They ask, "Does he intend to go to the dispersion among the Greeks (Ἑλλήνων) and teach the Greeks (Ἕλληνας)?" (7:35).[58] Because Jesus' dialogue partners are not portrayed as passive characters but are depicted as actively thinking and interacting with Jesus' message, one should ask, what had motivated the second question in 7:35? Even if they express an "open question without determination as to the answer,"[59] why did they think Jesus might go to the diaspora of the Greeks? What has Jesus said or done to elicit such a suggestion that he might go to the diaspora? The most likely explanation, at a narrative level, is that the Jews have been portrayed throughout John 1–7 in such a way that it is clear that they have been exposed to Jesus' teaching about his universal significance.[60] In other words, since they know Jesus' previous claims about his universal authority, they ironically ask whether his

---

[58] It is not always clear whether a group of words in ancient texts can be regarded as a question. See C. B. Randolph, "The Sign of Interrogation in Greek Minuscule Manuscripts," *Classical Philology* 5 (1910): 309–19. The case here is fairly clear. The first question begins with ποῦ and the second one with μή.

[59] Ulrike Swoboda, "Zur Bestimmung des Interrogativpartikels μή in Joh 7:35," *NovT* 58 (2016): 135–54, here 135.

[60] Carlos Sosa Siliezar, "A Threefold Testimony to Jesus' Universal Significance in the Gospel of John," in *El Evangelio de Juan: Origen, contenido y perspectivas*, ed. Bernardo Estrada and Luis Guillermo Sarasa, Teología Hoy 80 (Bogotá, Colombia: Pontificia Universidad Javeriana, 2018), 101–18.

next step in his earthly ministry is to go to the diaspora. This is an ironic question because evidently they do not believe Jesus will actually teach Ἕλληνας.

They were likely exposed to John's identification of Jesus as the "Lamb of God who takes away the sin of the world" because the interjection ἴδε (1:29) requires an audience who is the beholder and because John baptizes so that Jesus might be revealed to Israel (1:31).[61] John also gave direct testimony to them about Jesus' universal authority (3:31, 35).[62] At least one of the Pharisees, Nicodemus, was exposed to Jesus' teaching about his universal significance (3:1, 16–17, 19). Nicodemus is explicitly identified as "one of them" in 7:50. The Jews as a group were also exposed to Jesus' teachings about his universal significance. The miracle remembered in 7:22-23 indicates that those who ask the question in 7:35 about his ministry among Greeks are related to those who heard Jesus claim that *all* will honor the Son (5:23) and that *all* who are in the tombs will hear his voice (5:28). The next time a group of Jews is exposed to Jesus' teaching about his universal significance is in a synagogue in Capernaum (6:59).[63] They heard Jesus saying that he is the bread from heaven that gives life to the world (6:33) and

---

[61] Some priests and Levites from Jerusalem previously interrogated John (1:19, 24). They reported back to those Pharisees who sent them (1:22). Apparently, they fulfilled their mission because in 4:1 the Pharisees have already heard about John's ministry. Jesus himself tells the Jews that they sent to John and that he bore witness to the truth (5:33, 35; 10:41).

[62] The reading in 3:25 can be either "a Jew" (Ἰουδαίου) or "Jews" (Ἰουδαίων). The latter is found in 𝔓⁶⁶ (about 200 CE), while the former occurs in 𝔓⁷⁵ (early third century). The original reading of Sinaiticus has the plural form. A correction made to this codex by a second hand has the singular form. Bruce M. Metzger (*A Textual Commentary on the Greek New Testament*, 2nd ed. [Stuttgart: German Bible Society, 2007], 175) argues that the singular form was changed to the plural form because Ἰουδαίων is frequently used in the Gospel of John, making Ἰουδαίου the most difficult reading. However, one should also notice that the two nouns that accompany Ἰουδαίου have the same ending (Ἰωάννου, καθαρισμοῦ), making it possible that a scribe changed Ἰουδαίων to Ἰουδαίου by mistake. See also Johannes Beutler, "Jesus in Judea," *In die Skriflig* 49 (2015): 1–6.

[63] It is difficult to determine whether the "Jews" in 6:41-59 are included in the "Jews" mentioned in 7:35. Each group is located in a different geographical context (6:59; 7:14, 25). However, it is not impossible that groups of Jewish people traveled from Galilee to Judea and vice versa (4:45).

listened to a quotation from Isaiah 54:13 that Jesus used to remark that *everyone* who has learned from the Father comes to him (6:45). This previous knowledge that the narrator attributes to Jesus' dialogue partners clarifies that their question in 7:35 is ironic: "Does he intend to go to the Dispersion among the Greeks and teach the Greeks?" Although they do not actually believe Jesus will go to the dispersion among the Greeks and teach the Greeks,[64] the reader concludes that Jesus' message should be known elsewhere because he is the savior of the world. The reader is aware of Jesus' geographical movements from Judea to Samaria and from there to Galilee (John 3–4). The reader is by now used to Jesus interacting with people from different geographies and backgrounds: Nicodemus, a Pharisee in Jerusalem (3:1), a woman in Samaria (4:7), an official in Capernaum (4:46-54), a sick man by the Sheep Gate (5:2), and crowds from Galilee (6:2). The reader, therefore, can reasonably expect that Jesus' next geographical move will be to the diaspora of the Greeks. The identity of such Greeks, however, is not clear.[65] John might intentionally be opaque here so that the reader may identify these "Greeks" with Jews in the diaspora or gentiles living in the Hellenistic world.

After their questioning, the narrative changes abruptly to the "last day of the feast" (7:37). Instead of focusing on the identity of the "Greeks" in the ironic question of his interlocutors, Jesus invites *anyone* (τις) who thirsts to come to him (7:37).[66] Instead of him *going to* (πορεύομαι) the Greeks, anyone is invited to *come to* (ἔρχομαι) him and drink (7:37). Since there is no doubt that many Greeks would be present in the temple, especially during the last day of the feast, the great day,[67] Jesus' invitation is wide in scope. Jesus supports his

---

[64] Their question also reflects the limited grasp they have about Jesus' mission. Jesus came not only to teach but also to save the world (3:16).

[65] Hoskyns (*Fourth Gospel*, 319) suggested that the latter Christian mission to the gentiles was not grounded in Jesus' going to the Greek world during his earthly ministry, but instead depended on Jesus' death in Jerusalem (also Beutler, *Johannesevangelium*, 256; Zumstein, *Johannesevangelium*, 306).

[66] Lindars (*John*, 296) interprets that the fruitfulness of the gentile mission ironically put in the lips of Jesus' opponents in 7:35 finds expression in 7:37-52.

[67] According to Lindars (*John*, 298), the last day was "great" because it attracted large groups of people to Jerusalem.

invitation by referring to the "Scriptures" (7:38). Zechariah 14 is usually suggested as a text that helps explain John 7:38.[68] Since Zechariah is quoted in John 19:37, it is likely that this prophetic text influenced other parts of the Gospel.[69] This Old Testament text depicts an eschatological Feast of Tabernacles (Zech 14:16, 18, 19) that is going to be characterized by "living water" coming forth from Jerusalem (Zech 14:8). On that day, "the Lord will become king over all the earth" (Zech 14:9). The universalism of the last section of Zechariah, however, centers on Jerusalem: "All who remain of all the nations . . . shall also go up (ἀναβήσονται) . . . to do obeisance to the King, the Lord Almighty, and to keep the feast of Tabernacles" (Zech 14:16).[70] The striking turn in John 7:37 is that Jesus invites *anyone* who thirsts to come *to him* and drink.[71]

---

[68] Scholarly suggestions as to the source of the quotation include Pss 78:16, 20; 104:41; Isa 48:21; Neh 9:15; Ezek 47:1-10; Joel 3:18; Zech 14:8. I concur with Wheaton (*Feasts*, 137) that "Zechariah 14:8 is intrinsically likely since it expressly mentions Tabernacles, it contains the expression 'living water,' and it was associated with the . . . water ceremony in t.Sukk. 3.18." See also Dodd, *Interpretation*, 350; Michaels, *John*, 465; Paul S. Minear, "Diversity and Unity: A Johannine Case-Study," in *Die Mitte des Neuen Testaments: Einheit und Vielfalt neutestamentlicher Theologie*, ed. Ulrich Luz and Hans Weder (Göttingen: Vandenhoeck & Ruprecht, 1983), 162–75, here 169. Keener (*John*, 1:725) even considers that Zech 14 was a reading for Sukkoth, according to Tannaitic sources (t.Sukk. 3.18).

[69] Brown, *John*, 1:323.

[70] Larry Paul Jones, *The Symbol of Water in the Gospel of John*, JSNTSup 145 (Sheffield: Sheffield Academic, 1997), 151.

[71] The centrality of Jerusalem in relationship to God's universal significance has exceptions in the Old Testament. One of them is found in Isa 19:16-25. This text "talks about Yahweh cult in Egypt with an impact on the Egyptian population, causing them to turn to the God of Israel . . . ultimately causing people from all nations to turn to Yahweh," according to Hallvard Hagelia, "A Crescendo of Universalism: An Exegesis of Isa 19:16-25," in *Nomen et Nomina: Festskrift till Stig Norin, SEÅ 70* (Uppsala: Uppsala Exegetiska Sällskap, 2005), 73–88, here 73. Egypt will have access to the knowledge of God (v. 21) and will behave like Israel, i.e., swearing allegiance to the Lord (v. 18), offering sacrifices to the Lord in their own altar (vv. 19, 21), and making and honoring their vows to the Lord (v. 21). The Lord will listen to Egypt's cry and will send them a savior to deliver them (v. 20). Although Israel does not cease being the Lord's people, in this passage they are equal to other nations: "Israel will be the third with Egypt and Assyria" (v. 24). This striking description of Israel along other nations is divinely sanctioned. The Lord himself says, "Blessed be Egypt my people,

Imagery of light was also prominent during the celebration of the Feast of Tabernacles in Jerusalem. Jesus makes the topic of light the focus of a new set of discussions with people in Jerusalem (8:12).[72] The first reference to light in the Gospel of John is found in the prologue. The Word who took an active role in the creation of the world was the light of humanity (1:4). This light is the true light that comes to the world, shines in the darkness, and gives light to everyone (1:5, 9; 3:19). Jesus opens a new set of controversies stating, "I am the light of the world" (8:12; cf. Zech 14:7).[73] Although he is not of this world,[74] he came to offer the light of life to the world (8:12, 23)[75] and to declare to the world (τὸν κόσμον) what he heard from the Father (8:26).[76] The strong dualism found in 8:23, "you are from below; I am from above," might be intended to recall John's early testimony about Jesus' universal

---

and Assyria the work of my hands, and Israel my inheritance" (v. 25). It is possible to take the references to Egypt and Assyria in Isa 16:23 as representing all peoples of the world. Both were "mighty nations to the south-west and the north east Jerusalem and Judah" (Hagelia, "Crescendo," 85). Therefore, they might symbolize all nations, the whole world. The things narrated there will happen "in that day" (τῇ ἡμέρᾳ ἐκείνῃ, vv. 16, 18, 19, 21, 23, 24). This phrase is commonplace both in the Old Testament and in New Testament texts. It is found six times in the Gospel of John in different constructions (5:9; 11:53; 14:20; 16:23, 26; 20:19). It has a future sense in John 14:20, "In that day you will know that I am in my Father" (ἐκείνῃ τῇ ἡμέρᾳ), and in John 16:26, "in that day you will ask in my name" (ἐκείνῃ τῇ ἡμέρᾳ, cf. 16:23).

[72] The connection between 8:12 and the Feast of Tabernacles is allowed by Kai Akagi, "The Light from Galilee: The Narrative Function of Isaiah 8:23–9:6 in John 8:12," *NovT* 58 (2016): 380–93. Akagi, however, argues that the primary evocation in 8:12 is found in Isaiah 8:23–9:6, where the messiah comes from "Galilee of the nations."

[73] Keener, *John*, 1:739. The use of πάλιν might be a deliberate reference to 7:37, because this is the last time Jesus raised his voice (Schnackenburg, *John*, 2:189). If that is the case, the last day of the Feast of Tabernacles might be connected with the imagery of light. However, since "light" is used elsewhere in the Gospel of John in contexts where the Feast of Tabernacles is not in view, its use here should not be restricted to that festival (Zumstein, *Johannesevangelium*, 324).

[74] The phrase "this world" means "men in their alienation from God," according to Schnackenburg, *John*, 2:199.

[75] For Bultmann (*John*, 343), "The decisive feature [of Jesus as light of the world] is not the universalism but the dualism." The literary context, however, highlights Jesus' universal significance. Therefore, Jesus as the light of the world indicates his distance from the world and his salvific purposes for it.

[76] The noun "world" in 8:12 refers to the entire creation (Schnelle, *Johannes*, 204).

authority: "He who comes from above is above all" (3:31).[77] Since he is the light of the world, he came to judge the world (8:26).[78] This claim is illustrated by the restoration of a man born blind (9:1-41).[79]

Although with this miracle he gives sight only to a man in Judea, he says to his disciples that he is "the light of the *world*" (9:5).[80] Previous associations between light and life (1:4) and light and judgment (3:19-21)[81] prepare the reader not only for the miracle but also for Jesus' words about the blindness of his opponents.[82] Furthermore, the reference to the Sabbath (9:14) triggers evocations of the miracle Jesus performed in John 5. Jesus' claims that the Father has given him *all* judgment and that *all* who are in the tombs will hear his voice (5:28) were preceded by a miracle he performed during the Sabbath. Similarly, after restoring the sight of a man born blind, Jesus claims that he came into this world (τὸν κόσμον) for judgment (9:39).[83] The "light of the world" brings life to those who embrace him but pronounces judgment against those who reject him. Jesus' light allows those who believe to "see" but "blinds" those who reject him (9:39). The whole world is exposed to the light either for life or for judgment. Although the words in 9:39 refer primarily to the formerly blind man and to Jesus' opponents, "the statement is universal in its scope."[84] The reader is enlightened by the story and invited to

---

[77] Brown, *John*, 1:347; Michaels, *John*, 487.

[78] Since he is the light of the *world*, Jesus transcends the Jewish framework, according to Schnackenburg (*John*, 2:189).

[79] If the narrator intended to evoke Jesus' mission by indicating that the man was sent to wash in the pool of Siloam and by clarifying that Siloam means "sent" (9:7), the reader may relate this episode with previous references to Jesus' universal mission (e.g., 1:9, 29; 3:16-17; 4:34).

[80] For Barrett (*John*, 357), "light" is not "a metaphysical definition of the person of Jesus but a description of his effect upon the cosmos."

[81] Brown, *John*, 1:377; Michaels, *John*, 477.

[82] Lincoln, *John*, 281.

[83] Thompson, *John*, 219.

[84] Lindars, *John*, 351.

embrace Jesus' light.[85] The judgment of the world then is a "radical reversal of the human condition."[86]

PARABLES AND PREDICTIONS

There are two further episodes in John 5–12 that point to the comprehensive scope of Jesus' significance. The first is implicit and comprises two closely related parables followed by discussions during the Feast of Dedication (10:1-42) and a miracle in Bethany (11:1-57). The second is more explicit and includes Jesus' prediction that he will draw all people to himself (12:20-50). Although the phrase "truly, truly, I say to you" is used several times in the Gospel of John (e.g., 3:3; 5:19), it is significant to find it in the two episodes in 10:1, 7 and 12:24.

The Shepherd

The narrator informs the reader that Jesus uses a "parable" (παροιμία) to teach about his relationship with those who believe (10:6). The figurative speech about a shepherd and sheep who know his voice illustrates the idea that those who listen to Jesus' voice follow him (10:3, 27).[87] Jesus has previously indicated that whoever hears his word and believes in the one who sent him has eternal life (5:24), and he has also promised that the dead will hear his voice and that those who hear will live (5:25). The parable repeats Jesus' previous offer of eternal life to those who want to listen to and follow him. The initial parable in 10:1-5 about a shepherd and his sheep is developed in 10:7-18 by including imagery such as the robber and the door. Jesus compares himself with the door of the sheepfold (10:9). He indicates that if anyone enters by him, that

---

[85] Luc Devillers, "Jean 9, ou la christologie interactive de Jean," in *Studies in the Gospel of John and Its Christology: Festschrift Gilbert van Belle*, ed. Joseph Verheyden, Geert van Oyen, Michael Labahn, and Reimund Bieringer, BETL 265 (Leuven: Peeters, 2014), 227–38, here 238.

[86] Bultmann, *John*, 340.

[87] Shepherd imagery is found in Jewish and pagan Hellenistic contexts to portray God, gods, or rulers. See Bultmann, *John*, 364–71; Keener, *John*, 1:800–801; and Johannes Beutler, "Der alttestamentlich-jüdische Hintergrund der Hirtenrede in Johannes 10," in *The Shepherd Discourse of John 10 and Its Context: Studies by Members of the Johannine Writings Seminar*, ed. Johannes Beutler and Robert T. Fortna, SNTSMS 67 (Cambridge: Cambridge University Press, 1991), 18–32.

person will be saved (σωθήσεται) (10:9).[88] Since the only two previous references to Jesus' offer of salvation, found in 3:17 and 5:34, are clearly related to Jesus' universal significance, the use of σωθήσεται in 10:9 implicitly points to the same idea.[89] Jesus told Nicodemus that God sent his Son into the world in order that the world might be saved through him (δι᾽ αὐτοῦ) (3:17). Similarly, the parable of the sheep invites people to enter through Jesus (δι᾽ ἐμοῦ) in order to achieve salvation (10:9). The other reference to the verb σῴζω in 5:34 links Jesus' teaching with salvation.[90] Similarly, the sheep that listen to Jesus' words about his unique relationship with the Father obtain salvation. The parable also explains Jesus' mission in the world. He came to give life in abundance for his followers (10:10, 28) and to gather his people (10:11).[91]

So far, the parable provides only implicit instances of universal language. This continues in 10:16, where Jesus refers to "other sheep." Since some Jews did not believe in him (10:26) but others embraced his message (10:42), "his sheep" cannot be a particular ethnic group. It comprises people from the unbelieving world who hear his voice and follow him.[92] His other sheep do not belong to the current group of

[88] Michaels (*John*, 584) links 10:9 to 6:51; 7:17; and 8:51 and concludes that this is an open invitation to *anyone*.

[89] Schnackenburg, *John*, 2:292.

[90] The mention of Jesus' voice both in 10:3, 4, 5, 16, 27 and 5:25, 28, 37 points to the interpretation of the sheep following Jesus as their resurrection and ascension to the Father. Thus, Reinhartz, *Word*, 79, 95.

[91] The motif of "gathering" was found in the mission of the disciples in 4:36 (Reinhartz, *Word*, 77) and in the gathering up of leftover fragments in 6:12-13.

[92] Similarly, Reinhartz (*Word*, 74–76) takes the sheep as symbolizing humankind, the world. She also takes the "sheepfold" as the spatial dimension of the world. The use of "his own" in 10:3, 4 "implies a distinction between a general group of people who heard Jesus—the sheep—and those specific individuals whom he called by name and led out of the sheepfold" (75). She provides a helpful paraphrase of 10:1-2, "Truly, truly, I say to you, anyone who was not sent by the Father but entered the world a different way is the evil one, Satan. The one who was sent by God and became flesh is the savior of humankind" (96). A different opinion is held by John A. Dennis (*Jesus' Death and the Gathering of True Israel*, WUNT 2/217 [Tübingen: Mohr Siebeck, 2006], 346). For Dennis, "his own sheep" means "believers from Galilee and Samaria and 'other sheep' is equated with 'Israelites in the Diaspora.'" This, I think, downplays the prominent role of instances of universal language elsewhere in the Gospel.

believers, "this fold" (10:16). In the future, they will also listen to Jesus' voice, presumably through the testimony of his followers.[93] They will then be united with the current group of believers so that there will be one flock under the authority of one shepherd (10:16).[94] This universal outlook is based on the mission of the Son to the whole world.[95] The life that Jesus offers is not restricted to individual salvation and protection (10:29). It also comprises the unification in one flock of all those who believe.[96] The possibility that other people in the future will listen to Jesus' voice and believe in him stems from the universal authority of the Father. He is greater than all (ὁ πατήρ . . . μοι πάντων μεῖζόν ἐστιν)[97] and, therefore, gives the sheep to Jesus and protects them

---

[93] Schnackenburg, *John*, 2:299; Thompson, *John*, 227. Bultmann (*John*, 384) shares this opinion but he suggested 10:16 was a Christian interpolation.

[94] Scholars have interpreted variously this "other sheep": other Christians (e.g., Haenchen, *John 2*, 49), other Jews (e.g., J. Louis Martyn, "Glimpses Into the History of the Johannine Community," in *L'Évangile de Jean: Sources, redaction, théologie*, ed. M. de Jonge, BETL 44 [Leuven: Leuven University Press, 1977], 149–75, here 174), or gentiles (Hoskyns, *Fourth Gospel*, 378; Barrett, *John*, 376; Schnackenburg, *John*, 2:299; Lindars, *John*, 363; Lincoln, *John*, 298).

[95] Schnelle, *Johannes*, 234.

[96] Michaels (*John*, 589) resists the temptation "to read into the text any definitive assumption as to what the precise relationship between Jewish and gentile Christian congregations, or between Jews and gentiles in any single congregation should be." Instead, he observes that the emphasis in the Gospel of John is on unity in relationship to God, love for each other, and mission to the world (11:52; 17:11, 21, 23).

[97] The phrase, however, is variously preserved in the extant manuscripts. Most readings portray the Father as greater than something (μειζον, neuter) or someone (μειζων, masculine). He is greater than "any other power" (Codex A) or than "all others" (𝔓66). The Father can protect the sheep because there is no power or "shepherd" greater than him. These readings (A and 𝔓66) link "my Father" at the beginning of v. 29 with the following phrase using a masculine relative pronoun (ος). Other witnesses also have μειζον (neuter) or μειζων (masculine), but they use the neuter pronoun o (codices B* ℵ D) instead of the masculine ος. Here, there are two possibilities for translation. The first possibility is "My Father in regard to what he has given me is greater than all (others or things)" (Barrett, *John*, 381–82; Lindars, *John*, 370; Lincoln, *John*, 305). The other possibility is "as for my Father, what he has given me is greater than all" (Brown, *John*, 1:403; Michaels, *John*, 599n22). Since the differences between the readings depend on a few commonplace letters (ος or o, and ων or ον), the possibility of unintentional mistakes is very high. For current purposes, I follow the reading offered in NA28, selected by Metzger (*Commentary*, 198) as the reading

(10:29). Since there is nothing above the Father's authority, he alone, as the legitimate owner of the sheep,[98] can protect the sheep from anyone who threatens them.[99] The interpretation of the parable as indicative of Jesus' mission to the whole world in order to give life and unite those who believe in him is confirmed by the portrayal of the Father as the one who consecrated and sent Jesus *into the world* (10:36).[100] Jesus does not frame his mission in terms of his Father sending him to "his people" or "his disciples." Jesus was sent *into the world*.[101]

This section concludes with the narrator locating Jesus in a memorable place in the narrative. Jesus goes across the Jordan to the place where John had been baptizing (10:40), Bethany. Bethany is the place where the first public announcement of the universal significance of Jesus is found: "Behold, the Lamb of God, who takes away the sin of the world" (1:29).[102] The parable has indicated that Jesus achieves eternal life for his followers and the gathering of his sheep through his death (10:15, 17).[103] The location of Jesus across the Jordan might

---

that better explains the origin of the other readings. My translation, however, does not suggest that the sheep are greater than "all," because this would be bizarre in Johannine thought (Schnackenburg, *John*, 2:308). Rather, I follow this translation: "My Father in regard to what he has given me is greater than all (things)."

[98] Schnackenburg, *John*, 2:307.

[99] Bultmann (*John*, 386) compares 10:29-30 with 1:2, "in Jesus and only in him does God encounter man."

[100] Jesus then indirectly confirms that he is "the holy one of God" (6:69), according to Michaels, *John*, 605. For Edward W. Klink III (*The Sheep of the Fold: The Audience and Origin of the Gospel of John*, SNTSMS 141 [Cambridge: Cambridge University Press, 2007], 232) the "other sheep" are still unknown because it refers to "those who were to become the 'sheep.' . . . It was yet to be seen who would hear the voice of the Good Shepherd." Cf. also p. 238, "The Gospel envisioned an indefinite incorporation of future believers."

[101] Jesus' defense against the accusation that he makes himself God (10:33) includes a quotation from Ps 82:6 (LXX 81:6; John 10:34). The main topic of this psalm is God's judgment. In the last lines, the psalmist asks God to judge the earth, because he "will gain possession of all the nations (πᾶσιν τοῖς ἔθνεσιν)" (v. 8).

[102] Schnackenburg (*John*, 2:314) correctly observes that "the comparison with John the Baptist recalls yet again to memory the witness he bore to Jesus" (thus Michaels, *John*, 609) but fails to indicate that that witness was about Jesus' universal significance as the Lamb of God.

[103] Reinhartz, *Word*, 96.

be intended to evoke the designation of Jesus as a lamb who gives his life for the salvation of the world. John was introduced in the narrative as the one who gives testimony so that all might believe through him (ἵνα πάντες πιστεύσωσιν δι᾿ αὐτοῦ, 1:7). At the end of this section about Jesus as the shepherd, John's witness is recalled by many (πολλοί) who, through his testimony, come to believe in Jesus (ἐπίστευσαν εἰς αὐτόν) (10:42).

Jesus' parable about his care for his sheep and about the power of his word to give life to those who listen to him is illustrated in the miracle of the resurrection of Lazarus. This dramatic event, and the dialogues and teachings surrounding it, is tied to the previous restoration of a man born blind by some people from Judea who came to Bethany (11:19, 37). In both narratives Jesus tells his disciples that he is the light of the world (explicit in 9:5; implicit in 11:9).[104] Jesus also says that everyone (πᾶς) who lives and believes in him shall never die (11:26). This prompts Martha's confession of faith: "I believe that you are the Christ, the Son of God, who is *coming into the world*" (11:27).[105] It does not come as a surprise that the confession that brings life to Martha includes the declaration of Jesus' universal significance. Although there is no previous indication in the narrative that Martha was exposed to this element in Jesus' teaching, her confession matches the message of the Gospel so far: Jesus is the fulfillment of messianic expectation, that is, he is the Christ; he came from God, that is, he is the Son of God; his ministry is for the benefit of humanity, that is, he came into the world.

The resurrection of Lazarus brings preoccupation to religious leaders who fear "everyone (πάντες) will believe in him" (11:48). Although many actually believed in him on account of Lazarus (12:11), the use

---

[104] Reinhartz, *Word*, 94.

[105] Barrett, *John*, 397. The phrase might suggest Jesus' preexistence (Zumstein, *Johannesevangelium*, 429) or his incarnate status (Keener, *John*, 2:844). Brown (*John*, 1:425), however, links Martha's confession with people's expectations of a prophet who is to come into the world (6:14). Bultmann (*John*, 404) thought that, of all three confessions (the Christ, the Son of God, and the one coming into the world), the last is the most significant because it is an acknowledgment that "in Jesus the eschatological invasion of God into the world has come to pass."

of "all" is an ironic exaggeration,[106] perhaps spoken in exasperation.[107] On the one hand, they fear a Roman intervention if their own people believe in Jesus.[108] On the other hand, the reader may interpret the religious leaders' words in light of previous Johannine thought.[109] The Word is the true light that gives light to everyone (πάντα) (1:9). John came as a witness so that "all (πάντες) might believe through him" (1:7). The very reason why the Word came to the world was so that "whoever (πᾶς) believes in him" should have eternal life (3:16). The high priest Caiaphas tries to dispel their fears by judging that the death of a man would be beneficial for the whole nation (11:50). The narrator interprets these words as prophetic but expands their scope (11:51-52). Jesus will indeed die for the benefit of their nation (11:51),[110] but his death will result in God's children who are scattered abroad being gathered into one (11:52). The motif of "gathering" was introduced in Samaritan territory when Jesus included his disciples in his mission to the world (4:36). He told them that the one who reaps gathers fruit for eternal life (4:36). Jesus was also hailed as the prophet who is to come *into the world* right after the disciples gathered leftover fragments from the bread Jesus multiplied in Galilee (6:13-14). More recently, the reader has learned that Jesus has "other sheep" that he must bring

---

[106] Keener (*John*, 2:854) sees in 11:48 the fulfillment of John's witness (1:7-9) and a foreshadowing of the gentile mission (12:19-21). Dennis (*Jesus' Death*, 342) acknowledges the use of irony in this passage, but he seems to mute its full rhetorical import by restricting 11:47-52 to the "restoration of Israel." The language of 11:47-52 echoes Old Testament restoration theology (Barrett, *John*, 407). The Gospel of John, however, appropriates such a language to describe the gathering of believers who are children of God, born not of blood (1:13), into one. Christian appropriations of Jewish restoration theology are found in Jas 1:1; 1 Pet 1:1; Odes Sol. 10:5-6 (Barrett, *John*, 407). For Schnackenburg (*John*, 2:350), "The old image of the gathering of the scattered Israelites is taken up into the universal perspective of all those chosen by God, particularly the Gentiles."

[107] Lindars (*John*, 405) indicates that these words "could be taken as an ironical forecast of the future universal following of Christ."

[108] Haenchen, *John 2*, 75. They seem to tolerate the Roman yoke, although they ironically regarded themselves as free people (8:33). See Schnackenburg, *John*, 2:348.

[109] The reader would notice irony in these words, according to Barrett, *John*, 405; Lincoln, *John*, 330; Michaels, *John*, 649.

[110] Schnelle, *Johannes*, 255.

so that there will be one flock (10:16).[111] Since the motif of gathering has to do with Jesus' mission to the world, the prophecy of Caiaphas should be taken as a prediction of the mission of the disciples among those who were outside "the people," "the whole nation" (11:50).[112] They too will become "children of God" (11:52).[113]

The narrator is the only one who uses the expression "children of God" in the Gospel of John, and he uses it twice in 1:12 and 11:52,[114] where he provides his own interpretation of the significance of Jesus' earthly ministry (1:12) and death (11:52). The introductory section of the Gospel claimed that all who did receive him and believed in his name received the right to become children of God (1:12). This status is not associated with physical birth but stems from the will of God himself (1:13).[115] Through the testimony of the disciples after Jesus' death, many others will believe and will become children of God (11:52).[116] The contrast between "the people" and "nation" in 11:50, 52 and "the

---

[111] Dennis (*Jesus' Death*, 342) also links 11:47-52 to 2:19-21; 4:36; 6:13-14; 9:1-41; 10:16. Dennis takes the man born blind as "symbolic of the true Israel" (343). However, the noun "man" is intentionally ambiguous to indicate that Jesus is capable of restoring the sight of any man (cf. 1:4, τῶν ἀνθρώπων). Actually, the restoring of this man's sight is preceded by Jesus' claim that he is the light of *the world* (9:5; see 1:9). He does not claim to be the "light of Israel," although he brought light and life also to his Jewish people.

[112] Bultmann, *John*, 411. Bultmann also ruled out the idea suggested by B. Sundkler and A. Fridrichsen, *Contributions à l'étude de la pensée missionnaire dans le Nouveau Testament*, Arbeiten und Mitteilungen aus dem Neutestamentlichen Seminar zu Uppsala 6 (Uppsala: A. B. Lundequistska Bokhandeln, 1937), 40–41, that Israel should be the instrument of salvation for the whole world (411n3).

[113] Haenchen, *John 2*, 75: "The death of Jesus therefore has universal meaning in the sense that it benefits all Christians."

[114] Michaels (*John*, 654) observes that the phrase has an article in 11:52 but lacks it in 1:12.

[115] Elsewhere, the Gospel of John challenged the soteriological value of ethnic descent from Abraham (8:34, 39) (Keener, *John*, 1:819). Jesus has even disputed the claim by some Jews that God is their Father (8:41, 42).

[116] Scholars interpret "children of God" here as referring to Jews in the diaspora (John A. T. Robinson, "The Destination and Purpose of St. John's Gospel," *NTS* 6 [1960]: 117-31, here 127), gentiles (Brown, *John*, 1:440), or Jews and gentiles (Thompson, *John*, 255; Keener, *John*, 857n204; Lincoln, *John*, 330–31). For Lindars (*John*, 407), "children of God" in 11:52 is an instance of universal language.

scattered children of God" in 11:52 likely indicates that "children of God" is not restricted to Judaism.[117] The narrator, commenting on the significance of the prophecy of Caiaphas, uses the present tense to indicate that Jesus' death will result in the gathering of those who are scattered abroad. The universal significance of Jesus includes his own Jewish people, but it is not restricted to them.[118] The earliest reception of this idea is found in 1 John 2:2, "He is the atoning sacrifice for our sins, and not for ours alone, but for the whole world."[119]

The Greeks

The last episode of the first major section of the Gospel takes place in Judea (12:1-50). This episode is climactic because the reader encounters a voice from heaven glorifying the Father's name (12:28). This is the only time God speaks publicly in the Gospel of John.[120] Jesus moves from Bethany to Judea, six days before the Passover (12:1). The audience is a large crowd of the Jews (12:9), many of whom believed in

---

[117] Michaels, *John*, 588–89n90.

[118] As previously observed, Dennis (*Jesus' Death*, 341–49) emphasizes the point that Jesus' mission is the restoration of Israel (Judea, Samaria, Galilee, and the Diaspora). Although he acknowledges that John used the Jewish motif of "dispersion" to talk about all those who are estranged from Jesus and in need of being united with him (346), his reading of 1:11-12 leads him to conclude that "John's fundamental concern . . . was Israel's . . . restoration as such and not a Gentile mission" (348). Dennis interprets 1:11-12 as Jesus coming to *Israel*, but only those from *Israel* who respond to faith will become God's children, "the restored Israel" (349). Since these verses are framed by clear instances of creation (1:3, 10) and by an emphatic negation that God's children are not related to "blood, will of the flesh or will of man" (1:13), I suggest it is not accurate to indicate that John's "fundamental concern" is the restoration of Israel over against a gentile mission. God is concerned with the whole world because he is its Creator (1:3, 10). Therefore, he gave universal authority to his Son to bring salvation to the whole world he has created (1:29; 3:16), including his Jewish people. The "fundamental concern" of the Gospel of John is God's whole humanity. People from Judea, Samaria, and Galilee are part of this world that rejected its Creator but are invited to embrace the Son.

[119] Michaels, *John*, 654. This presupposes that the Gospel of John was written previous to the Johannine letters. For a different opinion, see Udo Schnelle, "Die Reihenfolge der johanneischen Schriften," *NTS* 57 (2011): 91–113.

[120] Michaels, *John*, 694. God's declaration of his beloved Son at his baptism is not portrayed as a public event in John 1:33-34.

Jesus (12:11). The focus of the following paragraphs will be on those verses that highlight the universal significance of Jesus.

Once Jesus enters Jerusalem, the crowd hails him as King of Israel and quotes words from Psalm 118:25-26 (John 12:13). This Old Testament text lacks instances of universal language in its larger context. The narrator, however, interprets the event by remembering prophecies from Zechariah (John 12:15).[121] Since the larger context of Zechariah 9:9 has a universal outlook, the narrator "corrects the crowd's limited nationalistic perceptions."[122] In other words, the narrator and Jesus himself accept the acclamation "King of Israel,"[123] but their use of Old Testament quotations signals that Jesus' kingship is not restricted to his Jewish people. This is the same Old Testament prophet Jesus used to interpret his offer of life during the Feast of Tabernacles (7:37-38). Zechariah predicts that "the Lord will become king over all the earth" (Zech 14:9) and all the nations will go up to Jerusalem to keep the eschatological Feast of Tabernacles (Zech 14:16).[124] This time the narrator refers to Zechariah 9:9 to interpret the entrance of the king sitting on a donkey's colt (John 12:15). The surrounding context of this Old Testament text has instances of universal language.[125] The prophet

[121] This is, however, a condensed quotation, according to Thompson, *John*, 265. The Gospel of John preserves key words from Zech 9:9 ("daughter Zion" and "look, your king is coming!") to turn attention away from the donkey and back to the proclamation: "Blessed is the one coming . . . the king of Israel" (Michaels, *John*, 677). This quotation from Zech 9:9 evokes the universal authority (*l'autorité universelle*) of the Messiah, according to Jean Zumstein, "Au Seuil de la passion (Jean 12)," in Verheyden, van Oyen, Labahn, and Bieringer, *Studies in the Gospel of John and Its Christology*, 275-288, here 280.

[122] Mary L. Coloe, "Gentiles in the Gospel of John: Narrative Possibilities—12.12-43," in *Attitudes to Gentiles in Ancient Judaism and Early Christianity*, ed. David C. Sim and James S. McLaren, LNTS 499 (London: Bloomsbury T&T Clark, 2013), 209-13, here 212.

[123] Michaels, *John*, 678.

[124] The scriptural citation in John 12:15 also resembles Zeph 3:16. Coloe ("Gentiles," in Sim and McLaren, *Attitudes to Gentiles in Ancient Judaism and Early Christianity*, 213) rightly observes that in Zephaniah "the coming of the king is to have implications well beyond Israel's nationalistic hopes [Zeph 3:8, 9]."

[125] Barrett (*John*, 420) observes, "Universalism is already implied in Zech. 9:9." Similarly, Lincoln, *John*, 344. Schnackenburg (*John*, 2:376) attends to the context of the quotation but highlights the topic of peace instead of the universal significance of

predicts that God's reign will extend "over the waters as far as the sea" (Zech 9:10)[126] and the house of Judah will be a blessing among the nations (Zech 8:13). The centrality of Israel is prominent in this Old Testament prophecy. Many peoples (λαοὶ πολλοί) and many nations (ἔθνη πολλά) will come to Jerusalem seeking the face of the Lord Almighty (Zech 8:22). Even ten men from all the languages of the nations will take hold of the hem of a Judean man, saying, "We shall go with you, for we have heard that God is with you" (8:23).[127]

The positive reception of Jesus in Jerusalem increases the fear of the religious leaders (cf. 11:48-49). The Pharisees claim with exaggeration that "the world (ὁ κόσμος) has gone after him" (12:19).[128] At the same time, this exaggeration is ironic.[129] Its deeper meaning is that Jesus will effectively become the savior of the world.[130] It prepares the reader for the next incident.[131] Some of the Greeks who went up to worship at the feast wanted to see Jesus (12:20-21).[132] These might be gentiles of Greek

---

God. For a thorough study of Isa 52–53 in John 12, see Daniel J. Brendsel, "Isaiah Saw His Glory": The Use of Isaiah 52–53 in John 12, BZNW 208 (Berlin: de Gruyter, 2014).

[126] Coloe, "Gentiles," in Sim and McLaren, Attitudes to Gentiles in Ancient Judaism and Early Christianity, 213.

[127] Coloe ("Gentiles," in Sim and McLaren, Attitudes to Gentiles in Ancient Judaism and Early Christianity, 215) notices that Zech 8:23 resembles the Greeks coming to Philip seeking Jesus.

[128] Apparently, the scribe behind Codex D recognized this exaggeration by adding ολος. For Hoskyns (Fourth Gospel, 422), this reading "brings out the author's meaning." Schnackenburg (John, 2:525n53) explains the addition of ολος as influenced by passages such as 1 John 2:2; 5:19.

[129] Lincoln, John, 345. Thompson (John, 266) sees the use of "world" here as derogatory (cf. Keener, John, 2:871, "the rabble"). If that is the case, the religious leaders might be thinking about the gentile world (see Zumstein, Johannesevangelium, 449). However, there are few clues in the text as to embrace this interpretation as highly likely. Michaels (John, 682) finds the same ironic exaggeration in 3:26, "All are coming to him."

[130] Beutler, Johannesevangelium, 355; Lindars, John, 425.

[131] Schnackenburg, John, 2:378.

[132] Brown (John, 1:466) pays attention to the larger Johannine context and interprets "to see" as "to believe in." However, since there is no personal interaction between Jesus and the Greeks, it is not clear whether they believed or wanted to believe in him. Barrett (John, 427) comments that the meeting did not take place because Jesus will draw the Greeks to himself only after his glorification.

birth who were attracted to the worship of Israel[133] or Jews from the Hellenistic diaspora.[134] On the one hand, a more precise term for Hellenistic Jews would be Ἑλληνισταί, as in Acts 6:1.[135] On the other hand, the Gospel of John intentionally avoids a term that might point to the religious status of the "Greeks,"[136] such as "proselytes" (προσήλυτοι or σεβόμενοι). The lack of any clear clue to interpret the "Greeks" in a particular direction might be intentional. The Gospel of John might be referring not only to Hellenistic Jews but also to gentiles sympathetic toward the worship in Jerusalem.[137] The use of the noun "Greeks" then might indicate that they represent the larger Greek world.[138]

Gentile visitors to Jerusalem were admitted to the outer court of the Temple, likely the same place that Jesus cleansed earlier in the Gospel of John (2:13-19).[139] Gentiles were allowed to "worship" in the temple but were not allowed to eat the Passover lamb.[140] This time, however, they are attracted to Jesus, the Lamb of God who takes away the sin of the world (1:19), since they ask to see him (12:21).[141] The use of

---

[133] Hoskyns, *Fourth Gospel*, 423; Brown, *John*, 1:466; Schnackenburg, *John*, 2:381; Keener, *John*, 2:871; Coloe, "Gentiles," in Sim and McLaren, *Attitudes to Gentiles in Ancient Judaism and Early Christianity*, 214.

[134] Thompson, *John*, 268. H. B. Kossen proposes that they are Greeks from Asia Minor. See his "Who Were the Greeks of John xii 20?" in *Studies in John*, NovTSup 24 (Leiden: Brill, 1970), 97–110.

[135] Bultmann, *John*, 423n2; Lindars, *John*, 427; Lincoln, *John*, 348.

[136] Schnelle, *Johannes*, 267.

[137] Ruben Zimmermann, *Puzzling the Parables of Jesus: Methods and Interpretation* (Minneapolis: Fortress, 2015), 357.

[138] Bultmann, *John*, 423; Barrett, *John*, 420; Thompson, *John*, 267; Schnelle, *Johannes*, 266; Haenchen, *John 2*, 96.

[139] The Greeks possibly met the disciples in the court of the gentiles, but the Gospel of John does not provide explicit details about this (Schnackenburg, *John*, 2:382). They only prefigure the coming of gentiles to Jesus after the completion of his hour (Lincoln, *John*, 349).

[140] Schnackenburg, *John*, 381; Lincoln, *John*, 348; Michaels, *John*, 686. "For those afflicted with leprosy . . . or persons otherwise defiled were not permitted to partake of this sacrifice, nor yet any foreigners (ἀλλοφύλοις) present for worship (θρησκείαν), and a large number of these assemble from abroad (ἔξωθεν)" (Josephus, *J.W.* 6.427–428).

[141] They might have selected Philip because he was from Bethsaida in Galilee (12:21), a town associated with gentiles in Isa 9:1 (Hoskyns, *Fourth Gospel*, 423). Bultmann (*John*,

the verb προσκυνέω when the text says that they went up to worship (προσκυνήσωσιν) at the feast (12:20) recalls the discussion between Jesus and the Samaritan woman, when he told her that "the hour (ὥρα) is coming when neither on this mountain nor in Jerusalem will you worship (προσκυνήσετε) the Father" (4:21), and "the hour (ὥρα) is coming, and is now here, when true worshipers (προσκυνηταί) will worship (προσκυνήσουσιν) the Father in spirit and truth, for the Father is seeking such people to worship (προσκυνοῦντας) him" (4:23).[142] The evocation of the dialogue between Jesus and the Samaritan woman is stronger because Jesus says to Andrew and Philip that "the hour (ἡ ὥρα) has come for the son of Man to be glorified" (12:23).

The Greeks' request prompts Jesus' words about the fulfillment of "the hour" and his glorification (12:23).[143] Jesus uses the imagery of a grain of wheat that falls into the earth and dies to talk about his own forthcoming death (12:24). The imagery, however, also relates death with "much fruit."[144] Thus, Jesus' death will bring his glorification, that is, many people coming to him.[145] Previously, Jesus told his disciples that he sent them to reap the fruit of his own labors in Samaria (4:36-38).[146] The one who reaps gathers fruit for eternal life (4:36). The association between "fruit" and Jesus' death was not evident in 4:36-38, but now the association is explicit using figures of speech in 12:24 and straightforward language in 12:33.[147]

---

423) observes that Philip and Andrew are the only two disciples among the twelve with Greek names, and wonders whether they were missionaries among gentiles after resurrection. At another level, it is possible that the two disciples were able to translate into Aramaic what pilgrims wanted to say in Greek, according to N. Clayton Croy, "Translating for Jesus: Philip and Andrew in John 12:20-22," *Neot* 49 (2015): 145–74.

[142] Schnackenburg, *John*, 2:381.

[143] "The approach of the Gentiles marks the glorification of Jesus" (Hoskyns, *Fourth Gospel*, 423).

[144] Schnackenburg (*John*, 2:383) talks about "rich missionary fruit." Similarly, Lindars, *John*, 429.

[145] Lincoln, *John*, 349. "The universality of the significance of the death of Jesus . . . is the answer to the request of the Greeks to see . . . Him" (Hoskyns, *Fourth Gospel*, 424).

[146] Michaels, *John*, 689.

[147] Cf. Zimmermann, *Parables*, 358: "The parable [John 12:24] works on a time lapse principle as there is actually a considerable amount of time between the dying of the grain and the bearing of fruit. . . . [T]he present time is time that should be filled with the disciples' mission to woo the people in the Gentile world."

Furthermore, Jesus' forthcoming death is related to the judgment of the world. Although Jesus is in Jerusalem talking to a crowd (12:29, 34), he announces judgment of *the world* (τοῦ κόσμου) because its ruler is going to be cast out (12:31).[148] This is an illegitimate ruler because he is a thief and a robber (10:1). This "ruler" is a "stranger" (10:5), and the sheep are not going to listen to his voice (10:5, 8). He steals what belongs to the rightful owner of creation and kills and destroys instead of giving life (10:10). Jesus, on the contrary, will lose his life in this world so that many may have eternal life (12:25). The obedience of the Son "explains the universal significance" of his death.[149] The judgment of the world is the victory of Jesus over the illegitimate ruler of creation. His death frees the world from his tyranny and enables humanity to embrace the giver of life. The glorification of Jesus, which includes his death, effects the end of the old and deadly world (judgment of the world), a universal change of rule (judgment of the prince of this world), and, therefore, the enthronement of Jesus, who brings a new world order.[150]

Jesus' death is the hour of his glorification because this event will precipitate a crisis in the world (12:31). He will be lifted up from the earth, and he will attract *all people* (πάντας)[151] to him (12:32).[152] The

---

[148] Elsewhere in the Gospel, judgment has been comprehensive in scope (Barrett, *John*, 426).

[149] Hoskyns, *Fourth Gospel*, 425.

[150] Schnelle, *Johannes*, 269; Schnackenburg, *John*, 2:393; Lindars, *John*, 433. For Michaels (*John*, 696), the phrasing of the "driving out" of the ruler of this world (12:31) recalls John the Baptist's earlier proclamation of Jesus as the Lamb of God who "takes away" the sin of the world (1:29).

[151] Some witnesses, including 𝔓⁶⁶ and the original reading of Sinaiticus, have the neuter plural. If this is the original reading, the neuter might have the sense of a general masculine reference (Brown, *John*, 1:468). Haenchen (*John 2*, 98) has a surprising comment here: "The word 'all' is here an error." For him Jesus will draw *only* those whom the Father has given him. Michaels (*John*, 698), similarly, comments that the "apparently universal scope of 'all' is striking." He finds a solution to his surprise by interpreting that *all* refers to people from different ethnic groups rather than individuals. I agree with Coloe ("Gentiles," in Sim and McLaren, *Attitudes to Gentiles in Ancient Judaism and Early Christianity*, 214) who interprets that πάντα ("all things") points to the "cosmic dimension of Jesus' mission."

[152] The active voice ἑλκύσω in reference to Jesus reminds the reader of the active voice ἑλκύσῃ in reference to God in 6:44 (Beutler, *Johannesevangelium*, 363; Zumstein, *Johannesevangelium*, 461; Barrett, *John*, 427).

word *all* indicates the scope of Jesus' death.[153] He will die for the benefit of all people because God created *all things* through the Word (1:3)
and he loves the whole world.[154] The universalism consistently found
throughout the Gospel (e.g., 1:9; 3:16; 4:42; 12:19) finds here an unmis-
takable expression.[155] Jesus' death has cosmic dimensions because no
one will escape from his light. Those who will reject it will be judged,
but those who accept it will receive eternal life.[156]

The Greeks who want to see Jesus are part of all those who will
be drawn to the exalted Jesus.[157] As Moses lifted up the serpent in the
wilderness, the Son will be lifted up, that "whoever (πᾶς) believes in
him may have eternal life" (3:14-15). The universal implications of Jesus'
glorification do not mean that every person will believe in him. Some
people refused to believe in him even after witnessing some signs
(12:37). The narrator finds in Isaiah the explanation for such unbelief.
The first text quoted is Isaiah 53:1. The context of this passage resonates with Johannine thought.[158] The Isaianic servant is rejected by all
men (πάντας ἀνθρώπους) (Isa 53:3), faces death (53:7-8, 11-12), and
suffers because of his people's sin (53:4-6). However, he will be exalted
and glorified (52:13). The larger context of the prophecy includes several instances of universal language. The offspring of the servant will
inherit the nations (ἔθνη) (54:3). God will be called in all the earth
(πάσῃ τῇ γῇ) (54:5). The Lord will reveal his arm before all the nations
(πάντων τῶν ἐθνῶν), and all the ends of the earth (πάντα τὰ ἄκρα
τῆς γῆς) will see "the salvation that comes from God" (52:10). Many

---

[153] It refers to both Jews and gentiles, according to Zumstein, *Johannesevangelium*, 463.

[154] Thompson, *John*, 271, 272.

[155] Beutler, *Johannesevangelium*, 363; Schnackenburg, *John*, 2:393.

[156] Donatien Mollat, *Études Johanniques*, Parole de Dieu (Paris: Éditions du
Seuil, 1979), 27.

[157] Lindars, *John*, 434.

[158] Similarly, Coloe, "Gentiles," in Sim and McLaren, *Attitudes to Gentiles in
Ancient Judaism and Early Christianity*, 219: "The exact citation of the LXX version of
Isa. 53.1 offers a significant insight into the evangelist's consistent universalist theme."
The several resonances of Isa 52:13–53:12 in John 12 are explored in Jonathan Lett, "The
Divine Identity of Jesus as the Reason for Israel's Unbelief in John 12:36-43," *JBL* 135
(2016): 159–73, here 163–66. However, Lett does not highlight the universal significance
of the Isaianic Servant.

nations will be astonished at him (52:15).[159] God himself has blinded their eyes and hardened their hearts (John 12:40).

This climactic section that portrays Jesus in Jerusalem announcing a forthcoming crisis for the world, a voice from heaven announcing the glorification of the Father's name, and a group of Greeks wanting to see Jesus concludes with clear instances of universal language (12:44-50).[160] The importance of Jesus' own claim that he came *into the world* is highlighted by the use of the verb "to cry" (12:44, 46). Jesus not only said he came into the world, he actually cried out those words. Although the prophecy of Caiaphas was exclusively concerned with the fate of "the people" and "the whole nation" (11:50), Jesus' speeches in Jerusalem concern the whole world. Echoing his previous claim that he is the light of the world (8:12; 9:5), Jesus cries out saying, "I have come into the world (τὸν κόσμον) as light, so that whoever (πᾶς) believes in me may not remain in darkness" (12:46). The reference to the light recalls the judgment that Jesus brings to those who do not believe in general (9:39-41) and to the ruler of this world in particular (12:31).[161] It also highlights the positive effects of the light, that is, giving people the opportunity to realize darkness and to achieve salvation.[162] Jesus also states his mission as "coming in order to save the world" (12:47). The language is reminiscent of 3:16-17. Since God loved the world, he sent his Son in order that the world might be saved through him.

The universalistic ring of this Johannine episode is even clearer if the larger context of Isaiah 53:1 (quoted in John 12:38) is recognized.[163] The wider context of John 12:38 resonates with the suffering servant of Isaiah. Key Johannine terminology such as the verbs δοξαθῆναι and

---

[159] This larger universalistic context also includes a previous text quoted in John 6:45: "They will all be taught by God" (Isa 54:13).

[160] For Zumstein ("Seuil," in Verheyden, van Oyen, Labahn, and Bieringer, *Studies in the Gospel of John ad Its Christology*, 275, 286), John 12:44-50 is the final synthesis of Jesus' message, and functions almost as an epilogue.

[161] Lincoln, *John*, 360.

[162] Michaels, *John*, 715.

[163] Johannes Beutler, "Greeks Come to See Jesus (John 12,20f)," *Biblica* 71 (1990): 333–47. The importance of Isa 49 for the understanding of Jesus' mission in the Gospel of John is highlighted by Kossen, "Who Were the Greeks," in *Studies in John*, 103–4.

ὑψωθῆναι are found in the so-called fourth Song of the Servant.[164]
The role of the servant for the gentiles is explicit in Isaiah 42:1-4 and
49:1-6. The servant will be the hope for the nations (42:4) and be a light
for the nations until the ends of the earth (49:6).[165] The nations that do
not yet know the servant, in turn, will "see" and "hear" (Isa 52:15). Similarly, the Greeks in John 12 want to "see" Jesus, making the link with
Isaiah 52 even stronger.[166] These connections indicate that the "coming
of the Greeks to Jesus is the coming of those who had not seen, to
behold the lamb of God."[167]

SYNTHESIS

The first controversy between Jesus and religious leaders in John 5–9
is related to Jewish tradition. Although Jesus' opponents dispute his
authority to heal a man on the Sabbath (John 5), Jesus remarks that he
has received from the Father an unlimited measure of revelation that
allows him to engage the whole world, executing judgment and offering life. His comprehensive authority will result in all people honoring
him as they honor the Father. Jesus' universal significance also has a
future dimension. The dead will hear his voice and will resurrect either
for life or judgment. The narrator uses several strategies to convey the
comprehensive scope of Jesus' significance in John 5. First, the use of
future-tense verbs and phrases such as "the hour is coming" is intended
to highlight the future dimension of Jesus' universal significance. Second, Jesus uses Jewish tradition (the Sabbath) as a point of departure

---

[164] Beutler ("Greeks," 340) observes, "Among all Old Testament texts which in
one way or another contain δοξαθῆναι and ὑψωθῆναι, this text has the highest prob-
ability of standing behind John 12,32.34."

[165] Beutler, "Greeks," 341.

[166] Beutler, "Greeks," 343.

[167] Beutler, "Greeks," 346. For Andrew T. Lincoln (*Truth on Trial: The Lawsuit
Motif in the Fourth Gospel* [Peabody, Mass.: Hendrickson, 2000], 255–56), Isaiah provides the larger cosmic framework for the Johannine trial. He suggests that this cosmic
trial is found during Jesus' earthly ministry and finds its climax in his interrogation
by Pilate. The Isaianic trial is universal in scope because it embraces the whole world
represented by the nations (40:5; 51:4-5; 52:10). Similarly, the "nations are represented
through the Samaritans who confess that Jesus 'is truly the Savoir of the world' (4:42)
and the Greeks who wish to see Jesus (12:20–22)" (Lincoln, *Truth*, 256).

to highlight his comprehensive scope as the giver of life and the one who executes judgment.

Jesus also has a discussion in a synagogue in Capernaum after providing food for a multitude (John 6). Contrary to his dialogue partners' arguments that the bread was for their parents, Jesus remarks that he is the bread from heaven that was given for the life of the whole world. His authority to give life extends to the future because he will raise people up on the last day. The narrator uses two strategies to highlight Jesus' universal significance in John 6. First, he portrays people in Galilee acclaiming him as the prophet who is to come *into the world*. Second, he depicts Jesus creatively using an Old Testament quotation (John 6:45; Isa 54:13) that highlights the universal significance of God. Although his dialogue partners also use the Old Testament in their discussions with Jesus, it is telling that the larger literary context of the text they use (Ps 78:24) lacks instances of universal language.

Another set of controversies with several groups begins with his brothers in John 7 and concludes with religious leaders in John 9. These discussions highlight Jesus' role as the light of the world who brings judgment and life. Throughout the story of the restoration of a man born blind, the narrator uses three strategies to remark on Jesus' comprehensive scope. First, he situates this section against the background of the Feast of Tabernacles. The eschatological celebration of this festival, as found in Zechariah 14, portrays a worldwide pilgrimage to Jerusalem and recognition of God as universal King. The narrator, however, has Jesus as the center of an encounter between God and humanity. Second, he portrays his brothers and religious leaders in an ironic way. His brothers invite Jesus to show himself *to the world*, although they did not believe in him. Some religious leaders ask an ironic question that expects a negative answer, that is, whether he will go to the dispersion of the Greeks and teach the Greeks. Third, the narrator has Jesus quoting from Zechariah 14 to support his open invitation to anyone who wants to come to him.

The discourse about the shepherd and the sheep in John 10 also highlights the comprehensive scope of Jesus' significance. Jesus is the shepherd who offers life in abundance to humanity and who gathers his sheep. He has other sheep that will listen to his voice and will become part of the only fold secured by the Father's hand. The positive portrayal of Jesus giving life and gathering believers shows that the ruler of this world is a stranger who illegitimately entered the world to steal and destroy. The following encounter between Jesus and Martha and Lazarus illustrates Jesus' power to give life (John 11). They listen to Jesus' voice, and they both receive life. Religious leaders, however, fear *everyone* will believe in him. Throughout the account set in Bethany, the narrator uses three strategies to convey the universal significance of Jesus. First, he uses parables that point to Jesus as the rightful owner of creation who will unify in himself those who believe in him. Second, he uses irony to show that the religious leaders' fear of this will be fulfilled in Jesus attracting *all* peoples to himself, although some will reject him as the revelation of God. Third, the narrator himself makes an intervention to interpret Caiaphas' words. The narrator indicates that Caiaphas was prophesying that Jesus will die to gather into one God's children scattered abroad.

The last and climactic episode of the first major section of the Gospel gives a prominent place to instances of universal language (John 12).[168] These instances are used to highlight that Jesus' death, which is his glorification, will result in all people being attracted to him. Jesus' death and resurrection expands the scope of his work as the one who brings life and executes judgment. Jesus' death will bring much fruit because many will believe in him, the illegitimate ruler of this world will be cast out, and the world will be judged. The narrator again uses three strategies to highlight the comprehensive scope of Jesus' significance. First, Scripture is quoted by the crowds in Jerusalem, the narrator, and Jesus himself. However, only the larger context of the quotations attributed to Jesus and the narrator have instances of universal language. Such quotations are used to interpret the events taking place in Jerusalem but also to highlight Jesus' universal significance as King and bringer of judgment for the world. Second, the narrator introduces for the only time in his narrative a peculiar group of characters. A group of Greek people in Jerusalem asks to see Jesus. Third, he concludes this major section with Jesus crying that he *came into the world* as light. It is highly significant that the first major section of the

---

[168] The first major section of the Gospel (John 1–12) is usually known as "the book of signs." The second section is traditionally called "the book of glory" (John 12–21).

Gospel (John 1–12) begins with a clear instance of universal language, that is, the role of the Word in the creation of the world (1:3, 10), and concludes with Jesus crying about his mission to the whole world (12:46-47).

II

3

THE WITNESS TO A DIFFERENT WORLD

The largely public controversies and discourses in John 5–12 were intended to highlight Jesus' authority to engage the whole world because he has received from the Father an unlimited endowment of revelation. The following teachings and prayer in John 13–17 take place in a more private setting, where the narrator deepens his portrayal of Jesus' universal significance in substantial ways. First, the comprehensive scope of Jesus' significance secures his unique relationship with God because his authority over all flesh will result in the glorification of the Father. Second, Jesus' victory over the world legitimizes the all-encompassing mission of the disciples, who are expected to give testimony by loving each other, living in unity, and engaging the world with life and light. Third, the Spirit will further Jesus' ministry through the disciples by convicting the world of sin, righteousness, and judgment. The Spirit, through the work of the disciples, is a witness to a different world characterized by love, unity, and light.[1] Humanity, then, can realize that its world, dominated by hate, disunity, and darkness, can be transformed into what God expected his creation to be in the beginning.

---

[1] Cf. Sjef van Tilborg, *Reading John in Ephesus*, NovTSup 83 (Leiden: E. J. Brill, 1996), 167, "Jesus' death is not in contradiction with his life's mission: to be in this cosmos a witness of a different world."

The Last Teachings to the Disciples

Before facing his passion, Jesus pronounces two farewell discourses[2] that include important instances of universal language.[3] The first discourse, in John 13–14, is bracketed by the narrator's indication that the Father had given all things into the hands of his Son (13:3) and by Jesus' claim that his obedience to his Father is intended so that the world may know his love for the one who sent him (14:31).[4] The second discourse, in John 15–16, concludes with a triumphant note: "I have overcome the world" (16:33). The narrator and Jesus himself are the only two characters who use universal language in the farewell discourses. The only exception is Judas' confusion about whether Jesus will manifest himself to the world (14:22).

Jesus' Authority in the World

Instances of the universal authority of the Son are found in the first farewell discourse of Jesus in John 13–14 in two scenes where he washes the disciples' feet and teaches about the mission of the Spirit in the world through his followers. John 13–14 moves from particular to

---

[2] Scholars agree that John 13–16 is a complete example of the farewell genre. For example, John C. Stube, *A Greco-Roman Rhetorical Reading of the Farewell Discourse*, LNTS 309 (London: T&T Clark, 2006).

[3] Some scholars distinguish between Jewish opposition in John 5–12 and the world's opposition in John 14–17, and suggest that "the world" in the farewell discourses and Jesus' final prayer refers to widespread gentile disbelief that the putative Johannine community faced. Lars Kierspel (*The Jews and the World in the Fourth Gospel: Parallelism, Function, and Context*, WUNT 2/220 [Tübingen: Mohr Siebeck, 2006], 179n108) cautions against this identification of different opponents in light of his narratological study of Ἰουδαῖοι and κόσμος.

[4] The first farewell discourse (John 13–14) begins with a prelude in the form of a dramatic act (13:1–30) that prepares the reader for Jesus' interaction with his disciples in 13:31–14:31. See Francis J. Moloney, *Johannine Studies 1975–2017*, WUNT 372 (Tübingen: Mohr Siebeck, 2017), 405–26. The literary unity of John 13–17 has been highlighted by a number of scholars. For example, see Yves Simoens, *La gloire d'aimer: Structures stylistiques et interprétatives dans le Discours de la Cène (Jn 13–17)*, AnBib 90 (Rome: Biblical Institute Press, 1981), 52–80; Wayne Brouwer, *The Literary Development of John 13–17: A Chiastic Reading*, SBLDS 182 (Atlanta: Society of Biblical Literature, 2000); and L. Scott Kellum, *The Unity of the Farewell Discourse: The Literary Integrity of John 13.31–16.33*, JSNTSup 256 (London: T&T Clark, 2004).

universal. First, Jesus interacts with a particular group of Jewish people in a specific Jewish place; he washes the feet of an intimate group of disciples in Judea and predicts that Judas will betray him. Second, Jesus frames the interpretation of that act of service using instances of universal language:[5] the ruler of *this world* is behind Judas Iscariot's actions (13:2; 14:30),[6] Jesus is leaving *this world* (13:1),[7] and he has loved his disciples *in the world*.[8] Thus the narrator sets a particular act of service in the cosmic dimension.[9]

Jesus' act of service is motivated by his knowledge that the Father "had given all things (πάντα ἔδωκεν) into his hands (εἰς τὰς χεῖρας)" (13:3). The emphases of this declaration are better appreciated when compared with John the Baptist's testimony in 3:35, "the Father loves the Son and has given all things (πάντα δέδωκεν) into his hand (ἐν

[5] J. Ramsey Michaels, *The Gospel of John*, NICNT (Grand Rapids: Eerdmans, 2010), 724. This "cosmic tale," studied by Adele Reinhartz (*The Word in the World: The Cosmological Tale in the Fourth Gospel*, SBLMS 45 [Atlanta: Scholars Press, 1992], 4), is "universal in location and has eternity as its time frame" (36). Reinhartz contends that "by universalizing the specific temporal and spatial boundaries of the historical [i.e., the historical Jesus] and ecclesiological [i.e., the putative Johannine community] tales," John invites readers "to see themselves as its addressees" (38).

[6] The ruler of this world is a reference to Jesus' main opponent in the Gospel, i.e., the devil. Thus, Reinhartz, *Word*, 23, 91–92.

[7] Jesus previously indicated that he came *into the world* in order to *save the world* (12:46-47). The presence of the pronoun τούτου in κόσμου τούτου emphasizes the "distinction between the world, and the disciples," according to C. K. Barrett, *The Gospel according to St. John: An Introduction with Commentary and Notes on the Greek Text* (Philadelphia: Westminster, 1978), 438.

[8] The phrase "to the end" means "fully" or "completely," but in light of John 15:13, the meaning here is closely related to Jesus' death (19:30). See Andrew T. Lincoln, *The Gospel according to Saint John*, BNTC 4 (New York: Hendrickson, 2005), 365; Barnabas Lindars, *The Gospel of John: Based on the Revised Standard Version*, NCB (Grand Rapids: Eerdmans, 1981), 448; Marianne Meye Thompson, *John: A Commentary*, NTL (Louisville: Westminster John Knox, 2015), 284; Edwyn Clement Hoskyns, *The Fourth Gospel*, ed. Francis Noel Davey (London: Faber and Faber, 1967), 436; Michaels, *John*, 722; and Craig S. Keener, *The Gospel of John: A Commentary* (Peabody, Mass.: Hendrickson, 2003), 2:899.

[9] John 13:1-13 is taken as the "prologue" to the second part of the Gospel by Xavier Léon-Dufour, "Situation de Jean 13," in *Die Mitte des Neuen Testaments: Einheit und Vielfalt neutestamentlicher Theologie*, ed. Ulrich Luz and Hans Weder (Göttingen: Vandenhoeck & Ruprecht, 1983), 131-41, here 131, 134.

τῇ χειρί)."[10] The similarities are striking.[11] Most notably, the love motif has a prominent place in both declarations. The Father loves the Son (3:35), and the Son has loved his disciples (13:1). The demonstration of the Father's love for his Son is the granting of authority over the whole world. This may imply, although it is not yet clearly seen in the narrative, that Jesus' love for his disciples will include their authority to be his witnesses for the benefit of the world. However, the evidence of their authority over the world should not be in the form of public demonstrations of power over humanity but in the form of acts of service, as when Jesus washes his disciples' feet.[12] The overall meaning of both declarations (3:35; 13:3) is also similar. On the one hand, the former text refers to the authority Jesus has to give life. Whoever believes in the one who has all things in his hand has eternal life (ζωὴν αἰώνιον) (3:36). On the other hand, the latter text may refer to Jesus' authority to give light to the world that is in darkness. Jesus came into the world as light (ἐγὼ φῶς εἰς τὸν κόσμον ἐλήλυθα), so that whoever believes in him may not remain in darkness (12:46). His authority to give life and light to the world stems from his role in creation. Life was in the Word (1:4) and the life was the "light of humanity" (1:5).[13] Jesus is the way, the truth, and the life, and "no one (οὐδείς) comes to the Father except through" him (14:6). There is yet a third similarity between 3:35 and 13:3. Both texts use the adjective πάντα (all). Since this adjective has no restriction in the two contexts, it may point to Jesus' unlimited and "world-encompassing authority" over his whole creation.[14]

---

[10] Similar ideas are also found in 5:20; 6:37, 39; 10:29; 12:32, according to Thompson, *John*, 285; Barrett, *John*, 439.

[11] The differences between 13:3 and 3:35, as shown below, are minimal. The verb in 3:35 is perfect tense but the verb in 13:3 is aorist. The noun "hands" is plural in 13:3 but singular in 3:35. The verb is followed by a dative pronoun that refers to Jesus in 13:3 but a genitive pronoun modifies "hand" in 3:35. Barrett (*John*, 435) observes that the expression in 13:3 is awkward because "either αὐτῷ or εἰς τὰς χεῖρας would have sufficed alone." The use of the pronoun and the prepositional phrase in 13:3 may be for emphasis.

[12] The expression of love is a concrete act of sacrifice and service, according to Moloney, *Johannine Studies*, 133.

[13] The phrase πρὸς τὸν θεὸν ὑπάγει in 13:3 evokes ἦν πρὸς τὸν θεόν in 1:1, according to Michaels, *John*, 724n20.

[14] Michaels, *John*, 724. The idea of the Father giving all things into the hands of the Son contrasts with the devil inciting Judas to betray Jesus (13:2-3). Jesus' universal

The disciples recognize the authority of the Son in their reference to Jesus as "Lord" (13:6, 9, 13, 14; cf. 13:25, 36, 37; 14:5, 8, 22).[15] Jesus acknowledges the accuracy of the disciples' epithet by saying that they are right (13:13) and by using the noun "Lord" (13:14).[16] The correct interpretation of Jesus' lordship, however, is shaped by his act of service for his disciples and by his discourse about his relationship with the Father. Jesus' universal authority over humanity is demonstrated in a dramatic act of service. The washing of the disciples' feet shows that Jesus has authority even over his own life, to lay it down for the salvation of the world (see 10:18).[17] Contrary to popular expectations, the one with authority expresses his power by taking the role of a servant.[18] After washing his disciples' feet, Jesus interprets the scope of his authority. He can bring life and light to the whole of creation, but he is not greater than the one who sent him (13:17). Jesus has everything in his hands but the Father is greater than the Son (14:28). Jesus' authority is not a challenge to the authority of the Father, but it is fully expressed in his complete obedience to the one who sent him.

Since Jesus soon will depart from this world, his larger concern for the world will be carried out by the Spirit through the disciples. The dramatic condition of humanity demands the disciples' engagement with the world.[19] Humanity will see Jesus no more because he

---

authority stems from his unique relationship with God, but Judas' actions are induced by the devil. The devil can influence Judas, but he has no claim on Jesus (14:30).

[15] Keener (*John*, 2:900) suggests that "Jesus takes his position as Lord of all things" in 13:3.

[16] Raymond F. Collins, "'You Call Me Teacher and Lord—and You Are Right. For That Is What I Am' (John 13,13)," in *Studies in the Gospel of John and Its Christology: Festschrift Gilbert van Belle*, ed. Joseph Verheyden, Geert van Oyen, Michael Labahn, and Reimund Bieringer, BETL 265 (Leuven: Peeters, 2014), 327–48, here 327.

[17] Lincoln, *John*, 366; Lindars, *John*, 449.

[18] The host of a meal was presumably in authority over his house and household, and, therefore, it was not his duty to wash his guests' feet himself. Slaves or servants were provided for such a task. See Richard Bauckham, *The Testimony of the Beloved Disciple: Narrative, History, and Theology in the Gospel of John* (Grand Rapids: Baker Academic, 2007), 192.

[19] Previously, Jesus has indicated that the world does not know the Spirit (14:17). He also has accused his opponents of not knowing the Father (8:55). The narrator anticipated very early in the narrative that the world did not know the one through

will depart this world to the Father (13:1; 14:19).[20] Therefore, they will be unable to achieve the eternal life that is obtained only by seeing Jesus, knowing him, and receiving his words (1:12; 6:40, 64). Similarly, humanity cannot receive the Spirit because it neither sees him nor knows him (14:17). Therefore, people cannot experience the new birth that gives them entrance into the kingdom (3:5), they remain in darkness (8:12; 12:46), and they are controlled by the ruler of this world (12:31). The world may think that their present reality, dominated by darkness and death, is the only possible way of living. However, the world's present reality is not eternal or absolute. The only hope for the world remains with the disciples, who embody a different reality.

The disciples are witnesses in the world to a different reality because they enjoy a privileged position in relationship to Jesus, the Spirit, and the Father. They know the Spirit because he dwells with them (14:17). The disciples will also see Jesus after his departure from the world (14:19) because they will later encounter the risen Lord (20:20). This unique position allows them to live in a distinctive way as a testimony to the world.[21] Their mutual love will signal that they are distinctive people: "by this all people (πάντες) will know that you are my disciples, if you have love for one another" (13:35). As in 13:3, the word πάντες here in 13:35 does not seem to have restrictions in its current literary context, and, therefore, it potentially refers to "everyone in the world."[22] The sacrificial service demonstrated in the washing of the disciples' feet should be the

---

whom the world was created (1:10). The ability to know Jesus leads to knowledge of the Father (14:7), freedom (8:32), and eternal life.

[20] The negative portrayal of the world in the farewell discourses is pervasive. For example, in John 14:6 ("no one comes to the Father except through me"), "the context makes clear that 'no one' includes everyone. The assumption is that all people are separated from God," according to Craig R. Koester, "Jesus as the Way to the Father in Johannine Theology (John 14,6)," in *Theology and Christology in the Fourth Gospel: Essays by the Members of the SNTS Johannine Writings Seminar*, ed. Gilbert Van Belle, J. G. Van der Watt, and P. J. Maritz, BETL 184 (Leuven: Leuven University Press, 2005), 117–33, here 117.

[21] Rudolf Bultmann, *The Gospel of John: A Commentary*, trans. G. R. Beasley-Murray, R. W. N. Hoare, and J. K. Riches, The Johannine Monograph Series 1 (Eugene, Ore.: Wipf & Stock, 2014), 528.

[22] Michaels, *John*, 760–61. Ernst Haenchen (*John 2: A Commentary on the Gospel of John, Chapters 7–21*, ed. Robert W. Funk with Ulrich Busse, trans. Robert W. Funk, Hermeneia [Philadelphia: Fortress, 1984], 118), however, thinks that "John does not

measure of the disciples' love for each other. This specific kind of love will function as a "sign to the world"[23] that points to Jesus' love for the world.[24] Since Jesus has already anticipated that whoever receives his disciples receives him and his Father (13:20), those from the world who will embrace the disciples' testimony will also have the opportunity to become children of God (1:12). Therefore, humanity can receive Jesus and the Father by embracing God's representatives in the world (13:20).

This reading is evident for the reader, who has access to the narrator's introductory assertion about Jesus departing out of this world to the Father (13:1), the disciples' position in the world (13:1), and Jesus' universal authority granted by his Father (13:3). The disciples, however, seem confused. Five of them ask clarification questions about Jesus' teaching (13:25, 36, 37; 14:5, 8, 22).[25] The last question in the farewell discourses is posed by Judas.[26] He asks, "How is it that you will manifest yourself (ἐμφανίζειν σεαυτόν) to us, and not to the world (τῷ κόσμῳ)?" (14:22). Since he has been exposed to Jesus' previous teaching, he may know that Jesus' ministry is universal in scope.[27] On the one hand, Jesus previously told his disciples that he is "the light

---

have in view the worldwide church, but the small band of disciples for whom this Gospel was written."

[23] Lindars, *John*, 464. Bultmann (*John*, 527), expresses this idea as "the new world" becoming "reality in the community."

[24] Thompson, *John*, 301. The love among the disciples "is to bear witness to the love of God for the world and so to offer eternal life to *all men*," according to Hoskyns, *Fourth Gospel*, 451 (emphasis in original).

[25] Those asking questions include the disciple Jesus loved (13:23), Simon Peter (13:36-37), Thomas (14:5), Philip (14:8), and Judas (14:22). Judas' question can be taken as climactic because it is the last question that a disciple will ask Jesus during his earthly ministry. The group of disciples will later want to ask a question, but, before they do, Jesus will provide an answer (16:17-19).

[26] Although Judas "acts as an individual, he fulfils a collective/representative role" in this narrative, according to Catrin H. Williams, "Judas (Not Iscariot): What's in a Name?" in *Character Studies in the Fourth Gospel: Narrative Approaches to Seventy Figures in John*, ed. Steven A. Hunt, D. François Tolmie, and Ruben Zimmermann, WUNT 314 (Tübingen: Mohr Siebeck, 2013), 550–53, here 551.

[27] At the narrative level, then, it is not correct to characterize Judas' question as "foolish" (contra Bultmann, *John*, 622). Cf. Michaels, *John*, 789: "Judas's question is the best anyone has asked yet." Even his own brothers, who did not believe in him, encouraged Jesus to go to Judea to "show yourself (φανέρωσον σεαυτόν) to the world

of the world" (9:5). On the other hand, Jesus has recently stated that he will manifest himself (ἐμφανίσω . . . ἐμαυτόν) to those who are loved by his Father (14:21), that he will come to his disciples (14:18), and that the world will not see him (14:19). Since the Father will love those who keep Jesus' commandments (14:21), and since at least the new commandment has been given only to the disciples (13:34), Judas supposes that Jesus will only manifest himself to them. Jesus' reply to Judas ("if anyone loves me, he will keep my word") extends the possibility of loving him to "anyone" (ἐάν τις, 14:23).[28] The world will then learn to love Jesus through the disciples. Then Jesus will reveal himself to the world through the disciples because they will bear witness to Jesus' crucifixion and resurrection to those who were not present in Jerusalem during his passion. This includes the circle of disciples but is not restricted to them. Those who so embrace Jesus will experience the love of the Father (14:23). Since God has loved the world (3:16), the Father can manifest his love to those who love the Son (14:23).[29] Jesus' reply to Judas also highlights his teachings. Instead of using the plural "commandments" (14:21),[30] he refers more broadly to his "word" (14:23). His teachings about the Father during his earthly ministry is one of the most important commandments to the world: to receive him as the revelation of God (12:49-50).[31]

(τῷ κόσμῳ)" (7:4) (see Williams, "Judas," in Hunt, Tolmie, and Zimmerman, *Character Studies in the Fourth Gospel*, 55).

[28] Jörg Frey correctly observes that although "not all humans come to belief and to the realization of God's love yet in spite of the experience of hatred and hostility against the community (Jn 15,18ff), the positive and salvific aims of Jesus' mission (Jn 3,17) and God's love (3,16) are clearly retained in a strikingly undualistic manner." See his "Love-Relations in the Fourth Gospel: Establishing a Semantic Network," in *Repetitions and Variations in the Fourth Gospel: Style, Text, Interpretation*, ed. Gilbert van Belle and P. J. Maritz, BETL 223 (Leuven: Peeters, 2009), 171-98, here 186.

[29] Bultmann (*John*, 488) sees no contradiction between the Father's love for the world in 3:16 and Jesus' love for his own in 13:1, since he indicates, "Of course the love of the Son, like that of the Father, is directed towards the whole world, to win everyone to itself; but this love becomes a reality only where men open themselves to it."

[30] This observation leads Lindars (*John*, 482) to conclude that Jesus in 14:23 "does not deny the universal manifestation at the Parousia."

[31] Haenchen (*John 2*, 127), however, takes Judas' question and Jesus' reply as indicative of a "closed community" behind the Gospel: "It follows from this remark that

The confusion of the disciples (esp. Judas) about Jesus' manifestation to the world is further dispelled at the end of the first farewell discourse (John 13–14), since Jesus indicates that he obeys the Father so that the world may know (γνῷ) that he loves the Father (14:31).[32] Jesus' works and words during his earthly ministry were intended to benefit not only his close circle of disciples but also the whole world. The first set of farewell discourses (John 13–14) then concludes with a clear instance of universal language in 14:31 that is linked to previous statements about Jesus being the savior of the world (4:42) and its life and light (6:51; 8:12).[33]

The Disciples' Fruit and the Spirit's Work

The second group of farewell discourses in John 15–16 also comprises several instances of universal language that point to the worldwide missionary work of the disciples. The Spirit dwelling among them allows Jesus' followers to be witnesses to the whole world of a new reality made possible through him.

Jesus continues his farewell discourses by comparing himself with "the true vine," his Father with the "vinedresser," and his disciples with "branches" (15:1-2, 5).[34] The meaning of the "fruit" (καρπόν, 15:2, 4, 16;

---

the Johannine community knew itself to be a 'closed community' more or less. It is not informed by the [awareness] that it ought to evangelize the world; rather, its mission has internal [boundaries]."

[32] The world is under the authority of the "ruler of this world" (14:30) and, therefore, is in darkness. Jesus' obedience to the Father demonstrates to the world the unique relationship to him. Jesus' obedience signals his authority over creation (13:3) to give light to the world (12:46). The world may know that Jesus loves the Father (14:31) by attending to the testimony of the mutual love that characterizes the disciples.

[33] Michaels, *John*, 797.

[34] The image of a "vine" was widely applied to Israel in Jewish tradition (Jean Zumstein, *Das Johannesevangelium*, ed. Dietrich-Alex Koch, KEKNT [Göttingen: Vandenhoeck & Ruprecht, 2016], 562; Thompson, *John*, 323n112). It was also connected to the Son of Man in Ps 79:14-16 LXX, according to David W. Wead, *The Literary Devices in John's Gospel*, Theologische Dissertationen 4 (Basel: Friedrich Reinhardt Kommissionsverlag, 1970), 92. In John 15, the "true vine" is not the disciples but Jesus himself. If John intends to evoke Jewish traditions about Israel and the vine, Jesus here takes the place of Israel or embodies the people of God, as he becomes the center of the community of those who believe in him (Schnelle, *Johannes*, 316; Johannes Beutler,

καρπὸν πολύν, 15:5) that the disciples ought to produce (15:16) is not immediately clear. The most likely conclusion following a sequential reading that illuminates our present passage with clues found in John 4 and John 12 is that "fruit" should be other people, especially those who were not traditionally associated with Judaism, believing, following, and abiding in Jesus through the testimony of the disciples.[35] The first use of the noun "fruit" in the Gospel of John is found in the story of Jesus with his disciples right after his dialogue with a woman from Samaria: "The one who reaps is receiving wages and gathering fruit (καρπόν) for eternal life" (4:36).[36] This "fruit," taken in its literary context, refers to many (πολλοί) Samaritans believing (ἐπίστευσαν) in Jesus through the testimony of the Samaritan woman (4:39).[37] Those from Samaria who believed asked Jesus to "abide" (μεῖναι) with him, and he stayed (ἔμεινεν) there with them two days (4:40). This "abiding"

Das Johannesevangelium: Kommentar [Freiburg: Herder, 2013], 422). However, the lack of an explicit quotation from the Old Testament in John 15:1-11 may indicate that the figure of the vine is used because it was widely known in the ancient Mediterranean world in a number of cultural milieus. The faithful disciples are compared with fruitful branches. Barrett (*John*, 473) interprets that the unfruitful branches are "apostate Christians" and also suggests that they might represent unfruitful Israel. Barrett, however, does not explain how Israel was unfruitful. The interpretation that better fits the literary context (cf. 15:5) is that the disciples are the branches (Lindars, *John*, 488). In the Gospel of John, those who embrace and believe in the Word receive the right to become God's children (1:11). Jesus' disciples are "chosen," "appointed," and "sent" to bear much fruit (15:16).

[35] The "fruit" here represents the "effective missionary work" of the disciples, according to Hoskyns, *Fourth Gospel*, 476. Haenchen (*John 2*, 131) takes "fruit" in 15:2 as some sort of individual "spiritual" progress (cf. Bultmann, *John*, 533, "the life of faith"). Barrett (*John*, 474) embraces an interpretation of 15:2 that focuses on community, the "bearing of fruit is simply living the life of a Christian disciple . . . perhaps especially the practice of mutual love." Raymond Edward Brown (*The Gospel according to John*, 2 vols., AB 29 [Garden City, N.Y.: Doubleday, 2000], 2:676) allows two interpretations: spiritual progress and missionary enterprise. Keener (*John*, 2:997), however, rejects the missionary interpretation because the immediate context suggests to him "moral fruit." However, 15:16 clearly links the sending of the disciples and the bearing of fruit (Hoskyns, *Fourth Gospel*, 476). The verb "to go" in 15:16 points to the missionary activity of the disciples (Schnelle, *Johannes*, 319; Michaels, *John*, 816).

[36] Barrett, *John*, 478.

[37] The adjective πολύν is used several times in the Gospel to indicate people who believe in Jesus: 2:23; 4:1, 39, 41; 7:31; 8:30; 10:42; 11:45; 12:11, 42.

of Jesus produced even more fruit because the narrator informs the reader that "many more (πολλῷ πλείους) believed because of his word (τὸν λόγον αὐτοῦ)" (4:41). This leads the Samaritans to identify Jesus as the "savior of the world" (4:42). Jesus then gave a previous example (4:35-42) of what he now demands from the disciples (15:1-17). His followers are pruned through Jesus' word (τὸν λόγον) so that they may bear much fruit (πολύν καρπόν) that should abide (μένῃ) (15:3, 16).[38]

The other previous instance of the noun "fruit" in the Gospel of John is found in Jesus' reply to Andrew and Philip after they told him that some Greeks (Ἕλληνες) who went up to Jerusalem to worship requested to see him (12:20-26).[39] Jesus foresees that his forthcoming death will bear much fruit because he will draw all people to himself (12:32-33). Jesus compares himself with a grain of wheat that falls onto the earth, dies, and bears much fruit (πολὺν καρπόν, 12:24). The literary context requires that this "fruit" refers primarily to the Greeks who went up to Jerusalem to worship and, secondarily, to "all people" who are going to be drawn to the glorified Jesus (12:20, 32). This fruit that Jesus' death produces will bring honor to the Father's name (δόξασον, 12:28) because those who will believe in Jesus will abandon the authority of the "ruler of this world" (12:31).[40] The discourse about Jesus as the true vine has also as its core the glorification of the Father. The Father is glorified (ἐδοξάσθη) when the disciples bear much fruit because, presumably, those who will believe in Jesus through their testimony

---

[38] The idea of abiding figures prominently in John 15:1-16. The disciples should abide in Jesus (15:4, 5, 6, 7) and in his love (15:9, 10). Jesus abides in the love of the Father (15:10). Jesus' words should abide in the disciples (15:7). The fruit of the disciples' work should abide (15:16).

[39] Hoskyns, *Fourth Gospel*, 479.

[40] The world, then, will be judged through Jesus' death (12:31). The relationship between 12:24, 28 and 15:8 can be highlighted as follows:

12:24c πολὺν καρπὸν φέρει
12:28a πάτερ, δόξασόν σου τὸ ὄνομα
15:8a ἐν τούτῳ ἐδοξάσθη ὁ πατήρ μου
15:8b ἵνα καρπὸν πολὺν φέρητε

will abide with the Father and, consequently, will abandon the authority of the ruler of this world (15:8, 16).[41]

The missionary idea behind the noun "fruit" is further emphasized in 15:16, where Jesus indicates that the selection and appointment of the disciples is intended for them to "go and bear fruit." The verb "to go" (ὑπάγω) is used elsewhere in the Gospel of John in reference to Jesus' departure to his Father (e.g., 13:3).[42] However, it is also used in the story of the man born blind in 9:7, 11. After putting mud in the man's eyes, Jesus commands him to go (ὕπαγε) and wash in the pool of Siloam. The narrator clarifies that Siloam means "sent" (ἀπεσταλμένος). This might evoke the sending of Jesus to the world (9:4), the sending of the Spirit (14:26; 15:26), or the sending of the disciples (4:38; see also 17:18; 20:21).[43] In light of this larger context, the use of "to go" in 15:16 may imply that the disciples can bear fruit only by *going* into the world. In distinction from Jesus, who attracts all people to himself (7:37; 12:32), the disciples bear fruit by going into the world as witnesses to Jesus. The disciples' separation from the world is not spatial but qualitative. They remain in the world (17:14-18) just as Jesus saved the world from inside it without being corrupted by it.

Paradoxically, the fruitfulness of the disciples in their missionary endeavors in the world is made possible by their separation from the world, that is, their purity. The somehow opaque reference to the cleanness of the disciples in the story of the washing of the disciples' feet in 13:8-11 is clarified in John 15:2-3.[44] The disciples have been cleaned by the word that Jesus spoke to them (15:3), and the Father prunes the

---

[41] The presence of the illegitimate ruler preceded that of Jesus. His reign brought darkness to the world. The world needs salvation from this ruler, and Jesus, the preexistent Word who created everything that exists, is the only one capable of bringing such salvation (Reinhartz, *Word*, 92).

[42] Brown (*John*, 2:665) observes that the verb "to go" is also used in Luke 10:3 to describe the mission of the seventy disciples.

[43] Michaels, *John*, 547.

[44] Scholars usually interpret the washing of the disciples' feet by referring to Jesus' death in John 19 (e.g., Larry Paul Jones, *The Symbol of Water in the Gospel of John*, JSNTSup 145 [Sheffield: Sheffield Academic, 1997], 196–97). For other possible interpretations, see Birger Olson, "The Meanings of John 13,10: A Question of Genre?" in Verheyden, van Oyen, Labahn, and Bieringer, *Studies in the Gospel of John and Its Christology*, 317–25, here 196–97.

branches so that they may bear more fruit (15:2). Their unity with Jesus allows them to bring much fruit (15:4, 5) that will glorify the Father (15:8). Their unity with God means their separation from the world. This separation will become even wider by the opposition of the world to the disciples. Jesus predicts that the world will be hostile to his followers.[45] The world hates the Father, Jesus, and the disciples (15:18, 24) and demonstrates its hate especially through persecution (15:20). Since the disciples do not belong to the world (15:19) but are part of a divine community, and since the world does not know the one who sent Jesus (15:21; 16:3), the world is antagonistic to the disciples.[46] The ignorance of the world even extends to their own reality. It does not know that it is dominated by darkness and sin. Therefore, Jesus also has demonstrated the Father's love for the world (3:16) by revealing its sin (ἁμαρτίαν) through his spoken words (15:22) and through his works performed during his earthly ministry (15:24). By implication, the disciples should show their love for the world by revealing the dramatic condition of humanity dominated by darkness, falsehood, and hate.

There is yet another element in the discourse about the true vine that might point to the universal significance of Jesus and the message about him. This is found in Jesus' assertion that he has loved his disciples as the Father has loved him (15:9). The demonstration of the Father's love for his Son is that he has given all things into his hands (3:35; cf. 13:3). Since Jesus shows his love for his disciples in the same way the Father showed his love for him, the disciples will receive from Jesus authority over the world as a demonstration of his love for them (cf. 20:22-23).[47] If this reading is correct, John 15:9 may point to Jesus'

---

[45] Kierspel (*Jews*, 178) rightly observes that "the world's hate and rejection of the *logos* . . . does not simply refer to the expulsion of Jewish Christians from the synagogue, but alludes to hostilities from Gentile opposition."

[46] Although "the world" here are those who do not believe in Jesus, there is an immediate identification with those associated with Judaism who reject Jesus claims. This is supported by the reference to "their law" in 15:25.

[47] Jacobus (Kobus) Kok, "The Plenipotentiary Idea as Leitmotiv in John's Gospel," *In die Skriflig* 49 (2015): 1–9. Kok suggests that in the Gospel of John "Jesus empowers the disciples to become authoritative representatives of himself and of the mission of God" (8). There are, however, "later heralds of the faith" who "can only recount, attest, and recall the revelation given by Jesus in 'signs' (and words), which

universal authority being extensive through the disciples' mission in the world.[48] At the same time, the disciples' love for Jesus should be modeled on the Son's love for his Father. Jesus obeys the Father so that the world may know that he loves the Father (14:31). Similarly, the disciples are invited to obey Jesus (15:10; see also 14:15, 21, 23-24) so that the world may know that they are truly his representatives on earth (13:35).

Their daunting global task is a divine appointment (15:16) that requires divine support. Jesus promises to send the Spirit of truth to help the disciples to bear witness about him (15:26, 27).[49] The recipients of the disciples' testimony in 15:27 ("you will bear witness") is implicit. The previous reference to "their law" in 15:25 points to those associated with Moses as the recipients of such a witness. However, the disciples' testimony is not limited to them. The hostile larger world will also be the recipient of the disciples' witness (13:35; 14:31).[50] This idea is further supported by previous instances of the testimony motif. The first one to give testimony in the Gospel of John was John the Baptist, who witnessed the Spirit descending from heaven and remaining on Jesus (1:32). He came to bear witness so that all (πάντες) might believe through him (1:7; cf. 5:33). The Samaritan woman, likewise, testified to her fellow Samaritans about Jesus (4:39). Jesus taught her that God is "Spirit" (4:24). Jesus himself has testified about the world that its works are evil (7:7). In light of this larger context, the seemingly incomplete thought in 15:27, "you also will bear witness," should be read "you also will bear witness [to the world]."

This is confirmed in 16:8-11, where the testimony of the Spirit is universal in scope since it is for the benefit of the world as a

---

becomes thereby 'present in their own day'" (Rudolf Schnackenburg, *The Gospel according to St. John*, 3 vols. [New York: Seabury, 1980], 1:524).

[48] Although the noun "world" is not used in 15:1-16, Jesus appointing his disciples so that they could go (ὑπάγητε) and bear fruit (καρπόν) in 15:16 might indicate that the disciples are meant to go "into the world" (thus Barrett, *John*, 478; Michaels, *John*, 816).

[49] Bultmann, *John*, 554: "The working of the Spirit is not unhistorical or magical, but rather requires the disciples' independent action."

[50] Bultmann, *John*, 566: "There is no longer any such thing as an unprejudiced Judaism or an impartial Gentile world within the circumference of the word of proclamation."

continuation of Jesus' task during his earthly ministry.[51] The Spirit will convict (ἐλέγξει) the world (τὸν κόσμον) concerning sin, righteousness, and judgment (16:8).[52] Although John never says that the Spirit is to be identified with "the light," he will carry on Jesus' task during his earthly ministry as the light of the world,[53] since his function is revealing that the world lives in darkness. Previously, it was stated that everyone (πᾶς) who does wicked things hates the light, "lest his works should be exposed (ἐλεγχθῇ)" (3:20). Jesus now repeats this same idea by indicating that the Spirit will expose the dramatic condition of humanity. Since John associates sin with unbelief (8:34-47), the Spirit will convict the world concerning sin because they do not believe in Jesus (16:9). Humanity lacks righteousness because it cannot see Jesus as the revelation of the Father (16:10).[54] The world is under judgment because it is under the authority of the ruler of this world (16:11).[55] However, the Spirit will convict the world concerning

---

[51] The range of action of the Spirit is significantly enlarged, for the benefit of the disciples (16:7) and for the benefit of the world (16:8) (Schnelle, *Johannes*, 324; cf. Michaels, *John*, 833). Since the world cannot receive the Spirit (14:17), his work of convicting the world should be carried out by the disciples (Barrett, *John*, 486–87). Reinhartz, *Word*, 38: "Though only a relatively small group of Jews in Galilee and Judea actually saw the historical Jesus, the paraclete is sent to the world as a whole, the disciples are sent out into the world, and Christ will return to the world." Also Keener, *John*, 2:1030.

[52] In distinction from the Synoptic Gospels, where the Spirit helps the disciples to defend themselves when on trial, John has him taking the offensive against the world. See Barrett, *John*, 487; and J. N. Sanders, *A Commentary on the Gospel according to St John*, ed. B. A. Mastin, BNTC (London: Adam & Charles Black, 1968), 351.

[53] The verb ἐλέγχω could indicate that Jesus will "bring to light the true meaning of these concepts [i.e., sin, righteousness, and judgment] in the world" (Lindars, *John*, 501). Lindars, however, thinks that this interpretation is problematic because "righteousness" should refer to God's not the world's (thus Keener, *John*, 2:1034). Brown (*John*, 2:705) suggests that Jesus' trial will be reversed and the world will be found guilty of sin because it does not acknowledge God's justice.

[54] The word "righteousness" may have legal overtones. If this is the case, the sense here is that the world has not been acquitted (thus Sanders, *John*, 351). If the sense of 16:8-11 is didactic, the idea may be that the Spirit will teach the world what righteousness consists of in relationship to Jesus' vindication (Beutler, *Johannesevangelium*, 438).

[55] The "judgment" of the ruler of the world in 16:11 echoes the "universal and timeless" divine judgment already introduced in 3:18-21, according to Lindars, *John*, 503.

sin, righteousness, and judgment. He is authorized to perform this task because the Father gave all judgment to the Son (5:22).[56]

The present status of the world, however, is not irreversible or permanent. Jesus' return to his Father has cosmic implications because his glorification will result in the ruler of this world being cast out (12:31-32).[57] A previous dialogue in John 8 between Jesus and some members of his Jewish people who believed in him (8:12-59) has striking resemblances with the role of the Spirit for the benefit of the world in John 16. On the one hand, Jesus challenges his audience to convict (ἐλέγχει) him of sin (8:46), but it is unable to do so because he was sent from the Father. On the other hand, Jesus is able to challenge his audience about its position in relation to the light (8:12), its lack of a proper relationship with God (8:32), and its alliance to the devil (8:44).[58] Jesus claims that his audience lives in darkness (8:12), alienated from the Father (8:19). Since the people do not realize their present condition, they will die in their sins (8:21, 24).[59] Jesus also asserts that they lack a right relationship with God. Since they practice sin, they are slaves to sin (8:34) and need freedom. Although they claim they belong to God (8:41, 47), their lies and desires to kill Jesus reveal that they do not know the Father (8:19, 41). They are not allied with God because they belong to this world (8:15, 23).

Notwithstanding this sharp portrayal of humanity, Jesus came to the world to take away its sin (1:29; see 8:32), to bring light to it (1:4, 9; 8:12), and to offer a proper relationship with God (14:6, 9; see 1:12). After his departure to his Father, the mission of the Son in the world is realized by the Spirit through the testimony of the disciples (16:8-10). The new community of disciples, where love is the main characteristic, is a testimony to the world of an alternative way of living under its true owner. After Jesus' departure from this world, the only way humanity will have to see a reflection of the Father's love is the community of

[56] The last intervention of the disciples in the farewell discourses is an acknowledgment that Jesus knows "all things" (16:30).

[57] Lindars, *John*, 504. Cf. Bultmann, *John*, 561n4: "cosmic drama."

[58] Jesus is "indeed King, who, though not of this world, has vanquished the ruler of this world and is therefore the one to whom all humankind owes allegiance" (Reinhartz, *Word*, 31).

[59] Thompson, *John*, 338.

disciples who live under the new commandment and in whom the Spirit now resides (14:16).

The universal scope of the Spirit's mission stems from Jesus' claim over all creation, "all (πάντα) that the Father has is mine" (16:15).[60] Once Jesus receives such "all-inclusive endowment"[61] from the Father, it belongs to him (16:15). Jesus is the rightful owner of everything that the Father has. Jesus is born into the world (16:21; cf. 1:9; 3:17; 16:28)[62] that belonged to him since the beginning in order to execute the salvation of a humanity that remains hostile to him. Therefore, those who embrace Jesus' message rejoice with the coming of the Son into the world but are sorrowful when he leaves it (16:20-21, 28). The world, however, receives with sadness the coming of Jesus into the world, because he exposes the sinfulness of humanity, and it rejoices when he leaves it (16:20). Notwithstanding this opposition from the world, the disciples will continue Jesus' work in the world. What they may achieve through their mission can only be "a part of what is given to Jesus by right."[63]

It is highly significant that John closes the farewell discourses with one of the clearest instances of universal language in his Gospel: "I have overcome the world (ἐγὼ νενίκηκα τὸν κόσμον)" (16:33).[64] This is the last teaching of Jesus to his disciples before his passion.

---

[60] John 16:15 is missing in 𝔓[66] and Sinaiticus. Since the previous phrase concludes with ὑμῖν (16:14) and the final phrase in 16:15 also concludes with ὑμῖν, it is likely that this is an unintended omission (Brown, *John*, 2:709; Lindars, *John*, 505–6). Keener (*John*, 2:1042) uses 5:20 to explain "all" in 16:15 in terms of revelation. Michaels (*John*, 837) restricts it to "truth" (16:13). However, John 3:31, 35 clearly portrays Jesus as having authority over the whole world (3:31, 35).

[61] Lindars, *John*, 506.

[62] Hoskyns, *Fourth Gospel*, 488.

[63] Lindars, *John*, 506.

[64] This is the only instance of the verb νικάω in the Gospel of John. However, the earliest written reception of this Gospel that we have available indicates that this idea was very influential. The first letter of John uses the verb five times to indicate that believers appropriate Jesus' victory over the world: "you, young men . . . have overcome the evil one" (2:13, 14), "little children, you are from God and have overcome [false prophets who deny Jesus]" (4:4), "everyone who has been born of God overcomes the world" (5:4), and "the one who believes that Jesus is the Son of God . . . overcomes the world" (5:5).

They will encounter him again only after his resurrection.[65] This way the farewell discourses are linked to the opening of the Gospel. The Word who took an active role in the creation of the world shines in the darkness, "and the darkness did not accept (κατέλαβεν) it" (1:5 RSV). The cosmic battle between Jesus and the ruler of this world had an anticipated outcome: the victory of the light over darkness, truth over falsehood, life over death, love over hate, joy over sorrow, peace over fear.[66] Along with his peace (14:27), his joy (15:11), and the Spirit that has been with him (1:32; 16:14), Jesus also gives to his disciples his victory (16:33).[67] The perfect tense νενίκηκα, (to conquer, overcome) "expresses certitude with regard to the future,"[68] and it is based on Jesus' earlier conviction that "all that the Father has is mine" (16:15). In this way, the reader is prepared to face the last section of the Gospel with a positive attitude. Although Jesus will be soon crucified, "his apparent defeat" is in fact a cosmic conquest.[69] Jesus will face trial by the Romans, false charges from religious leaders, and a shameful execution. However, the reader knows that he has already overcome the world, because his humiliation is in fact his glorification.

[65] Michaels, *John*, 856. Similarly, the first major section of the Gospel concludes with Jesus asserting that he came to save the world (12:47): "I have come into the world as light, so that whoever believes in me may not remain in darkness" (12:46)

[66] The phrase "overcome the world" draws "attention to the cosmic significance of the Passion," according to Lindars, *John*, 514.

[67] Bultmann, *John*, 594; Beutler, *Johannesevangelium*, 444; Michaels, *John*, 855. Schnelle (*Johannes*, 330) suggests that the narrator is addressing the reader here. Similarly, Zumstein (*Johannesevangelium*, 624) argues that the perfect tense of the verb "to overcome" refers to Jesus' crucifixion and, therefore, the narrator addresses the reader.

[68] Lindars, *John*, 514.

[69] Bultmann, *John*, 592. Jesus will defeat the ruler of the world (12:31; 16:11) and will conquer the world (16:33). "The conflict between God and his creation is solved (*ist gelöst*)" (Zumstein, *Johannesevangelium*, 624).

THE LAST PRAYER OF JESUS

The farewell discourses conclude with a prayer by Jesus.[70] This prayer includes important instances of universal language.[71] It states clearly that Jesus has universal authority, that he rules over all humanity, and that he is legitimized to give life and to execute judgment because he existed with God before the foundation of the world. Jesus' execution of his universal authority brings glory to the Father.

Jesus' prayer begins with him lifting up his eyes to heaven to implore to his Father. This movement signals a Johannine idea found elsewhere in the Gospel: there is an important distinction between "above" and "below" (e.g., 3:12). The reader is invited to consider Jesus' prayer from "above," from a heavenly perspective.[72] This prayer is also set in the larger context of Jesus' hour (17:1, ἐλήλυθεν ἡ ὥρα, "the hour has come"). Jesus will soon be arrested, judged, crucified, raised from the dead, and reunited with his Father.[73] The prayer then offers a window to a different reality that is framed by the glorification of the Father and shaped by the ideas of obedience, unity, and mission.

[70] This prayer has attracted a good deal of attention in Johannine scholarship. Previous studies have focused on its structure, genre, background, the glory and the name motifs, its position in the Gospel, its relationship to the Synoptic Gospels, or ideas about discipleship, unity, and Christology. See J. Becker, "Aufbau, Schichtung und theologiegeschichtliche Stellung des Gebetes in Joh 17," *ZNW* 60 (1969): 56–83; E. O. Tukasi, *Determinism and Petitionary Prayer in John and the Dead Sea Scrolls: Ideological Reading of John and the Rule of Community (1QS)*, LSTS 66 (London: T&T Clark, 2008); J. L. Boyle, "The Last Discourse (Jn 13, 31-16, 33) and Prayer (Jn 17): Some Observations on Their Unity and Development," *Bib* 56 (1975): 210–22; W. O. Walker, "The Lord's Prayer in Matthew and in John," *NTS* 28 (1982): 235–56; M. P. Hera, *Christology and Discipleship in John 17*, WUNT 2/342 (Tübingen: Mohr Siebeck, 2013); and J. F. Randall, "The Theme of Unity in Jn 17,20-23," *ETL* 41 (1965): 373–94.

[71] This is a neglected topic in previous research on John 17 even among those studies dealing with the topic of mission. See G. Segalla, *La preghiera di Gesù al Padre (Giov 17): Un addio missionario*, Studi biblici 63 (Brescia: Paideia, 1983); and C. D. Morrison, "Mission and Ethic: An Interpretation of Jn 17," *Int* 19 (1965) 259–73. Consider, for example, Wilhelm Oehler's claim that the Gospel of John is a "missionary document" except John 15–17, 21. See his *Zum Missionscharakter des Johannesevangeliums*, BFCT 42:4 (Gütersloh: C. Bertelsmann, 1941), 11–12.

[72] This emphasis is particularly noticeable in the tautology found in v. 7. See also Zumstein, *Johannesevangelium*, 639; Barrett, *John*, 506; Brown, *John*, 2:743.

[73] Michaels, *John*, 858; Brown, *John*, 2:740; Keener, *John*, 2:1052.

Jesus' Universal Authority

The unique relationship between the Father and the Son is manifested in Jesus' all-encompassing authority over people to give them life and to execute judgment (17:1-5). This is a faithful reflection of God's rule over all creation. Twice in this prayer, Jesus remembers that he enjoyed a distinctive relationship with the Father before the existence of the world (vv. 5, 24). The first reference highlights that Jesus and his Father shared the same glory (v. 5).[74] The second reference emphasizes that the Father loved the Son even before the foundation of the world (v. 24). This situates Jesus not only above creation but also apart from the created order, which is under his authority. Even before creation the Father and the Son shared the same glory and were united by love. Although the prayer does not explicitly mention the participation of Jesus in the creation of the world, the shared glory between them might imply that Jesus took an active role in the creation of all that exists. This idea was introduced earlier in 1:1-3, 10 where it is stated that the unique relationship between the Word and God was reflected in the act of creation. Similarly, the Father's love for the Son was closely linked to Jesus' universal authority previously in the Gospel: "The Father loves the Son and has given all things into his hand" (3:35). Jesus now prays that his Father has loved him "before the foundation of the world" (17:24), implying that, in his preexistence, he received authority to be involved in the work of creation.

This unique relationship allows the Father to grant to the Son authority over "all flesh" during his earthly ministry (17:2; cf. Luke 3:6).[75] In Jewish tradition, "all flesh" (πάσης σαρκός) was used in a universal

---

[74] The same idea with slightly different words is found in 12:28, according to the reading preserved in Codex D, εν τη δοξη η ειχον παρα σοι προ του τον κοσμον γενεσθαι. This longer reading, however, should be taken as influenced by Jesus' prayer in 17:5. Harmonization to the context is a frequent move observed in ancient manuscripts. See J. R. Royse, *Scribal Habits in Early Greek New Testament Papyri*, NTTS 36 (Leiden: Brill, 2008), 189–90.

[75] The unique relationship between the Son and the Father is preexistent. It is not only "the Word" who existed with God in the beginning, but the Son himself is said to have enjoyed a privileged relationship with the Father before creation. See Friederike Kunath, *Die Präexistenz Jesu im Johannesevangelium: Struktur und Theologie eines johanneischen Motivs*, BZNW 212 (Berlin: de Gruyter, 2016), 366.

sense, in reference to all humanity (e.g., Isa 40:5; 1QS 11:9; Sir 18:13) or "all creation" (e.g., Gen 9:16; Jub. 5:2).[76] According to the Gospel of John, some earthly rulers such as Pontius Pilate have received some authority from God (19:11). However, Jesus exclusively shares with the Father universal authority over "all flesh" (17:2). This is a privilege that no human or angelic being enjoyed according to Jewish tradition.[77] Although he became flesh (1:14), Jesus does not belong to the realm of creation because he rules supreme over all flesh.[78] However, he became flesh and came to his creation (1:14). His heavenly authority is then demonstrated during his earthly ministry. It "was precisely because the Son of God *became flesh* that He received *authority over all flesh*."[79]

Jesus will give life to all that the Father has given to him (17:2, πᾶν ὃ δέδωκας). Since the construction πᾶν ὃ in πᾶν ὃ δέδωκας is neuter singular (cf. 6:37, 39), it can be taken as a reference to creation.[80] It was already said of the Word that "life" was in him, and that the "life" was the light of humanity (1:4). Jesus now remarks here that he has authority to give life to creation, to the totality of humanity (17:2).[81] There is a shift from humanity (πάσης σαρκός) to creation (πᾶν ὅ, neuter singular), and then back to people (αὐτοῖς, masculine plural) in 17:2.[82]

---

[76] See Keener, *John*, 2:1053n37; Lindars, *John*, 518. Isaiah 40:5 is particularly relevant here: "The glory (ἡ δόξα) of the Lord (κυρίου) shall appear, and all flesh (πᾶσα σάρξ) shall see (ὀφθήσεται) the salvation of God, because the Lord has spoken (κύριος ἐλάλησεν)." C. H. Dodd (*According to the Scriptures: The Sub-structure of New Testament Theology* [London: Nisbet, 1952], 40) sees reminiscences of this passage in John 11:40 and perhaps 1:4.

[77] Bultmann, *John*, 492n3; Richard Bauckham, *God Crucified: Monotheism and Christology in the New Testament* (Grand Rapids: Eerdmans, 1998), 28–29; Keener, *John*, 2:1053n39.

[78] Bultmann, *John*, 493. Jesus, however, remains fully human according to John's perspective. See Marianne Meye Thompson, *The Humanity of Jesus in the Fourth Gospel* (Philadelphia: Fortress, 2001).

[79] Hoskyns, *Fourth Gospel*, 498 (emphasis in original).

[80] Thompson, *John*, 349.

[81] Lindars, *John*, 523; Barrett, *John*, 506.

[82] Thus, Barrett, *John*, 502. However, Barrett restricts the pronoun to "the small group of disciples" (cf. Michaels, *John*, 859). Similarly, Haenchen, *John 2*, 150 takes "all flesh" as an exaggeration and as a hyperbole. The larger Johannine context points to the idea that Jesus indeed has universal authority (3:35; 13:3) and offers eternal life to all

The Father gave "people" (αὐτοῖς, masculine plural) to the Son.[83] Earlier, the narrator indicated that "all things" (πάντα, neuter plural) were made through the Word (1:3) and that the Word came to "his own things" (τὰ ἴδια, neuter plural, 1:11).[84] But, at the same time, this Word was the "light of humanity" (ἀνθρώπων, 1:4) that gives light to everyone (ἄνθρωπον, 1:9). The Word was behind the creation of everything that exists and manifested his light to humanity, although only some received him (1:3, 9, 12). Similarly, Jesus has received universal authority from his Father because everything (πάντα ὅσα) that Jesus has comes from his Father, especially his words (17:7-8). He gives life to humanity, but the group of his disciples are the first recipients of eternal life (17:2). Through his words Jesus gives life to those who believe (17:2) or declares judgment to those who reject him (5:26-27).[85] Therefore, his authority is universal whether giving a positive verdict upon those who believe or a negative one upon those who embrace darkness.[86]

Given his universal authority, Jesus is in an appropriate position to glorify the Father. The ultimate goal of Jesus' own glorification is the glorification of his Father. The measure of glorification that the Father will receive from the Son is set by the authority Jesus received from God (ὁ υἱὸς δοξάσῃ σέ καθὼς ἔδωκας αὐτῷ ἐξουσίαν, "the Son may glorify you to the degree to which you have given authority to him," 17:1b-2a), since the comparative conjunction καθώς can be taken

---

people, including Samaritans (cf. 4:10), and extends judgment to those who embrace darkness (5:27).

[83] This reading (αυτοις) is supported by a correction to Sinaiticus and by Alexandrinus and Vaticanus. Earlier readings (αυτω, ℵ* 𝔓107) should be taken as a mistake given the use of the same pronoun αυτω twice in 17:2. The "resumption of a suspended case by a pronoun in another case" is a popular idiom (BDF, § 466). The "πᾶς is usually subject to" this kind of anacoluthon (BDF, § 466; see Haenchen, *John 2*, 151).

[84] Among those who interpret 1:11 in a "universal" sense are Bultmann, *John*, 56; Borgen, *Logos*, 17; and Urban C. von Wahlde, *Commentary on the Gospel of John*, vol. 2 of *The Gospel and Letters of John* (Grand Rapids: Eerdmans, 2010), 30.

[85] Brown, *John*, 2:740.

[86] Bultmann, *John*, 493-94; Lincoln, *John*, 434. See Andrew T. Lincoln, *Truth on Trial: The Lawsuit Motif in the Fourth Gospel* (Peabody, Mass.: Hendrickson, 2000), 257: "Jesus' sovereignty and the universal scope of his salvific judgment are brought together in his prayer [17:2], where the former is the precondition for the latter."

as "of extent or degree to which."[87] Therefore, if Jesus received universal authority over all flesh, it is expected that the Father will receive universal glory through the Son. The glory of the Father here is directly related to Jesus' execution of life and judgment over the whole world.[88]

However, the exaltation of Jesus cannot be achieved yet, and the glorification of the Father is not yet completely realized from the perspective of the prayer. Jesus cannot fully achieve this goal under the conditions of his earthly ministry. His full salvific ministry includes also his passion, resurrection, and ascension back to his Father. Until he is fully glorified with the authority he had before the creation of the world (17:5, 24), humanity cannot fully experience life and judgment. Jesus' glorification in heaven gives him full universal soteriological authority.[89] Therefore, Jesus asks to be glorified again with the glory he had before the foundation of the world but not for the sake of his own glory (17:1, 5, 24), since Jesus' exaltation will result in the glorification of his Father (17:1).

The exaltation of Jesus and the glorification of the Father began during his earthly ministry (1:14) and will continue after his return to heaven. An important component of Jesus' demonstration of his universal authority during his earthly ministry was the selection of his disciples. Since all (τὰ πάντα) that belongs to Jesus is from the Father, and since all that belongs to the Father belongs also to Jesus, he has authority to reveal himself to this group of disciples (17:10). They received God's words (17:8, 14), eternal life (17:13), knowledge of God's name (17:6, 26), and they also witnessed some of Jesus' works (17:8). Therefore, they enjoy a proper relationship with the only true God (17:3, 6, 21-23, 26), that is, a special relationship with the Father that makes them children of God (1:12). Jesus' ability to give life to whomever he

---

[87] BDAG, 493. A temporal relationship should be ruled out because the future action of the Son (ἵνα . . . δοξάσῃ) depends on the Father's previous action for the benefit of Jesus (ἔδωκας). The other option, suggested by BDAG, 494, is cause, "since, in so far as." However, this function is especially noticeable when καθώς begins a sentence. This is not the case here in John 17:2.

[88] Alfred Loisy, Le quatrième Évangile, 2nd. ed. (Paris: Émile Nourry, 1921), 441–42.

[89] Loisy, Évangile, 441–42; cf. Hoskyns, Fourth Gospel, 499.

wants is a clear manifestation of his universal authority (cf. 5:21).[90] The disciples bring glory to the Father through Jesus because they honor him as they honor the Father (5:23). Furthermore, the prayer also states that other people will also believe (17:20) through the testimony of the disciples (17:21, 23). The world that opposes God will be exposed to the testimony of the disciples about Jesus' unique relationship to his Father (17:21, 23). Other people, then, will also receive eternal life, will leave darkness, and will be called children of God (1:12). If the world recognizes that the Son is the revelation of the Father (17:21, 23), the world too has the possibility of reestablishing a proper relationship with its Creator and, therefore, the world too will bring glory to God through Jesus. Although Jesus prays for his disciples, indicating that the Father gave them to him (v. 9), there is immediately a shift from "the disciples" in verse 9 to "all things" in verse 10. There is a shift from masculine (v. 9, αὐτῶν) to neuter (v. 10, τὰ πάντα).[91] The use of neuter plural (τὰ πάντα) expresses that Jesus shares all things with the Father (17:10). This "community of possessions" entitles Jesus to claim that the disciples belong to him.[92] The neuter in verse 10 "has the effect of broadening the already remarkable claim" found in verse 9.[93] Just as the Son and the Father shared glory and love before creation (vv. 5, 24), during his earthly ministry, Jesus can also claim that "all mine are yours, and yours are mine" (v. 10).

The Mission of the Disciples

The basis of the disciples' worldwide mission in John 17 is Jesus' authority over all flesh. A clear demonstration of Jesus' universal authority is the selection of the disciples out of the world. They received revelation and, therefore, eternal life from Jesus. They remain different from the world but, at the same time, they are sent to engage the world in the

---

[90] The idea of predestination should not be included in 17:1-8 since this terminology is foreign to the Gospel of John. See also Zumstein, *Johannesevangelium*, 634.

[91] Michaels (*John*, 865) allows the possibility that this shift is influenced by 17:2, the closest Johannine context, as expressive of Jesus' universality. However, he prefers to look for a more distant context, i.e., the sheep from 10:14-15 (τῶν προβάτων, neuter plural). See Schnackenburg, *John*, 3:178–79; and Zumstein, *Johannesevangelium*, 642n94.

[92] Lindars, *John*, 523.

[93] Brown, *John*, 2:758. See also Barrett, *John*, 506–7.

same way Jesus was sent from the Father into the world. They also receive universal authority from Jesus that is expressed in their unity with the Father. Indeed, their unity has a missionary goal: so that the world may believe in Jesus. Their unity is of utmost importance due to the ethnic issues that surrounded social relationships in the first century.

On the one hand, the disciples are very different from the world. Just as the world did not know Jesus (v. 25) and rejected his claims, the world also is hostile to the disciples because they do not belong to this world (vv. 14, 16) dominated by darkness. Jesus is light and he does not belong to this world (vv. 14, 16). He comes from heaven, from his Father. Similarly, his disciples are children of God and belong to the light. However, they are not in heaven. They are in the world (v. 11). This is the place where they should be because they have a mission to fulfill. Jesus does not ask the Father to take them out of the world (v. 15). Jesus prays to his "holy" Father (v. 11; cf. 10:36) to sanctify them in the truth (vv. 17, 19)[94] and to keep them from the evil one (v. 15; cf. v. 11).[95] This sanctification is achieved in unity (v. 11).[96] They should remain as one among them, but also they should be united with Jesus and the Father.

On the other hand, the disciples have a mission in the world and for the benefit of the world. They are sent to the world in the same way that the Father sent the Son to his creation (17:18). The Father sent his Son to the world with authority over the created order (v. 2). Jesus received from the Father the authority to bring light to the world that leads either to eternal life for those who receive it or to judgment for

[94] Jesus relates "truth" to worship to God in his dialogue with the Samaritan woman. The "true" worshipers are those who will worship the Father in spirit and "truth" (4:23). Those who worship the Father must worship him "in spirit and truth" (4:24). During his earthly ministry, Jesus talks the "truth" which he heard from God (8:40). This sets him apart from the world because the world cannot receive the truth (8:45, 46; cf. 14:17). By asking that his disciples may be sanctified in the truth, Jesus is expecting they will be true worshipers who obey the truth.

[95] Prayers for protection from the evil one were common in Second Temple Judaism, as has been shown by Loren T. Stuckenbruck, "Evil in Johannine and Apocalyptic Perspective: Petition for Protection in John 17," in *John's Gospel and Intimations of Apocalyptic*, ed. Catrin H. Williams and Christopher Rowland (London: Bloomsbury T&T Clark, 2013), 200–32.

[96] The sanctification, setting apart, "is at the same time the preparation for [the disciples'] calling, his mission" (Bultmann, *John*, 389n5).

those who embrace darkness. Jesus has the power to give life (17:2) and to execute judgment (5:27).[97] Here in 17:18, the universal mission of Jesus is taken up by his followers.[98] They "come to occupy the position vis-à-vis the world that Jesus had."[99] The separation of the disciples from the world (sanctification) is actually "a consecration to a mission" (10:36).[100] They remain holy as long as they fulfil their mission to the world. The disciples have already been involved in Jesus' mission (4.38), but here they will engage the world after Jesus' departure to his Father.

Since the Father sent his Son with authority over "all flesh" (17:2), and since Jesus sends his disciples in the same way he was sent by his Father (17:18), it is reasonable to interpret that Jesus sends his disciples as representatives of God's authority over all humanity.[101] This is supported by 17:22, "the glory that you have given me I have given to them." In Jesus' prayer his glory is associated with his authority over creation. Since Jesus has authority over all flesh (17:2), he can ask his Father to be glorified (17:1) even with the glory he had with him before creation (17:5). The only way his disciples can undertake a mission to the whole world (17:18) is by having authority over all humanity. This is what Jesus does for his disciples: he gives them the glory that the

---

[97] Bultmann, *John*, 510.

[98] Barrett, *John*, 510; Bultmann, *John*, 510.

[99] Haenchen, *John 2*, 154. Frey ("Love-Relations," in Van Belle and Maritz, *Love-Relations in the Fourth Gospel: Establishing a Semantic Network*, 187) rightly observes that "the revelation of God's love is not confined to a definite group of disciples or to a sectarian community distant in some way from the world. Rather, it is open to the perception of the world. Thus, the world shall come to belief in Jesus' mission by means of the perception of the loving unity of the disciples (17,21)."

[100] Brown, *John*, 2:762; Ferdinand Hahn, *Mission in the New Testament*, trans. Frank Clarke, SBT 47 (Naperville, Ill.: Alec R. Allenson, 1965), 159–60; Lindars, *John*, 528; Lincoln, *John*, 438; Michaels, *John*, 872; Thompson, *John*, 355.

[101] This idea is explicit in Matt 28:18-20. There is debate whether John knew the Synoptic Gospels or the traditions that shaped them. The prayer (John 17) reflects a particular trajectory about the disciples' mission after Jesus' resurrection that does not contradict what we have preserved at the end of the Gospel of Matthew. Furthermore, the prologue has anticipated that "we all have received from his fullness" (1:16). This is perhaps an anticipated reference to the authority the disciples will receive from Jesus after his resurrection.

Father gave him (17:25).[102] This idea will be clarified by the investiture with authority over sin that the disciples will receive from the risen Jesus in 20:19-23. Jesus performs an act that resembles that of the Creator God (20:22) and immediately indicates that if they forgive the sins of "any," they are forgiven (20:23).[103]

The idea that Jesus sent his disciples into the world with authority over all humanity (17:18) is further supported by the love motif in this prayer. Jesus receives glory from the Father who loved his Son before the foundation of the world (v. 24). Remarkably, the Father loves believers even as he loved his Son (v. 23).[104] The same love that prompted the Father to give glory to the Son is the basis of his relationship with believers. Therefore, it remains possible that the Father demonstrates his love for his children by sending them as representatives of the Son's authority over all humanity (cf. 3:35; 13:3). However, this glory that the disciples receive in the form of authority over humanity does not mean independence from Jesus. The glory of Jesus was closely linked with his unity with the Father. The Son's exaltation allows the Father's glorification (17:1-5). Similarly, the universal authority the disciples receive from Jesus should nurture unity. The disciples should reflect among them the same unity that characterizes the Father and the Son (17:22). Those who will believe through the testimony of the disciples should

---

[102] Another aspect of Jesus' glory given to his disciples might be the privilege of suffering for God. According to Barrett (*John*, 513), Jesus' glory in the Gospel of John is associated with his "humiliation, poverty, and suffering" and, therefore, the disciples in John 17:22 do not receive a "promise of visible prosperity." Haenchen (*John 2*, 155) suggests that Jesus' glory here refers to the knowledge of his Father (cf. Bultmann, *John*, 515). Hoskyns (*Fourth Gospel*, 505) links 17:22 to 1:14 (thus Lindars, *John*, 530; Keener, *John*, 2:1063; Zumstein, *Johannesevangelium*, 653), Lincoln (*John*, 438–39) understands Jesus' glory primarily in terms of reputation and honor, and Michaels (*John*, 877) links it to mission. However, the commentator that comes closer to the idea I suggest *supra* is Thompson (*John* 356–57): "The disciples have a share in all that belongs to God and in all that God has given to Jesus."

[103] "The association of forgiveness of sin with the commissioning and sending of the disciples suggests . . . a missionological and kerygmatic context for the forgiveness of sins rather than one within the fellowship of the community" (R. Alan Culpepper, "Designs for the Church in John 20,19-23," in Verheyden, van Oyen, Labahn, and Bieringer, *Studies in the Gospel of John and Its Christology*, 501–18, here 517).

[104] Keener, *John*, 2:1063.

also be part of this divine unity (17:20-21). Ultimately, all believers are united with God in Jesus (17:21, 23). Since the prologue presupposes an original unity of humanity (1:3), Jesus' prayer to his Father envisions the unification of believers so that the world also may believe.

This unity has a missionary goal. The disciples are to become "the manifestation of the love and glory of God in the world."[105] Thus, the mission of the disciples in the world takes an active engagement with the world (17:20; cf. 15:17) and, at the same time, a passive demonstration of Jesus' relationship to God for the benefit of the world (17:21, 23). The disciples do "not take over . . . the duty to win the world solely by embarking on missionary enterprises"; they do so simply by their existence.[106] More precisely, the disciples' mission to the world is twofold: an active witness about the Word and a distinctive existence in unity among them and with the Father in the Son.

Jesus prays not only for his disciples but also for those who will believe in him through the word of those sent into the world (17:20).[107] The disciples are expected to teach what they learned from Jesus about his unique relationship with the Father. They will share what they received from Jesus: God's word (17:8) and God's name (17:6). They also will witness about Jesus fulfilling the works of his Father (17:6). Since knowledge and belief lead to the conclusion that God sent Jesus and that Jesus came from the Father (17:3), those who attend to the disciples' word[108] will know the only true God and, therefore, will obtain eternal life (17:3). The world, then, is offered the possibility of reestablishing a proper relationship with its Creator through the testimony of the disciples. Those who believe in Jesus through the

---

[105] Hoskyns, *Fourth Gospel*, 505.

[106] Bultmann, *John*, 510.

[107] "Since the words of Jesus and His sacrifice are of universal validity through the preaching of the disciples, the Lord extends His prayer to embrace the whole body of the faithful" (Hoskyns, *Fourth Gospel*, 505). Several commentators link 17:20 to the "other sheep" mentioned in 10:16 (e.g., Michaels, *John*, 874).

[108] The noun in 17:20 is singular, τοῦ λόγου, perhaps because the message of the disciples should be one and the same about Jesus' unique relationship with the Father. Notice also that the phrase εἰς ἐμέ at the end of 17:20 might be related to the noun (word *about me*) or to the participle (will believe *in me*). Cf. Brown, *John*, 2:769.

testimony of the disciples receive the right to become children of God (1:12), thus experiencing a new beginning (3:3, 5, 8).

The disciples' active witness to the world is supported by their unity as a powerful testimony to the world about the Son and his Father (17:21, 23). The followers of Jesus during his earthly ministry and those who will believe through their testimony (v. 20) should demonstrate this same unity (ἵνα πάντες ἓν ὦσιν, v. 21) that characterizes the relationship between the Father and the Son (v. 21). This unity might be called christological because it achieves perfection (τετελειωμένοι) when Jesus himself is in them (vv. 23, 26).[109] At the same time, the believers will be in the Son and in his Father (ἵνα καὶ αὐτοὶ ἐν ἡμῖν ὦσιν, v. 21).

During the first century, unity among believers was necessarily emphasized because people from different ethnicities were following the same Jesus. This might have created tensions (e.g., Acts 15:1-35; Gal 2:11-14). Since rivalries and issues between Jews and Samaritans were well known (John 4:9), the community of Jesus' followers should overcome such divisions and live in unity. If the disciples are going to engage the world (i.e., other Jews, Samaritans, and gentiles) expecting it to believe in Jesus, they should be prepared to welcome those new disciples from different ethnicities into a united community.[110] This unity among the disciples and between them and Jesus and the Father has then an explicit missionary purpose.

v. 21 ἵνα ὁ κόσμος πιστεύῃ ὅτι σύ με ἀπέστειλας
v. 23 ἵνα γινώσκῃ ὁ κόσμος ὅτι σύ με ἀπέστειλας καὶ ἠγάπησας αὐτούς

The world (ὁ κόσμος) that opposes God and his purposes (17:14) will have the opportunity to believe that the Father sent the Son (v. 21).[111] The verb "to believe" (here πιστεύῃ) figures prominently in the Gospel

---

[109] Those who do not believe have conflicting views about Jesus' identity and, therefore, experience division among them (e.g., 7:43; 9:16; 10:19). See also Keener, *John*, 2:1061.

[110] Keener, *John*, 2:1062.

[111] John 17:21 has three ἵνα clauses. The first two constitute the content of the prayer found in 17:20. The last one ("so that the world may believe") indicates the goal of the disciples' unity (Bultmann, *John*, 514n1; Brown, *John*, 2:770).

of John. Earlier, the narrator indicated that "all who did receive him, who believe (τοῖς πιστεύουσιν) in his name" become children of God (1:12). The world, then, might achieve through faith the same kind of relationship that the disciples enjoy with the Son and his Father. Just as Jesus' disciples believed that the Father sent him (17:8, ἐπίστευσαν ὅτι σύ με ἀπέστειλας; cf. 11:42), so too the world may believe (17:21, ἵνα ὁ κόσμος πιστεύῃ ὅτι σύ με ἀπέστειλας). Since the unity of the disciples will reflect Jesus' unity with his Father, "the world is challenged to decide between faith and unbelief."[112]

The world (ὁ κόσμος) will also have the opportunity to know (γινώσκῃ) that the Father sent Jesus (v. 23; cf. v. 25).[113] Both verbs ("to believe" and "to know") are found together in Peter's remarkable confession of faith: "We have believed, and have come to know, that you are the Holy One of God" (6:69). The verb "to know" is also found elsewhere in the Gospel. Although the world (ὁ κόσμος) did not know (ἔγνω) its own Creator (1:10; cf. 17:25), Jesus' sheep know (γινώσκουσιν) the Good Shepherd (10:14). Knowing Jesus means knowing his Father (14:7). Most significantly, eternal life is closely linked to knowledge in John 17: "This is eternal life, that they know (γινώσκωσιν) you the only true God, and Jesus Christ whom you have sent" (17:3). The world will also know that God loves the disciples just as he loved Jesus (v. 23). Since the Father shows his love for the Son through giving him glory (v. 24), that is, authority over all humanity to give eternal life (v. 2), and since the Father loves the disciples as he loved Jesus (v. 23), the world will recognize that the disciples, in unity with Jesus, have authority to give eternal life when testifying about him. This authority does not mean independence from the Father or the Son, but it is effective only in unity with them in the power of the Spirit.

SYNTHESIS

The narrator has taken the reader to a private encounter between Jesus and his disciples where the understanding of the comprehensive scope

---

[112] Barrett, *John*, 512.

[113] Bultmann (*John*, 518), finds no significant difference between "to know" and "to believe" in John 17:21, 23. Cf. Michaels, *John*, 878.

of Jesus' significance is deepened. "Jesus' speeches translate the particulars of the narrative about his life into notions of universal applications."[114] Specifically, the narrator discloses that the selection and sanctification of the disciples has a missionary purpose. The Spirit working through their testimony will further Jesus' mission in the world. The narrator also hints at the idea that the disciples will receive universal authority from Jesus to engage the world with life and light. The worldwide mission of the disciples is shaped by the anticipated victory of Jesus over the illegitimate ruler of this world. The narrator uses at least two strategies to highlight the universal significance of Jesus and the message about him in this section (John 13–16). The first strategy is the framing of the farewell discourses with clear instances of universal language (13:3; 14.31; 16:33). The second strategy is the careful portrayal of his characters. Jesus is depicted using several instances of universal language to explain the significance of his earthly ministry and forthcoming death. Judas, however, is depicted as a confused disciple who cannot grasp the relationship between Jesus' manifestation to them and his revelation to the world.

The sense of privacy that the reader experiences in his encounter with the farewell discourses is heightened in his reading of John 17. The narrator takes the reader to a very personal moment in Jesus' life where he prays to his Father. The reader listens only to Jesus' voice without any interventions from the disciples or the narrator. The strategic placement of John 17 at the conclusion of Jesus' earthly ministry and at the beginning of Jesus' passion and resurrection creates deep impact upon the reader. Through this prayer the reader learns (1) that the ultimate purpose of Jesus' universal authority is the glorification of the Father, (2) that others will believe through the testimony of the disciples, and (3) that the success of the disciples' mission in the world depends on their sanctification from the world. Jesus' prayer envisions the unity of all believers present and future with him and the Father. This vision coheres with the description found in the prologue of all humanity as having its origin in the Word.[115]

---

[114] Kierspel, *Jews*, 177.

[115] Cf. Thomas Wieser, "Community—Its Unity, Diversity and Universality," *Semeia* 33 (1985): 83–95, here 93: "The fact that Jesus' unity with the Father creates the

Overall, the farewell discourses and Jesus' prayer demonstrate that the Spirit is a witness to a different world, where the disciples take center stage.[116] Their unity among them and with Jesus and his Father is a powerful demonstration to a dispersed world dominated by darkness. Their active engagement with the world through mission is, paradoxically, only possible through their sanctification and separation from this world. Although the focus of this Johannine section is on Jesus' disciples, the goal of their privileged position in relationship to the Spirit is for the benefit of humanity. Ultimately, people from the world abandoning the ruler of this world and embracing God's revelation in Jesus are intended to bring glory to the Father.[117]

---

conditions for the unity within all humanity and of humanity with the Father, shows the universal dimension of this [John 17] unity."

[116] This "alternative world" is also anticipated by Jesus' actions during his earthly ministry. Jesus' signs reveal "what the state of affairs is in the world where Jesus comes from," according to Sjef van Tilborg, "Cosmological Implications of Johannine Christology," in *Theology and Christology in the Fourth Gospel: Essays by the Members of the SNTS Johannine Writings Seminar*, ed. G. van Belle, J. G. van der Watt, and P. Maritz, BETL 184 (Leuven: Leuven University Press, 2005), 483–502.

[117] Some scholars distinguish between editions in the text of the Gospel. There are, for example, the two-edition approach (e.g., Lindars, Ashton) and the three-edicion approach (e.g., von Wahlde). These scholars often assigned the work of the Spirit as present teacher to the suggested second or third editions of the text. Significantly, this study has uncovered that the universal theme comes through consistently in different sections in the Gospel.

4

THE FINAL COSMIC CONQUEST

The previous farewell discourses and prayer concluded with Jesus claiming that he has overcome the world (16:33) and praying for those who will believe through the testimony of his disciples (17:20). The last section of the Gospel of John then can be read from a cosmic perspective and in light of the missionary commissioning of the disciples. The knowledge the reader has accumulated so far about the universal significance of Jesus and the message about him aids in the interpretation of Jesus' passion in John 18–19 and resurrection in John 20–21.[1] The scenes of Jesus' interrogation highlight his testimony about the truth in pagan territory for the benefit of a gentile ruler. The discussions between Jesus and Pilate about authority accentuate the superior position of Jesus vis-à-vis the Roman emperor. The narratives of Jesus' crucifixion are shaped by two Old Testament quotations whose literary contexts portray the Lord's kingship over all the nations and over all the earth. The resurrection of Jesus demonstrates that he has indeed overcome the world. His manifestations to his disciples in Jerusalem and Galilee are followed by their being commissioned to go into the world to forgive sins and gather those who

---

[1] The earliest textual evidence for John 21 is found in the third century. Some scholars have dated $\mathfrak{P}^{66}$, a piece of papyrus that has John 21:1-9, to around 200 CE. Also, $\mathfrak{P}^{109}$ (third century) has John 21:18-20, 23-25.

will believe through their testimony. From a Johannine perspective Jesus' exaltation in his passion, resurrection, and ascension is indeed a cosmic conquest.

The Last Hours of Jesus' Earthly Ministry

Although the narrative of Jesus' passion includes clear indications of his close identification with the Jewish people, John also highlights the universal significance of Jesus and the message about him. This emphasis is constructed through focusing on Jesus' interlocutors and his place of interrogation, discussions about kingship and authority, and the title above his cross.

Jesus' Interrogation

As in previous Johannine scenes, the interrogation of Jesus moves from particular to universal. His passion is particular because several characters in the narrative identified Jesus ethnically with his Jewish people. Soldiers and officers from the chief priests and the Pharisees are looking for "Jesus of Nazareth" (18:5, 7; cf. 19:19).[2] Jesus embraces this designation with the affirmation "I am he" (18:5).[3] Elsewhere in the Gospel of John, Jesus is related to Galilee because he was welcomed by Galileans in Galilee (2:45) and performed miracles and taught there (2:1, 11; 4:3, 43, 46, 47, 54; 6:1; 7:1, 9; see also 21:2). Even peoples' doubts as to whether he is the Messiah because the prophet and the Christ are not meant to arise from Galilee (7:41, 52) reflect the popular perception that Jesus belongs to a particular geographical area. Even the first disciple Jesus called in Galilee, Philip, identifies Jesus as coming

---

[2] Those sent to arrest Jesus are identifying him "fully by name and locale" (Raymond Brown, *The Gospel according to John*, 2 vols., The Anchor Bible 29 [Garden City, N.Y.: Doubleday, 2000], 2:810; see also Ernst Haenchen, *John 2: A Commentary on the Gospel of John, Chapters 7–21*, ed. Robert W. Funk with Ulrich Busse, trans. Robert W. Funk, Hermeneia [Philadelphia: Fortress, 1984], 165).

[3] This is striking because place of origin was a "significant piece of information which served to communicate a person's worth, honor and status" (J. Ramsey Michaels, *The Gospel of John*, NICNT [Grand Rapids: Eerdmans, 2010], 890). See also Jerome H. Neyrey, "Space Out: 'Territoriality' in the Fourth Gospel," *HTS Teologiese Studies / Theological Studies* 58 (2002): 632–63, here 647.

from Nazareth (1:45-46). Pilate is another character in the passion narrative who identifies Jesus with his Jewish people. The Roman prefect informs Jesus that his own nation delivered him over (τὸ ἔθνος τὸ σόν, 18:35).[4] Pilate refers to him as "the king of the Jews" (18:39) and twice indicates to the Jews that Jesus is "your king" (ὁ βασιλεὺς ὑμῶν, τὸν βασιλέα ὑμῶν; 19:14, 15). In his response, Jesus does not dispute what is a correct observation: he is to be identified with Judaism.[5] Jesus' identification with his Jewish people, however, is not limited to his ethnicity.[6] The narrator interprets Jesus' own death as being for the benefit of his people (18:14; cf. 11:48, τὸ ἔθνος).[7] The narrator reminds the reader that Caiaphas advised the Jews that it would be expedient "that one man should die for the people (ὑπὲρ τοῦ λαοῦ)" (18:14). Previously, Caiaphas prophesied that "it is better that one man should die for the people (τοῦ λαοῦ), not that the whole nation (ὅλον τὸ ἔθνος) should perish" (11:50).

Notwithstanding Jesus' clear ethnic and soteriological identification with his Jewish people, the opening of the Gospel indicates that Jesus had an active role in the creation of the world and, therefore, his dominion is not limited to his Jewish people. Therefore, Jesus' passion should also be read from a universal perspective. This perspective is

---

[4] Similarly, the Samaritan woman previously asked Jesus, "How is it that you, a Jew (σὺ Ἰουδαῖος), ask for a drink from me, a woman of Samaria?" (4:9).

[5] One might perceive some distance between Jesus and his Jewish people in John 18:36, "If my kingdom were of this world, my servants would have been fighting, that I might not be delivered over to the Jews." At least in this specific example, Jesus refers to those religious leaders who used Judas in order to get to him (18:2-3). See also Andrew T. Lincoln, *The Gospel according to Saint John*, BNTC 4 (New York: Hendrickson, 2005), 462.

[6] Wayne A. Meeks rightly observes that in the Gospel of John "the Jews" usually "stand for the disbelieving world" and, therefore, the title "king of the Jews" "serves the evangelist's intent . . . to show that Jesus remains king of the disbelieving world as well of the believers." See his *The Prophet-King: Moses Traditions and the Johannine Christology*, NovTSup 14 (Leiden: Brill, 1967), 80.

[7] Craig S. Keener, *The Gospel of John: A Commentary* (Peabody, Mass.: Hendrickson, 2003), 2:1111; Michaels, *John*, 922. This link between 18:35 and 11:48 might indicate that "your nation" refers to Jesus' relationship to Judaism. However, it is clear in the narrative that a group of religious leaders actually handed Jesus over to Pilate. See also Zumstein, *Johannesevangelium*, 696.

initially elicited by the pagan setting of Jesus' final hours before his crucifixion. Three times the narrator reminds the reader that Jesus' interrogation took place in the governor's headquarters (τὸ πραιτώριον, 18:28, 33; 19:9). He has been teaching in the temple and the synagogues (18:20), but now he is giving testimony about the truth in gentile territory, the headquarters of the Roman prefect of Judea (18:28).[8]

Judea existed as an imperial province from 6 to 66 CE, and Pilate likely held office from 26 to 37 CE over a province that extended from Idumaea through Samaria.[9] Although the prefect's residence was in Caesarea Maritima (Josephus, *J.W.* 2.169–174), "during festivals the governor would make his way" to the praetorium "in case of civil unrest and to hear judicial cases" (Josephus, *Ant.* 20.106).[10] It has been suggested that the praetorium was a residence west of Jerusalem built by Herod (Josephus, *J.W.* 5.156–183).[11] Since this place was intended as a Roman administrative and judicial building, Jews considered it defiled. In Jewish tradition, for example, gentile residences were regarded unclean (Acts 10:28; cf. m. Ohal. 18:7).[12] Since John has portrayed his Jewish characters as keeping purification laws before the Passover in 11:55, the reference to the praetorium here is highly significant because John regards this place as pagan territory. Those who accuse Jesus lead him to the governor's headquarters but do not

[8] Andrew T. Lincoln, *Truth on Trial: The Lawsuit Motif in the Fourth Gospel* (Peabody, Mass.: Hendrickson, 2000), 256: "The climactic trial before Pilate . . . sets the lawsuit squarely on the world stage and in the context of the nations."

[9] Helen K. Bond, *Pontius Pilate in History and Interpretation*, SNTSMS 100 (Cambridge: Cambridge University Press, 1998), 1.

[10] Marianne Meye Thompson, *John: A Commentary*, NTL (Louisville: Westminster John Knox, 2015), 374–75.

[11] Cuthbert Lattey, "The Praetorium of Pilate," *JTS* 31 (1930): 180–82. Some scholars, however, have challenged this identification. For a summary of candidates, see Bargil Pixner, "Praetorium," in *ABD* 5:447–49.

[12] Michaels, *John*, 915; Barnabas Lindars, *The Gospel of John: Based on the Revised Standard Version*, NCB (Grand Rapids: Eerdmans, 1981), 555; C. K. Barrett, *The Gospel according to St. John: An Introduction with Commentary and Notes on the Greek Text* (Philadelphia: Westminster, 1978), 532; Brown, *John*, 2:845. Lincoln (*John*, 460) finds an irony here: the Jews are "so scrupulously concerned with ceremonial purity that they will not enter a Gentile house" but lack "any scruples about making use of its Gentile occupant in order to do away with Jesus."

enter them, "so that they would not be defiled (μιανθῶσιν)" (18:28). According to Deuteronomy 16:4, "no leaven shall be seen with you in all your territory for seven days," beginning from noon on the fourth of Nisan.[13] For example, if a Jew was defiled by touching a dead body, he had to eat Passover "in the second month on the fourteenth day at twilight" (Num 9:1).[14] Contrary to the refusal to enter the praetorium of those who accuse Jesus, John indicates that Jesus did indeed enter the governor's headquarters after Pilate called him inside (18:33). The importance of the location of Jesus' interrogation is signaled by nine references to "going in" and "going out" of the praetorium in the story of Jesus' interrogation.[15]

For present purposes, it is noteworthy that Jesus is portrayed giving testimony in a pagan place before Pilate, a gentile ruler.[16] Jesus is in a polluted place giving testimony about the truth to a representative of the Roman Empire.[17] Jesus indicates to Pilate that everyone (πᾶς ὁ)

---

[13] Brown, *John*, 2:846.

[14] Brown, *John*, 2:846; Barrett, *John*, 532.

[15] Jesus and Pilate enter the Praetorium (18:28). Then Pilate goes outside to ask for the particular accusation against Jesus (18:29). Pilate enters his headquarters again and talks to Jesus (18:33). Then he goes back outside to report to the Jews that he finds nothing against him (18:38). Pilate castigates and the soldiers mock Jesus, and then Pilate goes out again (19:4) and brings Jesus out (19:5). Pilate enters his headquarters once more to ask Jesus about his origins (19:9), and then he brings Jesus out (19:13). εἰσέρχομαι εἰς (18:28, 33; 19:9), ἐξέρχομαι (18:38) ἐξέρχομαι ἔξω (18:29; 19:4, 5), and ἄγω ἔξω (19:4, 13). Similarly, John carefully explains whether the disciples who went to the empty tomb remained outside or inside (20:5, οὐ εἰσῆλθεν; 20:6, εἰσῆλθεν; 20:8, εἰσῆλθεν; 20:11, εἰστήκει . . . ἔξω).

[16] Later Christian tradition remembered God as he who "gives life to all things" and "Christ Jesus, who in his testimony before Pontius Pilate made the good confession" (1 Tim 6:13). Cf. Thompson, *John*, 375.

[17] J. Duncan M. Derrett ("Christ, King and Witness [John 18,37]," *Bibbia e Oriente* 162 [1989]: 189–98, here 192, 198) links Jesus' testimony to Pilate to Isa 55:4. According to the prophet, David functions as a "testimony (μαρτύριον) among the nations (ἔθνεσι)" and as a "ruler (ἄρχοντα) and commander for the nations (ἔθνεσι)." The prophet predicts that "nations (ἔθνη) that did not know" God, the Holy One of Israel, shall call upon him and "peoples (λαοί) that do not understand him shall flee to him for refuge" because God has glorified (ἐδόξασέ) him. Derrett follows a clue found in E. W. Hengstenberg, *Das Evangelium des heiligen Johannes* (Berlin: G. Schlawitz, 1863), 3:225–28.

who is of the truth listens to his voice (ἀκούει μου τῆς φωνῆς, 18:37). The adjective πᾶς includes gentiles since it can be read as an invitation to Pilate to listen to Jesus' voice. This seems to be an allusion to his previous teaching about "sheep" (10:1-21).[18] Jesus already taught that he has "other sheep" that will listen to his voice (φωνῆς μου ἀκούσουσιν) so there will be one flock and one shepherd (10:16).[19] Here, however, Pilate does not wait for a reply to his question about Jesus' kingship and, thus, refuses to embrace the truth. During his earthly ministry Jesus moved confidently from Jerusalem to Galilee and Samaria because the whole world is his territory and he has shown solidarity with people from different backgrounds, having taken an active role in everything that exists (1:3, 10, 14; 17:5, 24). He is the light of humanity (1:4), the true light that gives light to every human being (1:9). For some readers, one of the implications of this scene may be that to give testimony about the truth, the messenger will sometimes have to defile himself by engaging pagans even in pagan territory.

Jesus' testimony in the interrogation scenes is framed by his use of the noun "world." Jesus does not restrict his mission to a particular religious group or geographical location. Jesus claims in front of the high priest (18:19) that he had spoken "openly to the world (τῷ κόσμῳ)" (18:20).[20] The choice of the noun κόσμος is significant because Jesus immediately indicates that he has taught in synagogues and in the temple, "where all Jews come together" (18:20).[21] His testimony, however, has also been for the benefit of Samaritans in Samaritan territory (4:7-26, 40-41)[22] and Greek pilgrims (12:20-36). Similarly, Jesus tells

[18] The prominence of shepherd imagery in Jesus' interrogation has been uncovered by M. W. G. Stibbe, *John as Storyteller: Narrative Criticism and the Fourth Gospel*, SNTSMS 73 (Cambridge: Cambridge University Press, 1992), 96–105.

[19] Lindars, *John*, 560; Lincoln, *John*, 463; Barrett, *John*, 538.

[20] From a Johannine perspective, Jesus has spoken openly, clearly, from a heavenly perspective. His words, however, had been heard as rather obscure because his dialogue partners are from this world. As Barrett (*John*, 528) notes, "It is unbelief that makes Jesus' words cryptic."

[21] For Brown (*John*, 2:826) the phrasing of Jesus' answer here presupposes a gentile readership.

[22] Rudolf Bultmann (*The Gospel of John: A Commentary*, trans. G. R. Beasley-Murray, R. W. N. Hoare, and J. K. Riches, The Johannine Monograph Series 1 [Eugene,

Pilate that he came *into the world* to bear witness to the truth (18:37). Yet although Jesus' testimony has been for the benefit of the "world," he tells Pilate twice that his kingdom does not belong to this hostile world (18:36); its origins are located in heaven. The content of Jesus' testimony during his interrogation comprises the basic teaching that he gave to his disciples, other Jews, and the Samaritan woman during his earthly ministry. This testimony includes his heavenly authority (18:36; 19:11; see 3:31) and his witness to the truth (18:37; see 4:23-24). Since Jesus has already indicated that his mission comprises giving testimony to the truth he heard from his Father (8:40), his encounter with Pilate is a further instance of his testimony to people of this world. Elsewhere in the Gospel of John, part of the revelation that allows people to establish a proper relationship with God is knowing that Jesus has come into the world, that he has come from the Father (11:27; 17:8, 21). Since recognizing that Jesus is the truth allows people to come to the Father (14:6), his testimony before Pilate was not only his defense against the charges brought against him but also an important component of his mission on earth.

The response from those gentiles who interacted with Jesus during his passion, however, was in line with the overall response of his Jewish people during his earthly ministry: opposition, rejection, and disbelief. Although it is obvious that Pilate was a pagan who represented Roman rule, his rhetorical question ("Am I a Jew?")[23] ironically brings him close to those he wanted to distance himself from, the Jews who

---

Ore.: Wipf & Stock, 2014], 646), Barrett (*John*, 528), and Keener (*John*, 2:1095), however, take "the world" as a reference to "the Jews." In contrast, Lars Kierspel (*The Jews and the World in the Fourth Gospel: Parallelism, Function, and Context*, WUNT 2/220 [Tübingen: Mohr Siebeck, 2006], 63, 105, 107–8) sees the reference to "the world" as neutral. The "world" is the object of Jesus' ministry (215). Lincoln (*John*, 454) takes the reference to the world as negative. However, the fact that those who had listened to Jesus' words can testify about him (18:21) might indicate that they are at least "potential disciples," according to Michaels, *John*, 904.

[23] The soldiers who mocked Jesus were also Romans (19:2), although John does not provide any information about their background. The designation οἱ στρατιῶται there is different from τὴν σπεῖραν and ὑπηρέτας found in 18:3, where the reference is to officers and servants of religious leaders.

brought Jesus to the praetorium.[24] Pilate's behavior is similar to the portrayal of some of the Jews in the Gospel.[25] Pilate ignores Jesus' origins, does not know the truth, and rejects Jesus' authority.[26] Pilate, and the empire which he represents "are part of the unbelieving 'world.'"[27] The opposition to Jesus does not stem from a particular ethnicity or geographical background. The Johannine irony is that the whole world opposes the one through whom everything was created. The irony of Pilate's question ("Am I a Jew?") is further enhanced by those Jews who claim, "We have no king but Caesar" (19:15). Pilate behaves like those Jews who opposed Jesus, but those Jews who wanted Jesus crucified behave like Romans under the authority of Caesar. They made themselves similar to Pilate, who wanted to be Caesar's friend (19:12).

The gentile response to Jesus is also found during his crucifixion. John highlights that Pilate wrote an inscription and put it on the cross (19:19). Although it is likely that he ordered his soldiers to prepare such an inscription, it is telling that John attributes to the representative of Roman rule the writing of a title that identifies Jesus as king (ἔγραψεν . . . ὁ Πιλᾶτος). Even after the opposition of chief priests, Pilate stood by the original inscription indicating that he indeed wrote it: "what I have written (ὃ γέγραφα) I have written" (19:22). Furthermore, at least four other gentiles are close to Jesus during his crucifixion (19:23). Four times John refers to Roman soldiers who crucified Jesus and took his garments (19:23), who cast lots to see who would take Jesus' seamless tunic (19:24), who did not break Jesus' legs (19:33), and one of whom pierced his side with a spear (19:34). Jesus came to his own territory and to his own creation, but his own people (both Jews and gentiles) did not receive him (1:11).

---

[24] The question expects a negative answer (Brown, *John*, 2:852; Barrett, *John*, 536; Thompson, *John*, 379).

[25] Lincoln, *John*, 462.

[26] Pilate's questions are similar to the Jews' doubts elsewhere in the Gospel of John about Jesus' identity, relationship with the truth, and origins. Pilate asks: οὐκοῦν βασιλεὺς εἶ σύ (18:37), τί ἐστιν ἀλήθεια (18:38), and πόθεν εἶ σύ (19:9; cf. 7:27-28). However, in distinction from the Jews, Pilate finds no guilt in Jesus (18:38).

[27] Bond, *Pilate*, 179, 189, 193. Bond also observes that Pilate answers his own question, "Am I a Jew?" The answer is yes, because he has "joined the unbelieving world—symbolized most starkly in Johannine thought by 'the Jews'—in rejecting Jesus."

Jesus' Authority

Jesus' interrogation and crucifixion might make it seem as if Jesus failed in his cosmic mission and that he was defeated by the world. However, through several rhetorical moves, the narrator highlights that Jesus' death was his victory over the world because his authority comes from heaven. In short, Jesus puts the Roman trial in cosmic perspective.[28] The first indication of Jesus' universal authority is his twofold claim that his kingdom is not of this world. Jesus clearly remarks that his is not a worldly kingdom because his authority is above and beyond this world (18:36). Jesus' reply to Pilate's question whether he was the king of the Jews (18:33) avoids a restriction of his kingdom to his Jewish people since Jesus claims that his "kingdom is not of this world (ἐκ τοῦ κόσμου τούτου)" (18:36). Elsewhere in the Gospel of John, the preposition ἐκ is used to explain origin (e.g., 1:13, 19, 46; 3:6). The source of Jesus' authority is not to be found in this world.[29] It is not of human origin.[30] Previously, Jesus said to some Jews that they are from "below" (κάτω), from "this world" (ἐκ τούτου τοῦ κόσμου) while he is from "above" (ἄνω) because he is not "from this world" (8:23). Jesus also says to Pilate that his kingdom is not from hence (ἐντεῦθεν) (18:36). Instead of the construction ἐκ τοῦ κόσμου τούτου, Jesus uses the adverb ἐντεῦθεν. Although he refers to "his kingdom," his previous prayer has clarified that "all mine are yours, and yours are mine" (17:10).[31] Therefore, his kingdom should be regarded as God's kingdom (cf. 3:3, 5, τὴν βασιλείαν τοῦ θεοῦ). Since Jesus' kingdom is not "from here," it is therefore "superior to all worldly dominion."[32] His kingdom does not come from Jerusalem or Rome but from his Father.[33] With this twofold reply (18:36), Jesus has "indirectly affirmed

---

[28] Lincoln, *John*, 468. See also Lincoln, *Truth*, 256: "God, through Jesus as God's authorized representative, is seen as judging the nations, represented by the official of the ruling Roman Empire."

[29] Bultmann, *John*, 654.

[30] Edwyn Clement Hoskyns, *The Fourth Gospel*, ed. Francis Noel Davey (London: Faber and Faber, 1967), 520.

[31] Bond, *Pilate*, 177n62.

[32] Bultmann, *John*, 654.

[33] Michaels, *John*, 923; Thompson, *John*, 380.

that he is a king."[34] Just as he entered the world to engage it, his kingdom has its origins in the Father and authorizes him to rule over the whole world.[35]

The second indication of Jesus' unique authority surfaces when compared with Pilate's own claims about his power. Pilate confidently asserts that he has power over Jesus' life (19:10) and has authority (ἐξουσίαν) to release or crucify him (19:10)[36] because he is a delegate of the Roman emperor (cf. 19:12).[37] Jesus opposes the idea of Pilate having any claim over him and asserts, "You would have no (οὐδεμίαν) authority (ἐξουσίαν) over me at all unless it had been given you (δεδομένον σοι) from above (ἄνωθεν)" (19:11). The use of the absolute "nothing" (οὐδεμίαν) along with the verb δεδομένον in the passive voice and the adverb ἄνωθεν make it all the clearer that Jesus is talking about an authority that goes above and beyond this world. Jesus is appealing to "God's sovereignty over *all things*."[38] This heavenly authority is greater than the authority of Pilate or of the Roman emperor. For the reader who has the advantage of the prologue (John 1) and Jesus' prayer (John 17), it is ironic that Pilate would claim that he has authority over someone who took an active role in the creation of the world (1:3, 10) and who has received authority from the Father over all flesh (17:2). "Pilate's unqualified claim to be above reason and justice, like an absolute monarch, makes him ascribe to himself almost the divine prerogative which is actually true of Jesus."[39]

---

[34] Bultmann, *John*, 654.

[35] There is no indication here (18:36) that Jesus' kingdom is "spiritual" or inward, manifested in each believer's heart. On the contrary, his kingdom is his authority over creation, even over Pilate as representative of the Roman Empire (19:11). Cf. Michaels, *John*, 922–23.

[36] Ironically, Pilate has been unsuccessful in his repeated attempt at releasing Jesus (18:38-40; 19:6). Thus, Michaels, *John*, 935.

[37] In distinction from the Synoptic Gospels that do not mention the emperor in the passion narrative, the Gospel of John refers to it three times. The first time Pilate indirectly refers to him (19:10). The other two times are explicit. The high priests press Pilate to demonstrate his friendship with the emperor (19:12) and claim that the emperor is their king (19:15). See Sjef van Tilborg, *Reading John in Ephesus*, NovTSup 83 (Leiden: Brill, 1996), 165.

[38] Michaels, *John*, 936n104.

[39] Lindars, *John*, 568.

The third indication that the passion narratives signal Jesus' universal authority is the reference to Caesar. Those who ask for Jesus' crucifixion see Jesus as a challenge to the Roman emperor, because they acknowledge the emperor as their own king. The high priests claim, "We have no king but Caesar" (19:15).[40] The religious leaders ally themselves with the empire and his ruler and, in doing that, reject Jesus' authority and kingship. Those who ask for Jesus' crucifixion see Jesus as opposing Caesar himself (19:12). They claim Pilate is Caesar's friend if he gets rid of the one who opposes the Roman emperor (19:12, ἀντιλέγει τῷ Καίσαρι). Pilate can keep his friendship with the emperor by rejecting the one who lays "down his life for his friends" (15:13). They gladly acknowledge the political authority of Caesar even upon Judea (19:15), but they fail to grasp and acknowledge the legitimate Son of God (19:7) who has shares in God's universal authority (3:31; 17:2).[41] Although Jesus has been identified as "king of the Jews" (18:33, 39; 19:14, 15), the phrase "of the Jews" is lacking in 18:37, when Pilate asks whether Jesus is a king.[42] Even those who ask for Jesus' crucifixion fail to accuse him of making himself "king of the Jews" and instead compare him with the most powerful person at that time, the Roman emperor (19:12). This is even clearer in the mocking of Jesus (19:2). Although the soldiers hail him as "king of the Jews" (19:3), the purple garment, the crown, "which may represent the imperial laurel wreath, and the greeting of the soldiers all suggest that Jesus is ridiculed here as a mock-Emperor" (19:2).[43] During his passion, Jesus never rejects explicitly the titles "king" and "king of the Jews."

[40] Judea was regarded an imperial province. Cf. Strabo, *Geogr.* 17.3.25: "The Provinces have been divided . . . as Augustus Caesar arranged them. . . . [H]e divided the whole of his empire into two parts, and assigned one portion to himself and the other to the Roman people; to himself, all parts that had need of a military guard (στρατιωτικῆς φρουρᾶς)" (LCL 267, 213). Cf. Thompson, *John*, 375.

[41] Although they claimed they "have never been in slavery to anyone" (8:3), the Jews here accept the kingship of Caesar. Cf. Michaels, *John*, 944.

[42] The adverb οὐκοῦν should be understood as introducing a conclusion: "So, you are a king." Cf. BDAG, 736; Brown, *John*, 2:853; and Michaels, *John*, 924n46. Lindars (*John*, 559), however, believes that this is a question that leaves the way open for affirmation.

[43] Bond, *Pilate*, 184. Tilborg (*Ephesus*, 214) understands the mocking of the soldiers as "the enthronement of Jesus as king." The soldiers pay homage to Jesus as they would offer their service to their king.

The fourth instance of Jesus' universal authority is conveyed through irony in the description of his judgment in John 19:13.[44] Previously, John has portrayed Jesus as authorized by his Father to bring judgment to his creation. He is the light of the world who exposes the evil works of humanity (3:19). Jesus judges the whole world (12:31; cf. 16:11). The Father has given "all (πᾶσαν) judgment" to the Son (5:22; cf. 8:6). Jesus has received authority (ἐξουσίαν) to execute judgment even upon those who are in their tombs (5:27, 29, 30). In light of this larger context of Johannine thought, it is ironic that Pilate sat down on the judgment seat and declared "behold your king!" (19:13).

Significantly, it is likely that the place of Jesus' judgment, where the "judgment seat" (Λιθόστρωτον) was located, is to be identified with the outer court of the gentiles in the temple (2 Chr 7:3; Josephus, *B.J.* 6.85, 189).[45] This is perhaps the same place that Jesus cleansed earlier in his ministry according to John 2:13-22. It is likely that those selling oxen, sheep, and pigeons "in the temple" (ἐν τῷ ἱερῷ, 2:13) would use the court of the gentiles for their business.[46] John explicitly indicates that Jesus' judgment took place about the sixth hour on Friday, the day before Passover (19:14). There is evidence that in the first century CE Jerusalem was visited by Jews from the diaspora and Greek pagans.[47] It can be suggested then that Pilate's words "behold your king!" (ἴδε ὁ βασιλεὺς ὑμῶν, 19:14) were heard by people beyond those identified with Judaism in Jerusalem. A gentile ruler (Pilate) sits in the court of

[44] Lincoln, *Truth*, 256: "Jesus . . . is seen as judging the nations, represented by the official of the ruling Roman Empire."

[45] Cornelius Vollmer, "Zu den Toponymen *Lithostroton* und *Gabbatha* in Joh 19,13: Mit einem Lokalisierungsversuch des Prätoriums des Pilatus," *ZNW* 106 (2015): 184–200, here 188–92. Josephus refers twice to the "stone pavement" (λιθόστρωτος) in his portrayal of the taking of Jerusalem by Titus. Cf. "Lucius promptly running up, Artorius plunged down on top of him and was saved; while he who received him was dashed by his weight against the pavement (λιθοστρώτῳ) and killed on the spot" (*J.W.* 6.189).

[46] Colin G. Kruse, *The Gospel According to John: An Introduction and Commentary*, TNTC 4 (Downer Grove, Ill.: InterVarsity, 2008); Jey J. Kanagaraj, *John: A New Covenant Commentary*, New Covenant Commentary Series (Cambridge: Lutterworth, 2013), 24.

[47] Martin Hengel, *The "Hellenization" of Judaea in the First Century after Christ* (London: SCM, 1989), 11, 13; cf. Acts 2:5-11.

the gentiles in front of pilgrims and visitors attracted to Jerusalem and proclaims that Jesus is king.[48]

Jesus' Name

The universal significance of Jesus in the passion narratives is also marked by the tile above the cross and by the larger literary context of two Old Testament quotations that John uses to frame Jesus' crucifixion (Ps 21:19; Zech 12:10).

The crucifixion scene is deeply ironic[49] because it portrays Jesus' exaltation through his humiliation.[50] Above his cross, Pilate writes an inscription in three different languages that reads: "Jesus of Nazareth, the king of the Jews" (19:19). The identification with Nazareth does not bring honor or reputation to him. This same identification prompted Nathanael very early in the Gospel to ask, "Can anything good come out of Nazareth?" (1:46). Early Christians, or at least Paul, were also identified in a disqualifying manner with Nazareth. The spokesman of the high priest Ananias referred to him as "a ringleader of the sect of the Nazarenes" (Acts 24:5). The irony in John 19:19 is about Jesus' origins. Although he is identified with Nazareth, he is from above, from heaven, because his origins are to be located with the Father before creation. The identification with Nazareth in this inscription might be a shameful identification, but, ironically, Jesus is being glorified and exalted on that cross.[51] The other instance of irony in the crucifixion scene is the restriction of Jesus' kingship and authority to Judaism.

---

[48] According to the account found in the Gospel of Luke, many visitors witnessed what happened to Jesus during his final days in Jerusalem (Luke 24:18). Cleopas, for example, refers to Jesus by using the title found on his cross: "Jesus of Nazareth" (Luke 24:19).

[49] Thus, J. Frey, "Jesus und Pilatus: Der wahre König und der Repräsentant des Kaisers im Johannesevangelium," in *Christ and the Emperor: The Gospel Evidence*, ed. Gilbert Van Belle and Joseph Verheyden, BTS 20 (Leuven: Peeters, 2014), 337–93, here 385.

[50] The mockery is obvious because crucifixion "was the most humiliating of Roman punishments, generally reserved for slaves or political agitators, usually from the lower classes" (Bond, *Pilate*, 192).

[51] A. Loisy, *Le quatrième Évangile*, 2nd ed. (Paris: Nourry, 1921), 484. Contra Lincoln (*John*, 475), who suggests that Pilate's statement "what I have written, I have written" shows that the title on the cross is "true and unalterable." Certainly, Jesus is

Pilate gives him a lesser title than he deserves: "king of the Jews." The link between Jesus' name and his kingship was anticipated during his triumphal entry to Jerusalem. Jewish pilgrims saluted Jesus as the one who comes "in the name of the Lord (ἐν ὀνόματι κυρίου)," who is "the king of Israel (ὁ βασιλεὺς τοῦ Ἰσραήλ)" (12:13). However, Jesus rules above the whole world because he took an active role in the creation of everything that exists (1:3, 10) and has received authority from the Father over all flesh (17:2).[52]

The interpretation of Jesus' humiliation as his exaltation is illuminated by at least two previous instances of the glorification motif in 3:14 and 12:32. During his earthly ministry, Jesus compared his forthcoming death with him being lifted up for the benefit of the whole world. He privately said to Nicodemus that the Son of Man must be lifted up (3:14) "that whoever (πᾶς) believes in him may have eternal life" (3:15). Similarly, he publicly said in Jerusalem that he will be lifted up from the earth so that he may "draw all people (πάντας)" to himself (12:32).[53] This wider Johannine context indicates that Jesus' exaltation through his humiliation on the cross was intended for the benefit of the world. He continues to exercise his universal authority even when he is hanging on a cross.[54]

---

the king of the Jews, but, ironically, he is the king of the whole world. Cf. Thompson, *John*, 398: "The one crucified as King of the Jews is king not just of the Jews."

[52] Per Jarle Bekken also sees irony in Pilate's presentation of Jesus as "the man" in John 19:5. He argues that Jewish eschatological hopes found in Philo (*Mos.* 1.290; *Praem.* 95) allow the reading of John 19:5 as "an ironic reversal of the mocking of a pseudo-Emperor, conveying the message that Jesus is the true king and 'Emperor' over against Caesar." See his *The Lawsuit Motif in John's Gospel from New Perspectives: Jesus Christ, Crucified Criminal and Emperor of the World*, NovTSup 158 (Leiden: Brill, 2015), 211.

[53] Thompson, *John*, 398, also notes this connection between 19:19 and 12:32.

[54] Bultmann, *John*, 669, links Jesus' kingship in 19:19 with him being the "savior of the world" (4:42). Thus, Hoskyns, *Fourth Gospel*, 528. Cf. Craig R. Koester, "Jesus as the Way to the Father in Johannine Theology (John 14,6)," in *Theology and Christology in the Fourth Gospel: Essays by the Members of the SNTS Johannine Writings Seminar*, ed. G. van Belle, J. G. van der Watt, and P. Maritz, BETL 184 (Leuven: Leuven University Press, 2005), 117–33, here 131: "The conviction that Christ dies for the sake of the world is underscored by the sign above the cross."

The crucifixion then serves the important purpose of exalting Jesus' name which is written in three different languages.[55] Those who were able to speak Aramaic, Greek, or Latin[56] were able to identify the man hanging on that cross as "Jesus of Nazareth, the king of the Jews" (19:19).[57] Jesus' name is repeated three times in three different languages while he dies in between two nameless malefactors. Pilate chose a multilingual inscription to reach as large an audience as possible.[58] Latin attributed Jesus' execution to Roman administration.[59] Greek, even in Judea, was a language used in everyday life. The language that is problematic, in historical terms, is Aramaic, since there is no other evidence that a Roman official used indigenous languages in inscriptions.[60] At the literary level, however, the inscription in Aramaic coheres with the repeated claim in the story of his passion that Jesus is the king of the Jews.[61]

---

[55] Although John does not specify the exact place where this inscription was located, he might be presupposing that his audience knew the traditions that shaped the Gospel of Luke about the inscription being located over Jesus' head (Luke 23:38). Thus, Brown, *John*, 2:901.

[56] Mixed-language inscriptions were commonplace in the first century CE. Cf. Rosalinde A. Kearsley, ed., *Greeks and Romans in Imperial Asia: Mixed Language Inscriptions and Linguistic Evidence for Cultural Interaction until the End of AD III*, Inschriften Griechischer Städte aus Kleinasien 59 (Bonn: Habelt, 2001). Kearsley finds that "mixed language usage was most frequent in the first two and a half centuries of the imperial period" (147). Some inscriptions used to honor individuals would use mixed language: "Roman citizenship may not have been an essential requirement in obtaining civic recognition" (151).

[57] Lincoln, *Truth*, 257: the fact that "the superscription . . . was in the world's three major languages, stresses Jesus' universal reign from the cross."

[58] Walter Ameling, "Neues Testament und Epigraphik aus der Perspektive der epigraphischen Forschung," in *Epigraphik und Neues Testament*, ed. Thomas Corsten, Markus Öhler, and Joseph Verheyden, WUNT 365 (Tübingen: Mohr Siebeck, 2016), 5–26, here 13–14.

[59] Ameling, "Epigraphik," in Corsten, Ohler, and Verheyden, *Epigraphik und Neues Testament*, 14.

[60] Ameling, "Epigraphik," in Corsten, Ohler, and Verheyden, *Epigraphik und Neues Testament*, 14. Ameling finds no evidence of Roman officials using, for example, "Germanisch, Keltisch, Syrisch, Punisch."

[61] For R. Alan Culpepper ("The Theology of the Johannine Passion Narrative: John 19:16-20," *Neot* 31 [1997]: 21–37, here 21), each language alludes to a particular "world": Aramaic refers to the religious world, Latin refers to the political world, and

Elsewhere in the Gospel of John, salvation is closely associated with Jesus' name. The first instance of Jesus name in this Gospel is found in the prologue: "Grace and truth came through Jesus Christ" (1:17). Those who believe in the name (τὸ ὄνομα) of the Word receive the right to become children of God (1:12; cf. 2:23).[62] At the end of Jesus' dialogue with Nicodemus, there is a clear reference to his crucifixion. Jesus compares his cross with the serpent in the wilderness (3:15-18). God loved the world (τὸν κόσμον), and those who believe in Jesus have eternal life (3:16-17). However, those who do not believe "in the name (τὸ ὄνομα) of the only Son of God" are condemned (3:18). Condemnation or salvation depends on rejecting or believing in Jesus' name. The very purpose of the Gospel of John is that the reader may believe that "Jesus is the Christ in order to have life in his name (ζωὴν τῷ ὀνόματι)" (20:31). During his earthly ministry, Jesus also instructed his disciples to pray in his name (14:13, 14; 15:16; 16:23, 24, 26).

This salvation through the exalted name of Jesus, however, was available only to those visitors in Jerusalem who were able to read Aramaic, Greek, or Latin. Many of the Jews, for example, were able to read this inscription (19:20-21). The inscription in three languages is "making the point that his is a universal reign over the whole civilized world."[63] This, however, raises the question of the literacy of the people visiting Judea for the festival.[64] The inscription would then highlight

Greek refers to the cultural world. It is not clear, though, whether this distinction was intended by John.

[62] "The Gospel of John maintains that human life is dynamic. . . . It also affirms that human beings are capable of change. . . . Change, indeed, transformation, is inherent in human experience, and it occurs in both positive and negative directions," R. Alan Culpepper, "'Children of God': Evolution, Cosmology, and Johannine Thought," in *Creation Stories in Dialogue: The Bible, Science, and Folk Traditions*, BibInt 139 (Leiden: Brill, 2015), 28, 29.

[63] Lincoln, *John*, 475. Similarly, Hoskyns, *Fourth Gospel*, 528: "The trilingual title summons the Gentiles to knowledge of Him" (cf. Keener, *John*, 2:1137). Barrett (*John*, 549), however, indicates that "if John saw any theological significance in the trilingual inscription [such as the universal offer of salvation] he does nothing to indicate it." This opinion misses the connections between 19:19 and 12:32.

[64] Ameling, "Epigraphik," in Corsten, Öhler, and Verheyden, *Epigraphik und Neues Testament*, 16.

the universal significance of Jesus at the reader's level,[65] but it might have been limited, at the narrative level, to those able to actually read this inscription. If the Gospel of John was read and heard for the benefit of mixed audiences composed of literate and illiterate people, the salvific power of Jesus' name exalted on his cross also reached out to those who were unable to read such title but now are able to listen to the reading of the Gospel.

The narrator of the Gospel directs the reader in the reading process by providing interpretations of the events he presents. One of the hermeneutical features he offers is the use of Old Testament quotations whose larger literary contexts point to the universal significance of the Lord. Jesus' crucifixion is framed by two references to Psalm 21:19 LXX and Zechariah 12:10 that, read in light of their larger literary contexts, point to Jesus' authority over the whole world. The evocation of the larger context of Psalm 21:19 in John 19:24 is elicited by two clear instances in the psalm that can easily be connected to the Johannine passion narrative[66] and by the use of Psalm 21 in the Synoptic passion narratives.

The quotation in John 19:24 is taken word for word from our reconstructed text of the LXX.[67] Furthermore, the mocking in Psalm 21:8 ("all who saw me mocked at me") can be compared with the soldiers' mockery of Jesus as king in John 19:2-3, and the kingship of the Lord (τοῦ κυρίου ἡ βασιλεία) in Psalm 21:29 can be tied to one of the most salient features of his passion, the kingship of Jesus (18:33, 36, 37, 39; 19:3, 14, 15, 19). These two thematic links between the larger context of

---

[65] The trilingual nature of the inscription describes the universal significance of Jesus, according to Roberto Vignolo, "Quando il libro diventa archivio—e quando deconstruire glorifica: Il cartello della croce (Gv 19,16b-22) come vettore cristologico e scritturistico della testimonianza giovannea," *RivB* 63 (2015): 465–512.

[66] Margaret Daly-Denton (*David in the Fourth Gospel: The Johannine Reception of the Psalms*, AGJU 47 [Leiden: Brill, 2000], 214–16), suggests that one of several candidates for "the Scripture" fulfilled in John 19:28 is Ps 21:16 and that the reference to Jesus' wounds in John 20:25 may be related to Ps 21:17. Justin (*Dial.* 97.3) clearly links Jesus' wounds with Ps 21:17. Daly-Denton also detects places outside the passion narrative where evocations of Ps 21 are sensed: e.g., 6:12 / Ps 21:27; 17:6 / Ps 21:23 (215–16).

[67] The group of Western manuscripts (R") has a transposition in the first phrase of this verse: ἑαυτοῖς τὰ ἱμάτιά μου.

Psalm 21:19 and the Johannine passion narrative are not idiosyncratic. The Synoptic references to Psalm 21:19 "are immediately followed by strong verbal allusions to other verses of the psalm in the account of the mockery of the bystanders."[68] This psalm was already part of Christian traditions about Jesus' death.[69] The Gospel of Matthew refers to the mocking of Jesus by the Romans (27:29, ἐνέπαιξαν; Luke 23:35, ἐξεμυκτήριζον; Ps 21:8, ἐξεμυκτήρισαν), the division of his garments by casting lots (27:35; Ps 21:19), people treating him with contempt (27:43; Ps 21:9), and his cry on the cross: ηλι ηλι λεμα σαβαχθανι (27:46; Ps 22:1, אלי אלי למה עזבתני). Similarly, the Gospel of Mark includes the casting of lots (Mark 15:24; Luke 23:34), the treatment with contempt (15:29), and the cry on the cross (15:34).

The thematic links between Psalm 21 and the Johannine passion narrative and the Synoptic use of this psalm in the crucifixion of Jesus encourage the reader to look at the larger literary context of Psalm 21. The first part of the psalm is a prayer of anguish. The one who suffers asks the Lord to save him from those who are being violent against him (Ps 21:1-21). The second part of the prayer is a hymn that the one who suffers sings to the Lord. The sufferer promises to "tell your name to my kindred (τὸ ὄνομά σου τοῖς ἀδελφοῖς μου)" (Ps 21:23). Through this prayer the sufferer has addressed his rescuer as "Lord," and, thus, it makes sense that the "name" (ὄνομα) in Psalm 21:23 is a reference to κύριος. Jesus has already prayed to his Father, according to John 17, indicating that he "manifested your name (σου τὸ ὄνομα)" to those who believed (17:6) and has "made known to them your name (τὸ ὄνομά σου)" (17:26), asking that he may "keep them in your name (ἐν τῷ ὀνόματί σου), which you have given me" (17:11) and reminding them that he kept the disciples "in your name (ἐν τῷ ὀνόματί σου),

---

[68] Daly-Denton, *David*, 209. Daly-Denton finds that "John's citation of Ps 21:19 exemplifies the principle that what is said is always heard against the background of the vast 'unsaid'" (213–14).

[69] The number of allusions to Ps 21 in the New Testament found by Dodd (*Scriptures*, 97) is impressive: Matt 6:13; 27:4, 43; Mark 9:12; 15, 24, 29, 34; Luke 6:20-21; 23:35; John 1:18; 19:24; Heb 2:12; 5:7; Rev 11:15. Dodd (*Scripture*, 97) comments, "The Psalm *as a whole* was clearly regarded as a source of testimonies to the passion of Christ" (my emphasis).

which you have given me" (17:12).[70] After the resurrection, Jesus asks Mary to go "to my brothers (τοὺς ἀδελφούς μου) and say to them: "I am ascending to my Father and your Father, to my God and your God" (20:17).

For present purposes, the most striking emphasis of Psalm 21 is its clear universal outlook.[71] This psalm concludes with a straightforward hope that nations will worship the Lord. Those who seek the Lord "shall live (ζήσονται) forever and ever" (21:27). All the ends of the earth (πάντα τὰ πέρατα τῆς γῆς) and all the paternal families of the nations (πᾶσαι αἱ πατριαὶ τῶν ἐθνῶν) shall remember, turn to, and worship (προσκυνήσουσιν ἐνώπιόν σου) the Lord (21:28; cf. 21:30) because kingship is the Lord's and "it is he who is master over the nations (αὐτὸς δεσπόζει τῶν ἐθνῶν)" (21:29).[72] All who descend into the earth (πάντες οἱ καταβαίνοντες εἰς τὴν γῆν) shall worship him (21:30). Even generations that are yet to be born will know the Lord because he has acted (21:30-31). The very last phrase of the prayer is "the Lord acted (ἐποίησεν ὁ κύριος)" (21:32). Remarkably, Pilate asks Jesus, "What have you done? (τί ἐποίησας;)" (18:35; cf. 6:30, τί ἐργάζῃ;). This is a motif in the Gospel of John. Jesus frames his earthly ministry as performing the works of his Father (τὰ ἔργα ἃ ποιῶ, 5:36; 7:21, ἔργον ἐποίησα; cf. 7:3, σοῦ τὰ ἔργα ἃ ποιεῖς).[73] Jesus tells his disciples that the works that he does (τὰ ἔργα ἃ ἐγὼ ποιῶ) in his Father's name (ἐν

---

[70] O. Merlier, "Ὄνομα et ἐν ὀνόματι dans le IVᵉ Évangile," *Revue des Études Grecques* 47 (1934): 180–204; Gerald J. Janzen, "The Scope of Jesus' High Priestly Prayer in John 17," *Encounter* 67 (2006): 1–26, here 22–24.

[71] Daly-Denton (*David*, 217) finds a reworking of Davidic ideology in Isa 55 that influenced John's presentation of Jesus: "It is the fact that God has glorified David . . . (Isa 55:5) . . . that assures his universal sovereignty. Similarly, throughout the account of 'the hour' of Jesus' glorification, his universal kingship is persistently underlined."

[72] The Old Latin (La), the Gallicanum Psalter of Jerome (Ga), and Cyprianus translate *dominabitur*, i.e., "to rule."

[73] P. W. Ensor, *Jesus and His "Works": The Johannine Sayings in Historical Perspective*, WUNT 2/85 (Tübingen: J. C. B. Mohr, 1996); F. Grob, *Faire l'oeuvre de Dieu: Christologie et éthique dans L'Evangile de Jean* (Paris: Presses Universitaires de France, 1986); M. Rae, "The Testimony of Works in the Christology of John's Gospel," in *The Gospel of John and Christian Theology*, ed. R. Bauckham and C. Mosser (Grand Rapids: Eerdmans, 2008), 295–310; A. Vanhoye, "L'oeuvre du Christ, don du Père (Jn 5,36 et 17,4)," *RSR* 48 (1960): 377–419.

τῷ ὀνόματι τοῦ πατρός μου) bears witness about him (10:25). Furthermore, the Father who dwells in the Son does his works (ποιεῖ τὰ ἔργα αὐτοῦ) (14:10). At the end of his ministry, Jesus can pray to his Father that he has completed all the works that the Father gave him to do (ἵνα ποιήσω) (17:4).

The universal significance of Jesus' death elicited by the larger literary context of Psalm 21 is further supported by the possible use of this psalm in the previous Johannine discourse in John 6. The portrayal of Jesus' passion in John 19:17-37 can be taken as a fulfillment of his discourse about the bread of life in John 6. Jesus indicates twice the universal significance of his death in relation to him being the bread from heaven: "the bread of God is he who comes down from heaven and gives life to the world (τῷ κόσμῳ)" (6:33); "the bread that I will give for the life of the world (τοῦ κόσμου) is my flesh" (6:51). This discourse has at least three literary links with Psalm 21.[74] The verb ἐνεπλήσθησαν ("they had eaten their fill," John 6:12) may be inspired by Psalm 21:27, "the needy shall eat and be satisfied (ἐμπλησθήσονται)." The crowds seeking Jesus (ζητοῦντες τὸν Ἰησοῦν), the bread of life, in John 6:24, may resemble from Psalm 21:27, "those who seek him (οἱ ἐκζητοῦντες αὐτόν) shall praise the Lord." Similarly, John 6:27, "work . . . for the food that endures to eternal life (εἰς ζωὴν αἰώνιον)," may be linked to Psalm 21:27: "their hearts shall live forever and ever (ζήσονται . . . εἰς αἰῶνα αἰῶνος)."[75] It is not idiosyncratic, then, that John may be using Psalm 21 in reference to the universal significance of Jesus' death, if he already evoked this same psalm to indicate that Jesus' flesh is given for the life of the world.

The other quotation that points to Jesus' universal significance occurs at the end of the portrayal of his crucifixion. The narrator uses Zechariah 12:10 to indicate that the piercing of Jesus' side was intended to fulfill Scripture (John 19:37).[76] Although the larger literary context

---

[74] It is not unusual that John alludes to an Old Testament text from which he has quoted elsewhere. For example, he quotes Ps 69 in John 2:17, and then he alludes to this same psalm in John 15:25; 19:28. Cf. Dodd, *Scripture*, 57–58.

[75] These observations are found in Daly-Denton, *David*, 215–16.

[76] The quotations might be taken from "an early Christian Greek translation of the Hebrew text," according to Maarten J. J. Menken, *Old Testament Quotations in the*

of this quotation does not portray the nations in a positive light, there is an emphasis on the Lord's universal authority.[77] The quotation is restricted to the phrase "they will look on him whom they have pierced" (Zech 12:10), but there is evidence that the larger context of this text was also influential in the composition of the Johannine passion narrative.[78] C. H. Dodd observed that in John 19:37 and Rev 1:7, "the whole context [from Zech 12:10] is one which drew the attention of writers in various traditions."[79] There is evidence that John knew other sections from Zechariah. For example, he quotes Zechariah 9:9 in John 12:15. The prophet has portrayed God promising to "pour out on the house of David . . . a spirit of grace and supplication" (Zech 12:10) and to open "on that day" (ἐν τῇ ἡμέρᾳ ἐκείνῃ) a fountain to the house of David "to cleanse them from sin and impurity" (Zech 13:1). Similarly, Jesus' side might be taken as an opened fountain of blood and water (John 19:34).[80] Furthermore, the mourn-

---

Fourth Gospel: Studies in Textual Form, CBET 15 (Kampen: Kok Pharos, 1996), 167–85, here 185. More recently, Wm. Randolph Bynum (*The Fourth Gospel and the Scriptures: Illuminating the Form and Meaning of Scriptural Citation in John 19:37*, NovTSup 144 [Leiden: Brill, 2012]) has argued for John's dependence on the Greek Minor Prophets Scroll (8ḤevXIIgr).

[77] After a throughout examination of Zech 12:10 in John 19:37, Bynum (*Scriptures*, 178) concludes, "John is sensitive to the scriptural context from which his citations come." Ruth Sheridan ("They Shall Look Upon the One They Have Pierced: Intertextuality, Intra-textuality and Anti-Judaism in John 19:37," in *Searching the Scriptures: Studies in Context and Intertextuality*, ed. Craig A. Evans and Jeremiah J. Johnson, LNTS 543 [London: Bloomsbury T&T Clark, 2015], 191–209, here 204) reaches the opposite conclusion: "The wider evocative context of Zech 12:10 has little relevance to John 19:37." This conclusion is based on a reading of John 19:37 that demands the Jews to be the subject of the verb "to see." This, however, is an unlikely interpretation of John 19:37, as it is shown below.

[78] Zumstein, *Johannesevangelium*, 734: "Es muss zugleich aus seinem alttestamentlichen Kontext und aus dem joh Kontext verstanden werden." Zumstein finds the larger context of Zech 12:10 in Deutero-Isaiah. Similarly, André LaCocque, "Zacarías 12, 10. '*Et aspicient ad me quem confixerunt*,'" in *Pensar la Biblia: Estudios exegéticos y hermenéuticos*, ed. André LaCocque and Paul Ricoeur, trans. Antonio Martínez Riu (Barcelona: Herder, 2001), 412; Carlos R. Sosa, "La influencia de Isaías II en Zacarías II," *Kairós* 37 (2005): 39–57, here 47–48.

[79] Dodd, *Scriptures*, 65.

[80] Lincoln, *John*, 482; Keener, *John*, 2:1156; Lindars, *John*, 591; Hoskyns, *Fourth Gospel*, 536. Michaels (*John*, 977) exercises restraint because the narrator is not explicit about such connections.

ing of the people of Israel in Zechariah 12:10-12 might be comparable to the "mourning" of two Jewish leaders, Joseph and Nicodemus, who took Jesus' body to bury it (19:38-42).[81]

The opening of the prophecy that includes Zechariah 12:10 portrays the Lord (κύριος) as the one who "stretches out heaven and founds earth and forms the human spirit within" (12:1). The prophecy concludes with the promise that "all who remain of all the nations (πάντων τῶν ἐθνῶν)" shall go up to worship "the king, the Lord (τῷ βασιλεῖ κυρίῳ) Almighty" (14:16). The prophecy also refers to a shepherd and his sheep.[82] The Lord became the shepherd of the flock and tended the sheep (11:7). However, the "shepherd" is struck and the sheep are scattered (13:7; cf. Mark 14:27). The Lord will bring judgment upon the shepherd and the sheep but some of the sheep will be tested and will say "the Lord is my God (κύριος ὁ θεός μου)" (13:9). John has already portrayed Jesus as the "good shepherd" who "lays down his life for the sheep" (John 10:11). The wolf scatters the sheep when they are being looked after by a hired hand (10:12). Jesus, however, brings the "other sheep" to form one flock under one shepherd (10:16). After resurrection, Thomas refers to Jesus as "my Lord and my God!" (ὁ κύριός μου καὶ ὁ θεός μου, 20:28).

Zechariah's prophecy concludes with hope: "On that day . . . the Lord (κύριος) will be king (βασιλέα) over all (πᾶσαν) the earth" (14:8-9). Most significantly for present purposes, "on that day the Lord will be one and his name one (ἔσται κύριος εἷς καὶ τὸ ὄνομα αὐτοῦ ἕν)" (14:9). In his prayer, Jesus has highlighted his unique relationship

---

[81] Michaels (*John*, 978) makes the connection but immediately cautions that such links are implicit "and the commentator's wisest course is to leave them at that." However, the Johannine use of Zech 14:8 in 7:38 and Zech 14:21 in 2:16 encourages the reader to look at the larger context of Zech 12:10 in connection with Jesus' passion. As Dodd (*Scriptures*, 67) has observed, "Although explicit quotations [from Zech 9–14] are not very thick on the ground . . . it appears highly probable that the whole was one of the Scriptures which from a very early time were adduced in illustration of the Gospel facts."

[82] For the importance of Zech 9–14 for the Gospel of John and other New Testament texts, see Sandra Hübenthal, *Transformation und Aktualisierung: zur Rezeption von Sach 9–14 im Neuen Testament*, Stuttgarter Biblische Beiträge 57 (Stuttgart: Katholisches Bibelwerk, 2006).

with his Father and the power of the Father's name to bring unity and salvation to those who believe. Jesus defines eternal life as knowing the "only true God" (τὸν μόνον ἀληθινὸν θεόν) and "Jesus (Ἰησοῦν) Christ" whom the Father sent (17:3). The Father gave his name (τῷ ὀνόματί σου) to Jesus (17:11, 12), and he manifested it to the disciples (17:6) and will continue to make it known to those who will believe (17:26; cf. 17:20). The prayer also highlights the close unity between the Father and the Son. They are one (ἡμεῖς ἕν) (17:22; cf. 17:11, ἕν . . . ἡμεῖς). The Father is in the Son, and Jesus is in the Father (17:21). Similarly, at the end of the discourse about the "good shepherd" Jesus remarks, "I and the Father are one" (ἐγὼ καὶ ὁ πατὴρ ἕν ἐσμεν, 10:30). Jesus also previously indicated that "when you have lifted up the Son of Man, then you will know that I am he (ἐγώ εἰμι)" (8:28).[83]

John quotes Zechariah 12:10 using the verb seeing in the future tense (ὄψονται) and without an explicit subject for such a verb (John 19:37). The same text was quoted in another early Christian text attributing the "seeing" to many more people than the soldiers in charge of Jesus' crucifixion (Rev 1:7; cf. Matt 24:30).[84] This shows that early Christian interpretations of Zechariah 12:10 universalized the text's audience.[85] The author of Revelation indicates that "every eye" and "all tribes of the earth" will see the one who was pierced (Rev 1:7). Since the verb in John 19:37 is in future tense, John might be pointing to people who will believe in the future.[86] The disciple who witnessed crucifixion (19:35, ὁ ἑωρακώς), Mary Magdalene (20:18, ἑώρακα), the gathered disciples after resurrection (20:20, ἰδόντες; 20:25, ἑωράκαμεν), and Thomas (20:25, ἴδω; 20:27, ἴδε) are among those who saw the crucified Jesus.[87] But much as Jesus' prayer anticipated future believers (17:20), the risen Christ blesses those who "have not seen (ἑώρακας) and yet

---

[83] Sheridan, "Intertextuality," in Evans and Johnson, *Searching the Scriptures*, 204, 209.

[84] In late Jewish tradition, those who "pierce" in Zech 12:10 are the nations (Tg. Neb. Zech 12.9; 13.1). See also Pierre Grelot, *Los targumes: Textos escogidos* (Navarra: Verbo Divino, 1987), 80; and Sosa, "Influencia," 47n31.

[85] Keener, *John*, 2:1156.

[86] Bynum, *Scriptures*, 178–79; cf. Lindars, *John*, 591: "The open side of Jesus . . . is the source of universal cleansing."

[87] Thompson, *John*, 405.

have believed" (20:29).[88] The invitation of John the Baptist to look at (ἴδε) the lamb of God who takes away the sin of the world remains open to those who read the Gospel of John.[89]

THE LAST ENCOUNTERS WITH THE DISCIPLES

The narratives of Jesus' resurrection and appearances to his disciples highlight Jesus' authority from the Father. This authority is not restricted to his select group of followers but extends even to those who will believe in the future. There are five clues in the narratives of Jesus' appearances in Jerusalem in John 20 that point to the authority of the risen Jesus: (1) his greetings of peace, (2) his commissioning of the disciples, (3) granting them authority to forgive sins, (4) his ability to bless even future believers, and (5) the purpose of the Gospel. The risen Lord's manifestation to seven of his disciples in Galilee in John 21, where he uses sheep and fish imagery, can also be read as portraying the comprehensive scope of the disciples' mission. Imagery about fishing and sheep is readily read in light of John 6 and John 10, where Jesus has stated that his significance extends to the world, even to the "other sheep." The cosmic conquest obtained on the cross is reclaimed by the disciples through their global mission.

The Authority of the Risen Jesus

The granting of peace to his fearful disciples is an indication of Jesus' authority. His greeting, "peace be with you" (εἰρήνη ὑμῖν, 20:21), echoes the farewell discourses that the disciples witnessed previous to Jesus' passion. Jesus indicated to them that his peace is different from the

---

[88] Menken, *Quotations*, 182, 184. C. Traets (*Voir Jésus et le Père en lui, selon l'évangile de saint Jean*, Analecta Gregoriana 159 [Rome: Università Gregoriana, 1967], 165) relates the "seeing" to the Roman soldiers and to all future gentile believers. Sheridan ("Intertextuality," in Evans and Johnson, *Searching the Scriptures*, 208), however, suggests that the subject of the verb "to see" is "the Jews." Her suggestion is not persuasive because the verb lacks an explicit subject, those who directly pierced Jesus are Roman soldiers under no Jewish influence, and the verb is in future tense.

[89] Cf. Bynum, *Scriptures*, 177; Zumstein, *Johannesevangelium*, 735. Indeed, the previous Old Testament quotation ("not one of his bones will be broken," 19:36) may be an allusion to the Passover lamb (Exod 12:46; cf. Ps 33:21). See Meeks, *Prophet-King*, 77. Dodd (*Scripture*, 98) indicates that Ps 33:21 "is slightly nearer to" John 19:36.

peace offered by the world (οὐ καθὼς ὁ κόσμος δίδωσιν, 14:27) because it stems from his victory over the world (ἐγὼ νενίκηκα τὸν κόσμον, 16:33).[90] Jesus' ability to grant peace signals that his authority has been vindicated.[91] The world, represented by Pontius Pilate, tried to show that it had authority over Jesus (19:10). Although he was executed under Caesar's friend, his resurrection demonstrates that Jesus has overcome the world. Jesus has conquered the world with his light (16:33; cf. 1:5). Jesus defeated death and, therefore, is authorized to bring peace to his fearful disciples. Although they still will face tribulation in the world (ἐν τῷ κόσμῳ θλῖψιν ἔχετε, 16.33), they have the assurance of Jesus' peace.

This assurance of Jesus' authority manifested through the granting of peace allows the disciples to embrace Jesus' commissioning. He sends those disciples who are behind closed doors (20:19) into the world. Jesus has the power to send his disciples as the Father sent the Son (καθὼς ἀπέσταλκέν με ὁ πατήρ, 20:21).[92] The Father's universal authority allowed the sending of his Son. Similarly, the authority Jesus has received from his Father permits him to send his disciples in the same way he was sent by the Father. Since the sending of the Son was intended to benefit the world, the sending of the disciples should be understood as comprehensive in scope. The Father consecrated the Son and sent (ἀπέστειλεν) him into the world (εἰς τὸν κόσμον, 10:36) in order to save the world (3:17; cf. 5:36; 6:57; 8:42; 11:42; 17:3, 8). The disciples then are sent to engage the world just as Jesus' mission concerned his whole creation.[93] This idea is clearer when compared with Jesus' prayer in 17:18.[94] Jesus prayed to the

[90] The many links between the resurrection narratives in John 20 and the farewell discourses are conveniently explained in Michel Gourgues, "Les échos du discours d'adieu dans les récits johanniques de christophanie pascale (Jean 20)," in *Studies in the Gospel of John and Its Christology: Festschrift Gilbert van Belle*, ed. Joseph Verheyden, Geert van Oyen, Michael Labahn, and Reimund Bieringer, BETL 265 (Leuven: Peeters, 2014), 485–99.

[91] Lincoln, *John*, 498.

[92] The conjunction καθὼς signals the parallelism between the way in which the Father sent the Son and the way the disciples are sent by Jesus (Thompson, *John*, 420). The verbs ἀπέσταλκεν and πέμπω are used as synonyms throughout the Gospel, according to Barrett, *John*, 569; Michaels, *John*, 1009; Keener, *John*, 2:1203.

[93] Lindars, *John*, 611; Schnelle, *Johannes*, 386; Zumstein, *Johannesevangelium*, 759.

[94] Bultmann, *John*, 692. Similarly, Zumstein, *Johannesevangelium*, 759n74.

Father saying, "As you have sent me into the world, so I have sent them into the world" (17:18). After the resurrection a similar idea is expressed: "As the Father has sent me, so I am sending you" (20:21).

17:18	καθὼς ἐμὲ ἀπέστειλας εἰς τὸν κόσμον
	κἀγὼ ἀπέστειλα αὐτοὺς εἰς τὸν κόσμον
20:21	καθὼς ἀπέσταλκέν με ὁ πατήρ
	κἀγὼ πέμπω ὑμᾶς

What is missing in John 20:21 is the phrase εἰς τὸν κόσμον, repeated twice in 17:18. In a sequential reading, however, it is possible to see Jesus' mission as intending to be meaningful to the world. Therefore, the natural implication when reading John 20:21 is that the sending of the disciples has similar cosmic overtones. During his earthly ministry, Jesus did not restrict his mission to a particular ethnic group or geographical area. The Father sent the Son "into the world." Accordingly, Jesus gave testimony to Jews, Samaritans, Greeks, and Romans (at least Pontius Pilate). Jesus also taught in synagogues, the temple, close to the sea of Galilea, and near a well in Samaria. The wider world (geographically and ethnically) was his mission field. It was in Samaria where Jesus said that his "food" is to do the will of him who sent him (4:34), and also where Jesus encouraged his disciples to see the fields ready for harvest (4:35), and where he sent his disciples to reap that for which they did not labor (4:38). After the resurrection, the disciples are sent not only to Judea but also to Samaria and, indeed, into the world.

The reading of John 20:21 in the light 17:18 may be clarified by looking at still another previous reference to Jesus' mission in John 3:17. At the conclusion of his dialogue with Nicodemus, Jesus says that God sent his Son into the world so that the world might be saved through him (3:17). The implication is that since Jesus was sent by his Father for the salvation of the world, the disciples should continue this all-encompassing soteriological mission.

3:17	ἀπέστειλεν ὁ θεὸς τὸν υἱὸν εἰς τὸν κόσμον
17:18	ἐμὲ ἀπέστειλας εἰς τὸν κόσμον
20:21	ἀπέσταλκέν με ὁ πατήρ

All three phrases are similar. The missing phrase in John 20:21 is again εἰς τὸν κόσμον, but by that point there is no doubt that Jesus' mission concerns the whole world. Therefore, it is possible to supply "into the world" in the narrative of the disciples' commission after the resurrection (20:21).[95] The sending of the disciples by the risen Jesus ensures that his universal mission will continue to be effective through them.

The disciples then will extend Jesus' life-giving work in the world,[96] and this mission will be possible through the work of the Spirit. Immediately after the commission of the disciples in 20:21, Jesus says, "Receive the holy Spirit" (20:22). Since the beginning of his earthly ministry, the Spirit has been with Jesus. John saw the Spirit descending from heaven and remaining in Jesus (1:32). Therefore, Jesus is authorized to baptize with the Holy Spirit (1:33). The Father gives the Spirit without measure and, because he loves the Son, he has given all things ($\pi\acute{\alpha}\nu\tau\alpha$) into his hand (3:34-35). The Spirit gives life (6:63), allows people to enter God's kingdom (3:5), and enables appropriate worship of the Father (4:23-24). Jesus has also stated that the role of the Spirit is to give witness about him (15:26-27). After his resurrection it becomes clear that this testimony is going to be effective through the work of the disciples (20:22). Since they have the Spirit, they will bear witness about Jesus (15:26-27). They will also bear witness about the Spirit, because the world does not know him (14:17). The anticipated role of the Spirit as convicting the world concerning sin, righteousness, and judgment demands that the mission of the disciples be intended for the whole world. The Spirit will point to the unbelief of the world and will judge the ruler of this world (16:8-11).

The giving of the Spirit by the risen Jesus is preceded by an act that recalls his universal authority. Jesus' act of breathing in 20:22 is a reminder of his role in creation and, thus, of his claim on everything that has been created.[97] Instances of creation imagery elsewhere in the Gospel are intended to highlight Jesus' authority over all flesh. The Word was in the beginning with God taking an active role in the

[95] Donatien Mollat, *Études Johanniques*, Parole de Dieu (Paris: Éditions du Seuil, 1979), 155.

[96] Thompson, *John*, 420, 422.

[97] Carlos Raúl Sosa Siliezar, *Creation Imagery in the Gospel of John*, LNTS 546 (London: Bloomsbury T&T Clark, 2018), 161–72.

creation of the world (1:1-3, 10). He is able to offer eternal life to the world because he is its light and its life (1:4-5, 9). After the resurrection, Jesus is again glorified with the glory he had with God before creation (17:5, 24). The glorified Jesus breathes the Spirit to his disciples and sends them as the Father sent him (20:22). This act that resembles the Creator God legitimizes Jesus granting his disciples authority to forgive people's sins.

During his earthly ministry, Jesus fulfilled the works of his Father (5:36; 17:4). With his ministry and crucifixion, he took away the sin of the world (1:29). And, with his resurrection, the results of his death are made available to the world through the work of the disciples in the power of the Spirit. The significance of Jesus will be extended through the disciples who have now authority to forgive and retain sins (20:23).[98] Immediately after breathing the Spirit on them, Jesus indicates to his disciples that if they forgive the sins of some (ἄν τινων), they are forgiven. Similarly, if they withhold forgiveness from any (ἄν τινων), it is withheld (20:23). The phrase ἄν τινων is found twice in 20:23 and has no specific restriction in the context. Therefore, it can be taken as "anyone" in the broadest possible sense. Furthermore, the verbs ἀφέωνται and κεκράτηνται are in the perfect tense, "implying a timeless state of affairs which will obtain in the future"[99] and, we may add, with future believers.

Jesus' presence in the world brought salvation and judgment. Those who were blind were able to see and those who said they were able to see became blind (9:39). Similarly, the Spirit gives the disciples power to bring light to those who are dead in their sins. Through forgiveness they can allow others to benefit from Jesus' death and resurrection. However, they also have the authority to judge those who reject Jesus by withholding forgiveness. Through the work of the disciples, the Spirit will convict the world of sin (16:8), and, therefore, Jesus' work of

[98] They do not "take away" the sin of the world (1:29) but have the authority to forgive or retain sins (Thompson, *John*, 423).

[99] Lindars, *John*, 612. Since the perfect tense in the apodosis of a general conditional has a future reference (BDF, § 344), the future αφεθησεται preserved in the original reading of Sinaiticus is not necessary. Notice also that the combination between aorist subjunctive (ἀφῆτε) and present subjunctive (κρατῆτε) may imply an act of forgiveness and a continued state of holding forgiveness (Brown, *John*, 2:1023).

taking away the sin of the world will become effective (1:29).[100] The disciples' mission is for the whole world, but not everyone exposed to the light will embrace it. The possibility of reading "anyone" in the broadest sense is enhanced when Jesus' commission to his disciples in this Gospel is compared with their commissioning in the Synoptic Gospels.[101] If John knew the traditions that shaped the portrayal of Jesus' resurrection in the other canonical Gospels, it is plausible that he knew the universal significance of Jesus linked to such accounts. Since there is no evidence that he contradicts the resurrection accounts found in the Synoptic Gospels, there is no reason to suggest John intended to subvert the Synoptic portrayal of Jesus' universal significance and the comprehensive scope of the disciples' mission.

The longer ending of Mark has the risen Jesus commanding his disciples to "go into all the world (τὸν κόσμον ἅπαντα) and proclaim the gospel to the whole creation (πάσῃ τῇ κτίσει)" (Mark 16:15). The disciples obeyed and preached the gospel "everywhere" (πανταχοῦ, 16:20). Matthew's account has creation being affected by Jesus' resurrection. After a great earthquake an angel from heaven rolled back the stone of Jesus' tomb (Matt 28:2). Matthew also portrays the risen Jesus in Galilee commissioning his disciples: "All authority (πᾶσα ἐξουσία) in heaven and on earth has been given to me . . . make disciples of all nations (πάντα τὰ ἔθνη)" (Matt 28:18-19). Jesus' universal authority warrants the universal mission of his disciples. In contrast, Luke has the risen Jesus in Jerusalem commissioning his disciples. A couple of visitors to Jerusalem interpreted that Jesus was the one to redeem Israel (Luke 24:21), but the risen Jesus himself commissions his disciples that "repentance for the forgiveness of sins should be proclaimed . . . to all nations (πάντα τὰ ἔθνη), beginning from Jerusalem" (Luke 24:47). John indeed chooses to portray Jesus performing an act that resembles that of the Creator God. This act would remind the reader of Jesus' claim on everything that has been created and, therefore, about his

[100] Michaels, *John*, 1014–15; Keener, *John*, 2:1206.

[101] Sosa Siliezar, *Creation*, 169–70. John 20:23 "has some similarities with the authorization of the disciples to bind or loose" in Matt 18:18, but the Gospel of John "broadens the notion from teaching authority in the church to mission in general" (Lincoln, *John*, 500).

universal mission. By performing such a peculiar act, Jesus implies that his followers' mission should also be universal in scope.

The authority of Jesus has been demonstrated through his granting of peace to the fearful disciples, through his sending of them as the Father sent him, and through his allowing his followers to forgive people's sins. His authority is further highlighted in his ability to bless future disciples and the efficacy of his life-giving power among future readers of the Gospel.

The fourth indication of the risen Jesus' authority is his blessing to others who will believe in him (20:29). Thomas believed in the risen Lord because he saw him (20:25, 29). However, Jesus blesses others who have not seen him: "Blessed are those who believe although they do not see" (20:29).[102] Since the other disciples have testified to Thomas about the resurrection of Jesus (20:25), Jesus' words may point to their testimony: "Have you believed their testimony because you have seen me? Blessed are those who have not seen and have believed their testimony" (20:29).[103] The relationship between the participles ἰδόντες and πιστεύσαντες may point to the future mission of the witnesses of the resurrection and to future believers who will believe through their testimony. The first participle is present (ἰδόντες) but the second one is aorist (πιστεύσαντες). The aorist can be taken as "timeless" and referring to John's audience composed of people who did not witness the risen Lord.[104] Since John "has the reader in mind . . . he gains the most universal reference by putting the final statement in the form of a beatitude."[105] The authority of Jesus is not only preexistent (1:1-5) or exercised during his earthly ministry (5:24; 6:63), but it even extends to the future. The risen Jesus has authority to bless (μακάριοι) the reader of the text who is located

---

[102] This refers primarily to the disciple who believed without seeing in John 20:8, according to Hans Förster, "Überlegungen zur Übersetzung von Joh 20,19 und 20,29," *Glotta* 92 (2016): 86–105.

[103] Lincoln, *John*, 503.

[104] Barrett, *John*, 574. For a different opinion, see Brown (*John* 2:1027), who retains the past tense of the aorist to indicate that "the evangelist is probably thinking of his own era when for many years there has been a group that has not seen but has believed."

[105] Lindars, *John*, 616.

several decades after his resurrection and even future disciples who will believe without actually seeing the risen Jesus.[106]

The narrator emphasizes this idea in his stated purpose for the writing of the Gospel (20:31). The narrator closes the stories of Jesus' appearances in Jerusalem by addressing the reader: "These are written so that you may believe that Jesus is the Christ" (20:31). "The book functions for its readers in precisely the same way that the epiphany of its hero functions within its narratives and dialogues."[107] The narrator envisions future believers who will "have life in his name" (20:31).[108] However, there has been debate whether the purpose of the Gospel allows the text to be a "missionary document" intended to gentiles or an "internal text" to enrich those who are already believers.[109] The decision is difficult.[110] The previous context, however, has Jesus blessing others who believe without seeing him (20:29). These other believers are set in contrast with Thomas, who believes in the risen Lord for the first time. Similarly, the Gospel as a whole includes a number of stories where diverse people are invited to believe for the first time such as Nathanael, Nicodemus, the Samaritan woman, a man born blind, and

---

[106] Lincoln, *John*, 504, "Faith is based on testimony and the Gospel narrative itself, with its witness to Jesus' signs . . . makes such faith available to later readers." Michaels (*John*, 1019) thinks that the readers addressed in John 20:29 are Jews and gentiles.

[107] Wayne A. Meeks, "The Man from Heaven in Johannine Sectarianism," *JBL* 91 (1972): 44–72, here 69.

[108] Haenchen, *John 2*, 212: "He hoped, as a result, that its reiteration would also awaken faith in Jesus among persons beyond the eyewitnesses."

[109] They base their interpretations on the verb "to believe" (πιστεύ[σ]ητε). The earliest reading is πιστευητε since it is found in the original reading of Sinaiticus and, possibly in 𝔓66. The reading πιστεύσητε is found in a correction to Sinaiticus and in Codex Alexandrinus. The aorist tense suggests that Jesus' signs are intended for readers to come to believe that Jesus is the Messiah, while the present tense addresses believers in need of a stronger faith. Cf. Bruce M. Metzger, *A Textual Commentary on the Greek New Testament*, 2nd ed. (Stuttgart: German Bible Society, 2007), 219.

[110] Commentators are divided. Present subjunctive: Barrett, *John*, 575; Lindars, *John*, 617; Lincoln, *John*, 506; Thompson, *John*, 430. Aorist subjunctive: Carson, *John*, 87-95; John A. T. Robinson, "The Destination and Purpose of St. John's Gospel," *NTS* 6 (1959–1960): 117–31. For Bultmann (*John*, 698), the distinction between present and aorist is "without significance" because a "precise circle of readers is obviously not in view" (cf. Michaels, *John*, 1022).

Martha. The testimony about Jesus is intended for "all" to believe in him (1:7).[111] Furthermore, believing in Jesus as Messiah and Son of God produces eternal life (20:31). If readers are already Christians, it is natural to suppose they are enjoying eternal life. Nonbelievers, however, need to experience eternal life for the first time. In light of this larger context, it makes sense that the narrator is addressing readers who will believe without actually seeing Jesus' signs.[112]

Previously, Jesus prayed remembering that the Father had given him authority over all flesh (πάσης σαρκός) to give eternal life (17:2, ζωὴν αἰώνιον). This eternal life is defined by Jesus as knowing (γινώσκωσιν) the only true God (τὸν μόνον ἀληθινὸν θεόν), and Jesus Christ (Ἰησοῦν Χριστόν) whom he has sent (17:3). Similarly, at the end of his story, the narrator relates Jesus' name, belief, and life (20:31). For him, life in the name of Jesus (ὀνόματι αὐτοῦ) is linked to believing in him as the Messiah (ὁ χριστός) and Son of God (ὁ υἱὸς τοῦ θεοῦ). Furthermore, the prologue promised that as many as (ὅσοι) did receive him, the Word gave them authority to become children of God, "to those who believe (τοῖς πιστεύουσιν) in his name (εἰς τὸ ὄνομα αὐτοῦ)" (1:12).[113] This same thought is also found at the end of Jesus' dialogue with Nicodemus, where the universal significance of Jesus is prominent: everyone (πᾶς) who believes (ὁ πιστεύων) may have eternal life (ζωὴν αἰώνιον) in him (ἐν αὐτῷ) (3:15), and God so loved the world (κόσμον) that everyone (πᾶς) who believes (ὁ πιστεύων) in him (εἰς αὐτόν) may have eternal life (ζωὴν αἰώνιον) (3:16).

The statement of purpose is linked to previous references to Jesus' identity. Nathanael identified Jesus early in the narrative as the "Son of God" and "king of Israel" (1:49), and a large crowd in Jerusalem later

---

[111] Thompson, *John*, 429.

[112] Cf. Adelbert Denaux, "The Twofold Purpose of the Fourth Gospel: A Reading of the Conclusion to John's Gospel (20,30-31)," in Verheyden, van Oyen, Labahn, and Bieringer, *Studies in the Gospel of John and Its Christology*, 519–36, here 528: "It is not impossible, then, that in writing his Gospel, the fourth evangelist intended to address not only a large audience of Christians . . . but also non-Christian readers, among whom particularly Jews, especially Hellenistic Jews form the diaspora and God-fearers, and even pagans."

[113] Bultmann, *John*, 699.

hailed him as the "king of Israel" (12:13). In his role as Son, Jesus "shares fully in the divine activity of giving life and judging" (5:25-26).[114] Martha also identified him as "the Christ, the Son of God, who is coming into the world" (11:27) in a context where Jesus' authority to give life was prominent (11:25). The most noticeable portrayal of Jesus in relation to God in this Gospel has been the Father and Son relationship.[115] The two designations (Christ and Son of God) have a Jewish background. However, "Son of God" would be "far more meaningful to a Hellenistic reader,"[116] without denying its clear Jewish milieu. John's "approval of the 'Lord and God' profession shows how he understood 'Son of God.'"[117] The conclusion of the Gospel effectively portrays the "final and unsurpassable self-disclosure" of God in Jesus.[118] The linking of the promised Christ and the preexistent Son of God in the earthly Jesus assures the "indissoluble unity of the lowliness (*Niedrigkeit*) and sovereignty (*Hoheit*) of Jesus Christ."[119]

The Commissioning of the Disciples

The commissioning of the disciples in Jerusalem in John 20 allows us to read Jesus' manifestation to seven of his disciples in Galilee as a further instance of their charge with a worldwide mission. John may have employed symbolism in the last chapter of his Gospel to portray the universal character of the disciples' mission.[120] In general, stories of individual encounters with the risen Jesus in the canonical Gospels highlight the proof of the resurrection, while the chief motif in the

[114] Thompson, *John*, 430.

[115] E. Zingg, *Das Reden von Gott als „Vater" im Johannesevangelium*, Herders biblische Studien 48 (Freiburg: Herder, 2006); T. E. Pollard, "The Father-Son and God-Believer Relationship according to St John: A Brief Study of John's Use of Prepositions," in *L'Évangile de Jean: Sources, rédaction, théologie*, ed. Martinus de Jonge et al., BETL 44 (Gembloux: J. Duculot, 1977), 363–69.

[116] Lindars, *John*, 617.

[117] Brown, *John*, 2:1060.

[118] Schnelle, *Johannes*, 395.

[119] Schnelle, *Johannes*, 395.

[120] Peter's confession that Jesus knows "all things" (πάντα σὺ οἶδας, v. 17) and the narrator's literary exaggeration that the world itself (τὸν κόσμον, v. 25) is insufficient to contain books about Jesus' manifestations to his disciples can be taken as instances of universal language.

corporate encounters with him is the missionary commission.[121] This is clearly seen in the Gospel of John. Jesus' encounter with Thomas highlights the proof of his resurrection (20:27), while Jesus' gathering with his fearful disciples is intended to send them on a mission (20:21). Since the encounter with the risen Jesus in John 21 is enjoyed by seven of his disciples (v. 2), the reader is initially inclined to find the missionary motif. In what follows, I offer a plausible reading of the first two scenes of John 21, considering our previous knowledge gained from a sequential reading of the Gospel of John.[122]

The encounter between Jesus and his disciples at the end of the Gospel is clearly a manifestation of the risen Lord. This is explicit in verse 14: "this was now the third time that Jesus was revealed to the disciples."[123] This comment connects John 21 with Jesus' encounter with his disciples in 20:19-23 and 20:24-29. There are other indications that highlight this as an encounter with the risen Jesus. Twice the narrator refers to the story as a manifestation (see ἐφανέρωσεν, v. 1). The narrator also indicates that Jesus "stood" (ἔστη) on the shore (v. 4). This verb has already been used in 20:19 to indicate that the risen Jesus came and "stood" (ἔστη) among his disciples. The motif of disciples not recognizing the risen Lord (οὐκ ᾔδει, 20:14) is repeated here (οὐ . . . ᾔδεισαν, 21:4). Similarly, the motif of people afterward recognizing the risen Jesus is found in 21:7, 12 and in 20:16.[124]

---

[121] Bultmann, *John*, 689.

[122] See also Culpepper, "Designs," in Verheyden, van Oyen, Labahn, and Bieringer, *Studies in the Gospel of John and Its Christology*, 379.

[123] The encounter with Mary Magdalene is not considered, not because she was not a disciple (contra Barrett, *John*, 582) but because the group of disciples was not with her (Lindars, *John*, 632; Haenchen, *John 2*, 221; Keener, *John* 2:1226n5; Lincoln, *John*, 514). Michaels (*John*, 1041–42), however, allows that the "two appearances a week apart in 20:19-23 and 26-29 respectively are actually one."

[124] The location of this encounter highlights that the risen Jesus is not only concerned with Judea but also with Galilee. He manifested himself to seven disciples by the Sea of Tiberias (21:1). Galilee was the place were Nathanael acknowledged Jesus as the Son of God and king of Israel (1:49; cf. 21:2). Galilee was also the place where Jesus performed his first two signs according to the Gospel of John (2:1; 4:46). The clearest link with the previous context, however, should be found in the story of the multiplication of bread in John 6. This miracle took place on the other side of the Sea of Tiberias (6:1). For Brown (*John*, 2:1067, 1098) "the name 'Tiberias' would have been more acceptable to a Greek-speaking audience than 'Gennesaret'" and "the catch of

The first scene centers on the topic of fishing. Peter is said to decide to go (ὑπάγω) fishing in the sea of Galilee, but his efforts were unsuccessful (21:3). Previously, Jesus told his disciples that he appointed them that they should go (ὑπάγητε) and bear fruit (15:16). Jesus also indicated that the disciples can do nothing apart from him (15:5).[125] Only if Jesus abides in the disciples, can they be fruitful (15:5). When the disciples bear much fruit they glorify the Father (15:8). In John 21, however, the disciples are unsuccessful since they caught nothing (21:3). In light of John 15:5, 8, 16, one might interpret their efforts as fruitless.[126]

The negative portrayal of the disciples' efforts is accentuated by a time reference: "that night" (νυκτί, 21:3).[127] Throughout the Gospel darkness is negative, but light is positive (e.g., 1:4-5).[128] Jesus himself has indicated to his disciples that the works of God should be completed "while it is day (ἡμέρα); night (νύξ) is coming, when no one can work" (9:4). The noun "work" is peculiarly Johannine and refers to Jesus' mission in the world. The completion of God's works brings glory to the Father (17:4). The fruitless situation of the disciples in John 21:3 changes radically when Jesus comes to them at "early morning" (πρωΐας, 21:4).[129] He asks them to cast the net on the right side of

---

fish [in John 21] is the dramatic equivalent of the command given in the Matthean account of the Galilean appearance: 'Go therefore and make disciples of all nations' [Matt 28:19]." Hoskyns (*Fourth Gospel*, 552) goes so far as to posit that the catch takes place in "Galilee of the nations" (Isa 9:1).

[125] Barrett, *John*, 582; Lincoln, *John*, 511; Michaels, *John*, 1030.

[126] This interpretation, however, is discarded by Lindars (*John*, 625) and Thompson (*John*, 437n67).

[127] Beutler, *Johannesevangelium*, 493; R. Alan Culpepper, "Inclusivism and Exclusivism in the Fourth Gospel," in *Word, Theology, and Community in John*, ed. John Painter, R. Alan Culpepper, and Fernando F. Segovia (St. Louis: Chalice, 2002), 85–108, here 101.

[128] Lincoln, *John*, 511.

[129] Although "early morning" can still be dark, the absence of a clarification such as "still dark" (σκοτίας, 20:1) might indicate that Jesus' manifestation to his disciples takes place when the light of a new day is just breaking. Notice also that the use of ἐφανέρωσεν in 21:1 (cf. 1:31; 2:11; 3:21; 7:4; 9:3; 17:6) has "the general connotation of emergence from obscurity" (Brown, *John*, 2:1067). If "early morning" in 21:4 also evokes the entrance of Jesus into Pilate's headquarters (Keener, *John* 2:1230), the reader might then be reminded of Jesus' interaction with a gentile.

the boat to find some fish (21:6). The result is a net difficult to handle because of the quantity of fish (ἀπὸ τοῦ πλήθους τῶν ἰχθύων, 21:6). The narrator even indicates that the net was full of large fish, 153 in total (21:11).

The only other reference to fish in this Gospel occurs in the feeding of a multitude on the other side of the Sea of Galilee (6:9, 11, ὀψάριον).[130] Two fish and five barley loaves become food for five thousand people. The fish, however, disappear from the story, and the loaves take center stage. Jesus asked his disciples to gather "the leftover fragments" (6:12), and they filled twelve baskets with "fragments from the five barley loaves left by those who had eaten" (6:13).[131] Jesus will later refer to the miracle by focusing exclusively on the loaves (6:26), and he will use the bread to teach about his mission (6:33), belief (6:47), and eternal life (6:50-51). The miracle in John 21 also refers to bread and fish (v. 9). Although the bread is mentioned twice (vv. 9, 13), the focus is on the fish. In distinction from the feeding of a multitude where Jesus uses bread to teach about eternal life for those who believe in him, here the reader is left without explicit explanations of the meaning of the fish. Previously, the bread was compared with Jesus' body (6:53). Here, the reader is invited to compare the multitude of fish with those who will believe through the testimony of the disciples (cf. Luke 5:10).[132]

---

[130] The noun ὀψάριον is used in John 21:9, 10, 13. The link between John 21 and John 6 is often noted by scholars: e.g., M. Hasitschka, "Die beiden 'Zeichen' am See von Tiberias: Interpretation von Joh 6 in Verbindung mit Joh 21,1–14," *SNTSU* 24 (1999): 85–102; M. Rissi, "'Voll grosser Fische, hundertdreiundfünfzig': Joh. 21,1–14," *TZ* 35 (1979): 73–89, here 75; Culpepper, "Inclusivism," in Painter, Culpepper, and Segovia, *Word, Theology, and Community in John*, 101; Esther Kobel, *Dining with John: Communal Meals and Identity Formation in the Fourth Gospel and its Historical and Cultural Context*, BibInt 109 (Leiden: Brill, 2011), 211–12; Zumstein, *Johannesevangelium*, 783.

[131] Lindars, *John*, 631, "Just as the leavings [in John 6] typify the universal feeding of the future, so the catch of fish [in John 21] typifies the universal population which is to be fed."

[132] Lincoln, *Truth*, 261, sees the miraculous catch of fish as "a sign of the success of their universal mission." This interpretation is supported by an early understanding of the 153 fish as indicative of diversity. According to Jerome, Greek zoologists had recorded 153 different kind of fish (Hoskyns, *Fourth Gospel*, 554; Lindars, *John*, 629; Bultmann, *John*, 709n2). Culpepper ("Inclusivism," in Painter, Culpepper, and Segovia,

The other element in the story found in 21:1-14 that receives emphasis is the net. Jesus asked his disciples to cast the net to the right side to get fish (v. 6); the disciples dragged the net full of fish (v. 8); Peter hauled the net ashore, full of large fish (v. 11). The narrator includes the suggestive indication that "although there were so many [153 fish], the net was not torn" (v. 11). For Schnelle, the number "symbolisiert Fülle und Universalität."[133] Since the topic of unity has figured prominently throughout the Gospel (cf. 10:16), the reader is invited to explore further the meaning of the narrator's comment in 21:11.[134] Before his arrest, Jesus prayed to his Father for the unity of the disciples. He prayed for his current disciples and for those who will believe "through their word" so that all of them may be one (17:11, 20, 21, 22). Their perfect unity will show the world that the Father sent and loved the Son (17:23). In light of the prayer, the net may suggest that those who will believe through the work of the disciples will remain united.[135]

The net is also important in the story because it occurs twice in connection with the verb ἕλκω (21:6, 11): "they were not able to haul (ἑλκύσαι) the net, because of the quantity of fish" and "Simon Peter . . . hauled (εἵλκυσεν) the net ashore." Jesus already taught in the discourse about the bread of life that no one can come to him unless the Father

---

Word, Theology, and Community in John, 101–2), links 21:11 to Matt 13:47, "a net that was thrown into the sea and caught fish of every kind." The implication of this interpretation is that "the disciples are to bring all people to Jesus, giving a final emphasis to John's affirmation of universal election" (Culpepper, "Inclusivism," in Painter, Culpepper, and Segovia, *Word, Theology, and Community in John*, 102; cf. Haenchen, *John 2*, 224). For a list of interpretations of the number 153, see Culpepper, "Designs," in Verheyden, van Oyen, Labahn, and Bieringer, *Studies in the Gospel of John and Its Christology*, 383–94. J. A. Romero ("Gematria and John 21, 11—the Children of God," *JBL* 97 [1978]: 263–64), argues that it represents the Hebrew phrase that correspond to "children of God" and, therefore, the "fish" collected by the disciples should convert to Christianity. Brown (*John*, 2:1075) concedes the likelihood that "the number may be meant to symbolize the breath or even the universality of the Christian mission."

133 "Symbolizes abundance and universality" (Schnelle, *Johannes*, 400).

134 Lindars, *John*, 629; Lincoln, *John*, 512.

135 Bultmann, *John*, 709; Culpepper, "Designs," in Verheyden, van Oyen, Labahn, and Bieringer, *Studies in the Gospel of John and Its Christology*, 381. The untorn net may also be related to the leftover broken pieces that are gathered in 6:12-13 so that nothing is lost (Michaels, *John*, 1037–38).

who sent the Son "draws (ἑλκύσῃ) him" (6:44).[136] After some Greeks were seeking Jesus in Jerusalem, he promises that when he is lifted up from the earth, he will draw (ἑλκύσω) all people (πάντας) to himself (12:32). These previous uses of the verb "to draw" provide "some basis for interpreting the fish as an image for persons being drawn to Jesus, and for interpreting the number 153 as symbolic of 'all persons.'"[137]

There is yet one more element mentioned in this miraculous catch of fish that deserves attention. The disciples meet Jesus on the shore, and they "saw a charcoal fire in place" (21:9). Since "seeing" is a prominent verb elsewhere in the Gospel, the reader is invited to focus on the charcoal fire that the disciples saw (βλέπουσιν). The previous reference to a charcoal fire is found in 18:8, when Peter was warming himself with some enemies of Jesus (18:18).[138] The charcoal in 21:9 may be a reminder of Peter's betrayal of Jesus and a preparation to his restoration in the following scene (21:5-22). Furthermore, I would like to suggest a link to the shepherd discourse in John 15:6. This discourse already helped us make sense of the unsuccessful fishing of the disciples. Here, I want to observe that the disciples are fruitful in their efforts after obeying the risen Jesus' command (21:6) but were unsuccessful when he was not present among them (21:3). The first thing they saw when they returned to shore was "a charcoal fire" (21:9), and the first thing they listen to is Jesus saying, "Bring some of the fish that you have just caught" (21:10). Jesus has already taught them that if they do not abide in him, they cannot bear fruit by themselves (15:4), because apart from Jesus they can do nothing (15:5). Therefore, "if anyone does not abide"

---

[136] Michaels, *John*, 1036.

[137] Culpepper, "Designs," in Verheyden, van Oyen, Labahn, and Bieringer, *Studies in the Gospel of John and Its Christology*, 381. This interpretation is fully developed by Ulrich Busse, "Die 'Hellenen' Joh 12, 20ff. und der sogenannte 'Anhang' Joh 21," in *The Four Gospels 1992: Festschrift Frans Neirynck*, ed. F. van Sagbroeck, C. M. Tuckett, G. van Belle, and J. Verheyden, BETL 3 (Leuven: Leuven University Press, 1992), 2083–100. Cf. Barrett, *John*, 580; Brown, *John* 2:1097; and Lincoln, *John*, 512–13. Michaels (*John*, 1036) finds the link between 21:11 and 12:32 unlikely because a different verb is used in 21:8 for the action of "dragging." However, John's variation in language shouldn't be surprising. Jesus' threefold command to Peter in 21:15-17 comprises, for example, language variation.

[138] Haenchen, *John 2*, 224.

in Jesus," he is "thrown into the fire, and burned" (15:6). Although the noun for fire (πῦρ) here is different from the noun for charcoal in 21:9 (ἀνθρακιάν), the image is suggestive. It helps the reader remember that fruitfulness in mission depends on the presence of the risen Lord among the disciples.

The second scene, Jesus' dialogue with Peter, can also be read in light of previous Johannine motifs, particularly in light of the shepherd discourse. This scene also suggests "the missionary and pastoral tasks of the church."[139] Three times Jesus asks Peter to take care of his people: "feed my lambs" (21:15), "tend my sheep" (21:16), and "feed my sheep" (21:17).[140] Jesus has already referred to his followers as his sheep.[141] They listen to the voice of the shepherd and follow him (10:3, 4, 27). Jesus is the good shepherd who lays down his life for the sheep (10:11, 17) and gives them eternal life (10:28). The wolf scatters the sheep (10:12), but the good shepherd gathers them and leads them where there is pasture (10:9). Jesus also refers to "other sheep" that are not of "this fold" (10:16). Jesus must bring them so that there may be "one flock, one shepherd" (10:16). This previous discourse may help us to read Jesus' dialogue with Peter. Jesus is asking Peter to take care of his disciples but also of those future believers who are going to become the "other sheep." The missionary enterprise of the disciples, however, will face opposition from the world. Jesus anticipated in the farewell discourses that the world will hate his followers (15:18). The straightforward reference to Peter's

---

[139] Culpepper, "Inclusivism," in Painter, Culpepper, and Segovia, *Word, Theology, and Community in John*, 101.

[140] There is a variety of vocabulary in the three confessions: "feed my lambs," "tent my sheep," and "feed my little sheep" (Brown, *John* 2:1104; Lindars, *John*, 633–34; Thompson, *John*, 442).

[141] Although the noun "lamb" (21:15) has not been used up to now, "it is clear that the same 'flock' is in view as in chapter 10, for the 'lambs' are Jesus' 'lambs'" (Michaels, *John*, 1044). Similarly, although the verb ποιμαίνειν "has not occurred before, it does evoke the image of the Shepherd (ὁ ποιμήν, 10:2, 11, 14)" (Michaels, *John*, 1044–45n90). See also D. Francois Tolmie, "The (Not So) Good Shepherd: The Use of Shepherd Imagery in the Characterization of Peter in the Fourth Gospel," in *Imagery in the Gospel of John: Terms, Themes, and Theology of Johannine Figurative Language*, ed. Jörg Frey, Jan G. van der Watt, and Ruben Zimmermann, WUNT 200 (Tübingen: Mohr Siebeck, 2006), 353–67, here 361–62.

death in 21:18 (see also 13:38) may be a reminder of the gentile opposition to the testimony of the disciples.[142]

SYNTHESIS

The climactic, but less explicit, expressions of Jesus' universal significance are found in the passion and resurrection narratives (John 18–21).[143] The idea that Jesus is the owner of creation who moves confidently in territory that has been his since the beginning, engaging people from different ethnic backgrounds, finds climactic expression in the scenes of his interrogation, where he is found in gentile territory, the praetorium, giving testimony to a pagan ruler, the Roman prefect of Judea. The clearest strategy John uses to convey the comprehensive scope of Jesus' significance during his passion is irony. Pilate occupies the judgment seat to judge the one who has received all judgment from the Father. Jesus was likely "judged" by Pilate in the outer court of the gentiles, the same place he cleansed very early in the Gospel of John. The one consecrated by the Father and sent into the world stands in defiled territory giving testimony about the truth. Jesus' Jewish people side with the world because they willingly accept the authority of Caesar.

The idea that Jesus has received an unlimited endowment of authority finds its culmination during his interrogation with Pilate. His kingship is above and beyond this world. Again, John expresses this idea using irony. Pilate claims that he has authority over the one through whom the world was created. Jesus is seen as opposing Caesar himself. The Roman soldiers mock Jesus as an emperor. The promised exaltation of the Son that will bring the glorification of the Father is fulfilled with Jesus' crucifixion. Jesus' name is ironically exalted because people from Aramaic, Greek, and Latin backgrounds were able to read the title on the cross. Two quotations from the Old Testament contribute to the portrayal of the crucified Jesus as conquering the world. The universal outlook that characterizes Psalm 21:19 and Zechariah 12:10 resonates with the Johannine portrayal of Jesus as king.

---

[142] Kierspel, *Jews*, 184–86.
[143] See Vignolo, "Quando."

The stories of Jesus' resurrection and encounters with his disciple are also climactic expressions of his universal significance. His resurrection signals that he has indeed defeated death. The persistent life motif in the Gospel of John is then confirmed in the resurrection of Jesus. The risen Jesus demonstrates his authority over the current group of disciples and even over future believers. The narrator envisions future believers who will be attracted to the risen king and portrays the risen Jesus with the authority to bless those future believers. The narrator also portrays the risen Jesus granting to his disciples a kind of peace that the world cannot give, bestowing upon them authority to forgive sins and commissioning them to engage the world. A strategy that John has used to illustrate this last point has been to use symbolic language in the manifestation of Jesus to seven disciples in Galilee. The reader can read this episode in light of previous information that the narrator has provided throughout the narrative. The large number of fish, the net, and the sheep are all images that point to the worldwide mission of the disciples who are responsible for keeping unity among those who will believe. The cosmic conquest obtained by Jesus through his passion and resurrection is made visible to the world through the missionary work of his followers who engage humanity in the power of the Spirit.[144] This, it seems, was understood by early readers of the Gospel of John: "For everyone who has been born of God conquers the world. This is the victory that has conquered the world—our faith" (1 John 5:4).

[144] Cf. Paul S. Minear, "Diversity and Unity: A Johannine Case-Study," in *Die Mitte des Neuen Testaments: Einheit und Vielfalt neutestamentlicher Theologie*, ed. Ulrich Luz and Hans Weder (Göttingen: Vandenhoeck & Ruprecht, 1983), 162–75, here 171: "Those who believe in him accept a mission from the same God to the same world."

III

5

THE ARTIFICER
OF A UNIVERSAL GOSPEL

Two issues have received particular attention in this study. The first
issue was the literary deployment of instances of universal language.
The result in this respect is better recapitulated by looking at three of the
major literary components of the text: point of view, narrative time, and
plot. The second issue was the rhetorical strategies John used to convey the universal significance of Jesus and the message about him. These
emphases were communicated in a variety of ways but three of them are
worth summarizing: his use of the Old Testament, geography, and irony.
The present chapter draws together elements from earlier chapters to
show that John was consciously and skillfully producing a text that can
be called "universal" in the sense expressed throughout this investigation.

Summary of Literary Components

Point of View

Each character that plays a role in the Gospel has a particular point of
view[1] within the narrative, including those who use universal language

---

[1] "Point of view is simply the way a story is told," according to James L. Resseguie, "Point of View," in *How John Works: Storytelling in the Fourth Gospel*, ed. Douglas

in the text. In his Gospel, John uses both "a literary point of view . . . which allows us to consider the life of Jesus from a point in time following the resurrection"[2] and a "heavenly" point of view that allows him to produce a "cosmological tale."[3] He opens the narrative sharing important information with the reader about Jesus' all-encompassing significance.[4] Since the Word was in the beginning with God, his authority cannot be restricted to a particular geographical area or ethnic group. The Word took an active role in the creation of everything that exists, and he is the source of life and light for the world. He came as flesh to territory that has been his since the beginning with an open invitation to humanity to become children of God.

The narrator intervenes several times to convey a universal perspective. He widens the prophecy of Caiaphas that was concerned with "the people" to clarify that Jesus' death will result in the gathering into one of God's children who are scattered abroad. The narrator sets the washing of the disciples' feet in cosmic perspective by heading this act of service with a statement about the Father giving all things into the hands of the Son. In the passion narrative, the narrator informs the reader that

---

Estes and Ruth Sheridan, SBLRBS 86 (Atlanta: SBL, 2016), 79–96, here 95. Attention to point of view helps us notice who uses universal language in the narrative and helps us uncover whether John provides evaluative statements about the importance of such a language (R. Alan Culpepper, *Anatomy of the Fourth Gospel: A Study in Literary Design* [Philadelphia: Fortress, 1983], 21, 32, 103).

[2] David W. Wead, *The Literary Devices in John's Gospel*, Theologische Dissertationen 4 (Basel: Friedrich Reinhardt Kommissionsverlag, 1970), 1.

[3] Sjef van Tilborg, "Cosmological Implications of Johannine Christology," in *Theology and Christology in the Fourth Gospel: Essays by the Members of the SNTS Johannine Writings Seminar*, ed. Gilbert Van Belle, J. G. Van der Watt, and P. J. Maritz, BETL 184 (Leuven: Leuven University Press, 2005), 483–502. Although "point of view" is a modern concept, Lucian, for example, discusses aspects of point of view in *Hist. conscr.* 49, when talking about a "bird's-eye view" that is omnipresent and omniscient, according to Resseguie, "Point of View," in Estes and Sheridan, *How John Works: Storytelling in the Fourth Gospel*, 79.

[4] This "reader" might be called the "implied reader," i.e., the reader who is present in the written text. This reader follows the clues provided by the narrator in order to properly interpret and disambiguate the text. See René Kieffer, "The Implied Reader in John's Gospel," in *New Readings in John*, ed. Johannes Nissen and Sigfred Pederson (Edinburgh: T&T Clark, 2004), 47–65; and Margaret Davies, *Rhetoric and Reference in the Fourth Gospel*, JSNTSS 69 (Sheffield: Sheffield Academic, 1992), 350–75.

the inscription on Jesus' cross was written in three different languages, implying that the benefits of Jesus' death are not restricted to Aramaic speakers from Judea. In the narratives of the risen Jesus' interaction with the disciples in Judea, he describes Jesus performing an act that resembles that of the Creator God when he breathed the Spirit into his disciples in order to recall his authority over creation. Similarly, in the narrative of the risen Jesus' encounter with seven of his disciples in Galilee, the narrator includes several evocative instances of symbolism (e.g., fish, net, sheep) that may point to the worldwide mission of his followers.[5] The narrator's intervention that produces the deepest impact is his direct address to the reader in order to make explicit the purpose of his Gospel. John wants to elicit faith in people who were not able to see Jesus during his earthly ministry so that they may experience eternal life. The Gospel of John as a text is an artifact that not only *informs* about the significance of Jesus as the giver of life but also *performs* such life-giving power for the benefit of other people beyond the original disciples of Jesus. In this sense, the Gospel of John is an apostolic document in that it functions as a witness to the world about Jesus' universal significance.

There are three characters in the narrative that use universal language in a positive way, that is, in line with the point of view of the narrator. John the Baptist recognizes Jesus as the one who takes away the sin of the world, who is above all things, and who has all things in his hand. The Samaritans declare that Jesus is indeed the Savior of the world. And Martha, a woman from Bethany, confesses that Jesus is the one who is coming into the world, implicitly suggesting that Jesus has a concern for the larger cosmos. Other characters seem to use instances of universal language in a neutral way because they do not understand fully what they say but do not necessarily oppose Jesus' message. The crowds close to the Sea of Tiberias wonder whether Jesus is the prophet who is to come into the world, Judas asks Jesus why he will not manifest himself to the world, and the disciples acknowledge that

---

[5] According to Jean Zumstein ("Intratextuality and Intertextuality in the Gospel of John," trans. Mike Gray, in *Anatomies of Narrative Criticism: The Past, Present, and Futures of the Fourth Gospel as Literature*, ed. Tom Thatcher and Stephen D. Moore, SBLRBS 55 [Leiden: Brill 2008], 121–35, here 125), John 21 "focuses on ecclesiology and on Peter's role as 'universal shepherd.'"

Jesus knows all things. Since the presentation of Jesus by the narrator clearly points to his comprehensive scope, these neutral or ambiguous uses of instances of universal language by the crowds, Judas, and the disciples should be resolved by the information the narrator has shared with the reader.[6] Despite confusion about Jesus' universal authority during his earthly ministry, it is clear for the reader, from a perspective after resurrection, that Jesus came to his own creation to engage the whole world with light and life.

The majority of characters in the narrative use instances of universal language in a negative way, with irony, to mock Jesus. This creates a deep impact on the reader, who should see beyond the irony and the mockery. Jesus' brothers encourage him to go to Jerusalem to show himself to the world, but the narrator clarifies that they did not believe in him. Some Jews ask the rhetorical question whether Jesus intends to go to the dispersion of the Greeks and teach the Greeks. The formulation of the question, however, expects a negative answer, revealing that they do not believe Jesus' ministry included the Greeks. A council gathered by chief priests and the Pharisees fears that *everyone* will believe in Jesus. This exaggeration ironically points to Jesus' claim that his glorification will attract all people to himself. Similarly, the Pharisees lament that *the world* has gone after him. In the passion narrative, some Jews reject Jesus' universal authority by embracing Caesar instead of Jesus as their king. Pilate also asks whether Jesus is a king,

---

[6] This way of reading the Gospel of John is related to what Zumstein ("Intratextuality," in Thatcher and Moore, *Anatomies of Narrative Criticism*, 121–35) calls "intratextuality." This designation explains the interplay of ideas within the text, its "internal connectedness" (122). Intratextuality encapsulates phenomena in the Gospel that "introduce, frame, present, interrupt or conclude" the text (123), such as the prologue (1:1-18), the statement of purpose (20:30-31) and the parentheses. This privileged information should control the interpretation of stories, dialogues, and discourses found in the text. The prologue indicates how the reader should engage the rest of the narrative (123). The purpose of the Gospel should point to the ultimate goal of instances of universal language (124). The parentheses explain and restrict the possible interpretations the reader finds in the narrative (127). See also John J. O'Rourke, "Asides in the Gospel of John," *NovT* 21 (1979): 210–19; and Gilbert van Belle, *Les parenthèses dans l'évangile de Jean*, SNTA 11 (Leuven: Leuven University Press, 1985). The narrator in the Gospel is "entirely reliable" and "he wins our trust from the outset and shapes our grasp of the whole" (Culpepper, *Anatomy*, 232; cf. 18, 233).

but he does not believe Jesus has the level of authority the Roman emperor had. The Roman soldiers mock Jesus as an emperor without realizing that he is the true king who rules over all humanity.

Jesus is by far the character who most often uses universal language. His first and last uses are implicit. The incident in the temple might point to Jesus as the place where a proper encounter between God and humanity takes place because such an act likely took place in the court of the gentiles.[7] His last encounter with his disciples in Galilee after the resurrection has instances of symbolism (i.e., fish, net, sheep) that might indicate that he sends them on a worldwide mission. In between these implicit instances, Jesus uses a number of clear references to his all-encompassing authority over creation, his soteriological work in favor of humanity, and the future work of the Spirit in the world through the disciples.

Jesus uses universal language publicly and privately in different geographical locations. In Judea, he said to Nicodemus that God loved the world, to some Jews who inquired about the healing of a man during the Sabbath that *all* will honor the Son, and to the Jews who witnessed the confession of the formerly blind man that he came into the world for judgment and that he has other sheep that he should bring to his flock. In Jerusalem, Jesus claims to be the light of the world, predicts that the ruler of the world will be judged, and announces that all people will be attracted to him in his glorification. He tells his disciples in Jerusalem that the world will know that he loves the Father and, after the resurrection, gives them authority to forgive peoples' sins. Additionally, Jesus uses instances of universal language in the temple. He announces in Solomon's Colonnade that his Father is greater than all and that the Father sent him into the world. Jesus even says in the high priest's courtyard that he has spoken openly to the world. He is also found using universal language in Galilee, Samaria, and in pagan territory (the praetorium). In a synagogue in Capernaum, Jesus

---

[7] Since it is believed that the Gospel of John was written a few decades after the destruction of the Jerusalem temple, it is remarkable that this text did not take this event as another reason to mark a clear distinction between Judaism and other nations. The Gospel of John seems to be, at least in part, a reflection about God's universal presence in Jesus.

claims to be the bread from heaven that gives life to the world and uses Scripture to indicate that all people will be taught by God. In Galilee, Jesus tells his brothers that he testifies about the world that its works are evil. In Samaritan territory, Jesus explains that true worship is not tied to a particular geographical location and invites his disciples to enter his worldwide mission. In pagan territory, the Roman governor's headquarters, Jesus tells Pilate that his authority and kingship are from above.

Attention to point of view has helped us uncover that instances of universal language are primarily, but not exclusively, available to the reader. On the one hand, the reader has access to each instance of universal language deployed in the Gospel, but there are a few that are exclusively available to those who read and listen to this text. The cosmic perspective provided by the prologue, the insight that a family relationship with God is not related to "blood or flesh," the universal implications of Caiaphas's prophecy, the cosmic dimensions of the washing of the disciples' feet, and the purpose of the Gospel all indicate that the narrator wants the reader to engage the narrative from a universal perspective that may challenge the reader's perception of reality or affirm the reader's current worldview. This privileged information helps the reader judge the appropriateness of the use of universal languages by the characters in the narrative.

Multiple characters are exposed to instances of universal language. They include those who eventually will respond positively to Jesus' message either as a group or individually: some of the disciples of John the Baptist, the formerly blind man, the group of Jesus' followers, and specific disciples such as Thomas, Peter, Andrew, and Philip. The disciples of Jesus are the characters most often exposed to instances of universal language. They learn that Jesus is the light of the world, that all that the Father has belongs to him, and that he has overcome the world. The disciples receive from Jesus a commission to engage the world in the power of the Spirit and receive universal authority to forgive the sins of many. The Spirit, working through them, will convict the world of sin, righteousness, and judgment. Andrew and Philip listen to Jesus saying that the death of a grain of wheat produces much fruit in a context where Greeks are present in Jerusalem. Thomas witnesses Jesus blessing future disciples who will believe without actually seeing

Jesus. Peter is charged with taking care of Jesus' sheep. These sheep seemingly will include Jesus' other sheep, who will believe through the testimony of the disciples. The disciples of John the Baptist learn that Jesus is above all and that the Father gave the Son all things into his hand. The formerly blind man, who presumably became a disciple, hears Jesus saying that he came into the world for judgment.

In addition to the disciples, some Jews, the Pharisees, religious leaders, the crowds, and Nicodemus have access to instances of universal language, although most of them do not accept the universal significance of Jesus and the message about him. Some Jews listen to Jesus' teaching about him receiving honor from all people, about his authority over all things, about the limitless endowment of revelation he received from the Father that legitimizes him to give life and execute judgment, and about his "other sheep" that he will gather. They even read the inscription on the cross that highlights Jesus' kingship. The group of Pharisees hears Jesus claiming that he is the light of the world who came into the world for judgment. Jesus himself testifies in front of the high priest and his officers that he has spoken openly to the world. Nicodemus, a religious leader from the Pharisees, receives clear teachings about God's love for the world and about salvation as a possibility open for everyone who believes. Jesus teaches the crowds about his all-encompassing mission in the world. He claims that he came to give life to the world, to save the world, and to enlighten humanity. Jesus teaches them that his glorification will draw all people to him and will result in the judgment of this world that includes the casting out of the illegitimate ruler of this world. Additionally, Jesus' brothers learn that Jesus testifies against the evil works of the world. However, there is no clear indication in the narrative that any of them accepted Jesus' message.

People whose ethnic background is different from Judaism also learn about Jesus' universal significance: the woman from Samaria, Greek worshippers in Jerusalem, Pilate, and the Roman soldiers. The woman from Samaria is offered a kind of water that anyone who is thirsty can drink and is taught about a kind of worship that is not tied to a particular geography or ethnicity. Worshippers in Jerusalem, who likely included gentiles, witness the temple incident where Jesus sets himself implicitly as the epicenter of a proper encounter between

God and humanity. They are invited, during the last day of the Feast of Tabernacles, to come to him and drink from the life-giving water he offers. Pilgrims from the pagan world are likely in the court of the gentiles when Pilate sits in the judgment seat and says to the Jews, "Behold your king!" Pilate had a private encounter with the "king of the Jews" where Jesus discloses that he came into the world, that his kingdom does not belong to this world, and that there is an authority in heaven superior to the Roman prefect. Additionally, the pagan Roman soldiers witness Jesus being mocked as an emperor in Pilate's headquarters. However, the only group of people not traditionally associated with Judaism who respond positively to Jesus' message are the Samaritans. This variety of characters may indicate that those who first received the Gospel of John were invited to see their mission in the world as comprising a variety of people from diverse backgrounds, although not all those exposed to their message would respond positively. In light of these observations, it is difficult to imagine a socially isolated community behind the Gospel of John that presumably was shaped by a text where people from a number of ethnic backgrounds play an important role.

Narrative Time

Our consideration of narrative time has uncovered that universal language is used previous to, within, and beyond the time of Jesus' earthly ministry.[8] The narrator informs the reader that the Word was with God before creation and took an active role in the creation of everything

---

[8] "When we read any narrative, we become involved in at least three different times: the time we spend reading, the time of the narrator and the time of the story," according to Davies, *Rhetoric*, 44. By narrative time, however, I refer to the movement in time reflected in the text of the Gospel of John. It is evident that John was not following modern conceptions of chronology, but it is certain that he understood linear temporalities such as "before" and "after." For him, Jesus' crucifixion is a decisive point that separates "before" from "after." This "massive event . . . warps the rest of the other narrative events toward it," according to Douglas Estes, "Time," in Estes and Sheridan, *How John Works*, 41–57, here 54. Culpepper (*Anatomy*, 53–54) distinguishes between "story time," i.e., "the passage of time during the ministry of Jesus as John records it," and "narrative time," i.e., the time within the narrative that "is determined by the order, duration, and frequency of events."

that exists. This points to the original unlimited claim of the Word on the whole world. Similarly, John the Baptist testifies that the Father has given all things into the Son's hand. The perfect-tense "has given" may point to the endowment Jesus received from God before his earthly ministry, when he existed with him in heaven. The Baptist's remarks are replicated by the narrator in his introduction of the washing of the disciples' feet: Jesus knew that the Father gave (aorist tense) all things into his hands. Jesus himself claims that what he reveals to the world is what he heard from the Father. The aorist "heard" may point to an endowment of revelation that Jesus received previous to his incarnation. In the prayer to his Father, Jesus recalls that he was given (aorist tense) authority over all flesh, that the Father gave (perfect tense) him everything, and that he shared (perfect tense) his glory with the Son. Since there are references to the preexistence of Jesus in this prayer, those past-tense verbs may point to a time previous to his incarnation.

There are copious references to Jesus' universal significance during his earthly ministry. Those are intended to highlight the close unity between the Father and the Son, the unlimited endowment of revelation Jesus received from the Father, his authority to engage humanity with light and life, and his open invitation to the world to believe in him. Similarly, there are several instances of universal language in the passion and resurrection narratives. The authority of Jesus during his crucifixion is highlighted by the ironic use of the kingship motif. The inscription on the cross proclaiming in three languages that he is king, the mockery of Jesus as emperor by Roman soldiers, and Pilate's proclamation of Jesus as king, all point to Jesus' authority displayed through his humiliation. The cosmic authority that Jesus has received from the Father is specifically seen in his unlimited endowment of revelation, his right to offer eternal life to the world, and his absolute power to execute judgment. Jesus indicates the results of his crucifixion several times during his earthly ministry by referring to this humiliating event as his glorification (12:32). Jesus' death will be for the life of the world (6:51), because when a grain of wheat dies it bears much fruit (12:54). Jesus' glorification will produce the unification of humanity, beginning with those who believe in him. Jesus will gather other sheep into one flock (10:16), he will gather into one the children of God who are scattered abroad (11:52) because he will draw all people to himself

(12:32). His crucifixion means judgment for this world in general and for the illegitimate ruler of this world in particular (12:31; 16:11). Therefore, Jesus can claim in advance that he has overcome the world (16:33).

The future dimension of Jesus' universal significance is prominent in the narrative. It comprises what will happen after his resurrection. The incident in the temple (2:19-22), his prediction that proper worship goes beyond ethnical distinctions (4:21), and the astonishing claim that all will honor the Son (5:23) seem to point to a future form of worship that can be fully achieved only after his resurrection through the mission of the disciples. Jesus also asserts that the hour is coming when the dead will hear Jesus' voice and *all* the dead will come out from their tombs (5:25, 28, 29). This seems to point to a distant future when Jesus' role as universal judge will have full effect. In the meantime, the disciples are charged with a worldwide mission that is grounded in the authority of Jesus (17:22; 20:21-23). During his earthly ministry, Jesus commissioned his disciples as witnesses for the world (17:18). However, they will be able to fulfill their task only when the Spirit comes to them after Jesus' resurrection (21:9, 11, 15, 16, 17). The Spirit will allow them to live a life of unity and love that will demonstrate to God's creation the kind of world that he intended in the beginning (13:35; 17:21). Therefore, they will be fruitful (15:2, 8, 16) in their witness to the world (15:27). All people coming to Jesus will be the fulfillment of Jesus' own blessing upon future believers during his earthly ministry (17:20) and after his resurrection (20:29).

Attention to narrative time reveals that the duration of instances of universal language in the narrative is generally brief. There are no examples where this topic is the point of a long discussion between Jesus and his opponents or the theme of an extensive teaching to his disciples. Most often, instances of universal language are not a point of contention between Jesus and other characters in the narrative. Those instances are intertwined with other topics such as Jesus' origins and identity. On the one hand, the narrator gives the impression that although this was an important topic in the preaching of Jesus, it did not generate important debates because Jesus' interlocutors generally misunderstood, ignored, or mocked his words and actions. On the other hand, prominent instances of universal language in the narrator's prologue and in Jesus' extended prayer are arguably only accessible to

the reader. Therefore, the proper understanding of the universal significance of Jesus and the message about him may be obtained only after
his resurrection by those who have embraced him as the life and light
of the world.

Plot

Focus on plot has led us to ask whether those characters in the narrative exposed to the universal significance of Jesus and the message
about him exhibit some change in their actions, thoughts, or personality.[9] A number of characters show no change even when they are
met with several instances of universal language. The narrator does not
record any reaction from the disciples as a group when Jesus includes
them in his mission in Samaria, when he claims to be the light of
the world, when confronted with a number of instances of universal
language in the farewell discourses, when the risen Jesus authorizes
them to forgive peoples' sins, or when they catch a large number of
fish that presumably points to their worldwide mission. Neither do
individual disciples exhibit any change after being confronted with
instances of universal language. Andrew and Philip do not react to
Jesus' teaching about the grain of wheat that dies in order to produce
much fruit. Thomas remains silent after Jesus blesses future disciples
who will believe without seeing him. Peter does not actively respond
to Jesus' charge to take care of his sheep. Similarly, some of the disciples of John the Baptist do not react to his presentation of Jesus as the
Lamb of God who takes away the sin of *the world*.

Others who do not show any change in their actions, thoughts, or
personality when confronted with instances of universal language are
worshipers in Jerusalem, the crowds, the Jews, and Nicodemus. Worshipers in Jerusalem witness the cleansing of the temple and Pilate's
presentation of Jesus as king. The crowds hear Jesus crying out that he

---

[9] "Plot" is understood as "the underlying *causality* of the story" (Kasper Bro
Larsen, "Plot," in Estes and Sheridan, *How John Works*, 97–113, here 98; see also Culpepper, *Anatomy*, 80). Therefore, "readers are not only reading a series of events . . . but
rather engage in a kind of detective work or emplotment activity where the reader
investigates the causality and direction of the events" (Larsen, "Plot," in Estes and
Sheridan, *How John Works*, 98).

came into the world as light in order to save the world. Jesus teaches the Jews that all will honor the Son as they honor the Father. Nicodemus learns that God loved the world and that anyone who believes in the Son has eternal life. The narrator, however, does not include any change in these characters after being exposed to this component of Jesus' teaching.

Several other characters do react to Jesus' teaching. Most often, however, those reactions are not directly related to Jesus' specific words about the comprehensive scope of his mission but are a response to a larger cluster of teachings. When Jesus teaches that all that the Father has given him will come to him and that everyone who looks on the Son will have eternal life, the crowds focus on Jesus' origins, asserting that Jesus is the son of Joseph. Jesus tells people that his flesh is for the life of the world, but the Jews dispute among themselves how Jesus can give them his flesh to eat. When Jesus tells the crowds that the judgment of the world will include the casting out of its illegitimate ruler and that his exaltation will draw all people to himself, the crowds ask how Jesus can say that the Son of Man must be lifted up. Jesus' teaching about himself as the good shepherd that includes references to other sheep creates division among the Jews. Some believe he has a demon or he is insane. Jesus teaches the Jews that the Father is greater than all things and that he is one with the Father. Some Jews try to stone Jesus because he claims unity with God. When Jesus discloses to the Pharisees that he came into *the world* for judgment so that those who do not see may see, they ask whether they are blind. Jesus' testimony in front of the high priest includes the assertion that he had spoken openly to *the world*, and one of the officers reacts by striking Jesus with his hand.

Other characters react with lack of understanding. Two of them (the Samarian woman and the disciples) move from misunderstanding to proper understanding, and one of them (Pilate) remains confused about Jesus' teaching. On the one hand, the Samaritan woman did not understand at first Jesus' offer of living water, but later she embraces Jesus' message and even goes back to her town testifying about him. The disciples witness the cleansing of the temple but grasp the full import of this action only after Jesus was risen from the dead. They show confusion during the farewell discourses, but later they acknowledge that

Jesus knows all things and came from God. On the other hand, Pilate misconstrues Jesus' teaching about his heavenly kingdom and his mission in the world. He asks whether Jesus is a king and inquires about the meaning of truth but does not understand Jesus' replies.

The narrator has recorded some reactions to instances of universal language used by other characters beyond Jesus. Some Jews fear that everyone will believe in Jesus. Caiaphas reacts to that exaggeration by prophesying that Jesus' death will be beneficial for the nation. The Jews say to Pilate that they have no king but Caesar, forcing Pilate to deliver Jesus to them to be crucified. The inscription on the cross was read by many Jews, prompting the chief priests to ask Pilate to change what was written on the inscription. When Jesus is presented as a mock emperor, the chief priests and officers reject him, asking that he be crucified. The only reaction that is not recorded in the Gospel is the reader's response to instances of universal language in the text. In light of the narrator's use of such language, it seems he expects those readers who are not sympathetic with Jesus to realize that the particular story of a Jew declared king of Israel and who died under Pontius Pilate has cosmic dimensions. Since he is the owner of creation who engages the whole world and has authority to bless even future believers, the reader cannot escape the all-encompassing claim Jesus has on this world. For those readers who are already believers, it seems the narrator expects them to participate in the worldwide mission of the disciples in the power of the Spirit that will bring glory to the Father.

A striking feature of the Johannine plot is Jesus' reaction to the use of universal language by other characters.[10] The crowds in Galilee start wondering whether Jesus is the prophet who is to come into the world. Jesus interprets that as the last step to their imminent recognition of his kingship. Jesus is forced to clarify why he will not travel to Jerusalem to show himself to the world, as his brothers were encouraging him to do. Jesus highlights that the world opposes him because he testifies about its works that are evil. The rhetorical question asked

---

[10] The Synoptic Gospels have few references to the noun "world": three in Luke and in Mark, and nine in Matthew. All of them are put in Jesus' lips with two exceptions in Matthew. The narrator uses the noun once in 4:8 and a second time in 13:35 in an Old Testament quotation.

by the Jews whether Jesus will go to the dispersion among the Greeks to teach them is not met with a direct answer. Instead, Jesus makes an open invitation to anyone who wants to drink to come to him. In distinction from the Jews' question that expects a negative answer, Judas asks Jesus why he will not manifest himself to the world. Jesus indicates that he is accessible to whoever loves him, including anyone from the world, but he will manifest only to those who keep his word. The only occasion when Jesus does not react to the use of universal language by other characters is before the resurrection of Lazarus. Martha confesses that Jesus is the one who is coming into the world. Although Jesus does not respond verbally to such a confession, he performs a miracle that demonstrates his divine authority to give life.

Focus on Johannine plot also reveals the concentration of instances of universal language in the narrative. There are two striking findings. The prologue (1:1-18) and Jesus' prayer (17:1-26) are by far the sections with the most instances of universal language. As much as 56 percent of the prologue has instances of universal language.[11] Similarly, as much as 46 percent of the prayer has instances of universal language.[12] This finding is significant because these two sections are important intratextual phenomena that control the interpretation of the rest of the narrative.[13]

[11] My calculations here are by no means precise; they are only estimates. I consider both implicit and explicit instances of universal language. If an instance is found in a particular verse, I take the whole verse as an instance of universal language. For example, Jesus closes his farewell discourses with the following words: "I have said these things to you, that in me you may have peace. In the world you will have tribulation. But take heart; *I have overcome the world*" (16:33). Although only the last sentence is an instance of universal language, for convenience in my calculations, I take 16:33 as an instance of universal language.

[12] The average found in the other sections of the Gospel is 12 percent. The sections that I include here are: 1:19–2:12; 2:13-25; 3:1-21; 3:22-36; 4:1-45; 4:46-54; 5:1-47; 6:1-71; 7:1–9:41; 10:1-42; 11:1-57; 12:1-50; 13:1–14:31; 15:1–16:33; 18:1–19:42; 20:1-31; 21:1-25.

[13] Jesus' prayer frames the meaning of the text because of its strategic literary position, the privileged place of Jesus' voice in the narrative, and the clear links between the prologue and John 17. Since Jesus is introduced very early in the narrative as the one who "explains God" (1:18), the reader should pay attention to the extended communication between the Son and his Father presented in John 17. In fact, the shared language between the prologue and the prayer makes John 18 the counterpart of John 1:1-18, according to Ernst Käsemann, *The Testament of Jesus: A Study of John in the Light of Chapter 17*, trans. Gerhard Krodel (London: SCM, 1968), 3. Furthermore,

There seems to be a deliberate attempt by the narrator to influence the interpretation of the meaning of the comprehensive scope of Jesus' significance in his Gospel. The second salient finding is that there is no detectable progression in the use of universal language. There are twenty-five instances in the first part of the Gospel (1:1–4:54), thirty-two in the second (5:1–12:50), thirty-one in the third (13:1–17.26), and twenty-two in the last part (18:1–21:25). This is a consistent motif used throughout the narrative. All in all, however, the universal significance of Jesus and the message about him is not the most important topic in the Gospel. It is only a supporting theme in John's larger presentation of Jesus as the revelation of the Father. Overall, the narrator devotes less than 13 percent of his Gospel (ca. 110 verses) to instances of universal language.

SUMMARY OF RHETORICAL DEVICES

Old Testament Quotations

Attention to the larger context of the Old Testament quotations used in the Gospel of John has uncovered a preference for those texts that highlight the universal significance of the God of Israel.[14] The first quotation in the narrative is used by John the Baptist, a character whose proclamation about Jesus' significance coheres with those of the narrator and of Jesus himself (John 1). The Baptist uses Isaiah 40:3 to identify his role as a witness. Since the larger context of Isaiah 40:3 resonates with the Johannine prologue, the reader is encouraged to look at Isaiah 40 as a whole in the interpretation of his proclamation

---

Jesus' prayer is carefully located because it concludes the farewell discourses (John 13–16) and introduces Jesus' passion and resurrection (John 18–21), according to Marianus Pale Hera, *Christology and Discipleship in John 17*, WUNT 2/342 (Tübingen: Mohr Siebeck, 2013), 15–18.

[14] After successfully challenging Rendel Harris' influential proposal that New Testament authors used a collection of isolated texts from the Old Testament to produce their quotations (*Testimonies*, 2 vols. [Cambridge: Cambridge University Press, 1916–1920]), C. H. Dodd observed that it makes better sense to suppose early Christians actually had access to larger sections of the Old Testament (*According to the Scriptures: The Sub-Structure of New Testament Theology* [London: Nisbet, 1952], 18). For Dodd, "the scripture which a writer has in mind is not necessarily limited to the amount which he quotes" (47n1; see also 59–60, 61, 65, 78, 82, 96).

about Jesus.[15] Isaiah predicts that all flesh shall see the salvation of God (40:5), portrays God as absolute Creator (40:22, 26, 28), and announces salvation and judgment for the nations (40:2, 15).[16] Similarly, John the Baptist announces that Jesus is the Lamb of God who takes away the sin of the world. In the Gospel of John, salvation or judgment are defined in relationship to Jesus. Those who reject the Son will see judgment but those who embrace Jesus will enjoy eternal life.

Jesus is portrayed using Isaiah 54:13 in his discussion with religious leaders in a synagogue in Capernaum (John 6). This is the first time that Jesus uses Scripture in the Gospel of John. Jesus uses Isaiah to support his contention that all those who obey the Father come to him in a context where he has identified himself as the bread for the life of the world. The Johannine innovation when using this text from Isaiah is remarkable. He omits the phrase "your children" found twice in Isaiah 54:13 in reference to Israel. Instead, Jesus says that *all* will be taught by God and *everyone* who learns from the Father comes to him. The justification for such a move seems to be found in the larger context of Isaiah 53:13. The prophet claims that the God of Israel shall be called upon in all the earth (54:5), predicts that proselytes shall be attracted to Jerusalem through God (54:15), and portrays David as a testimony and ruler for the nations (55:4). For John, all people will be attracted to Jesus during his exaltation in Jerusalem, and he will rule as a king even among pagans such as Pilate and the Roman soldiers.

Jesus quotes Zechariah 14 during the festival of Tabernacles to support his open invitation to all people to come and drink from him (John 7). This proclamation is made in Jerusalem at a time when many pilgrims and visitors would have been present in the temple. Zechariah portrays an eschatological Feast of Tabernacles with a worldwide pilgrimage to Jerusalem to worship the God of Israel (Zech 15:16, 18, 19). On that day

---

[15] For example, the prophet Isaiah predicts that the glory of the Lord will be seen. Similarly, the Johannine prologue indicates that "we have seen his glory" (1:14).

[16] Isaiah is one of the two (the other is Psalms) Old Testament books most often quoted or alluded to in the Gospel of John. Early copies of Isaiah show that scribes usually copied long sections, if not the whole, of this prophetic book: P.Beatty VI (pap. VII) + P.Mert. 12 + PSI XII 1273 (Isaiah); LDAB 3126 (probably originally containing the whole book of Isaiah). Cf. Alan Mugridge, *Copying Early Christian Texts: A Study of Scribal Practice*, WUNT 362 (Tübingen: Mohr Siebeck, 2016), 186–88, 196, 215.

there shall be light at evening time (Zech 14:6-7) and living water coming forth from Jerusalem (Zech 14:8). The kingdom of the Lord will be universal and his name will be one (14:9). However, in distinction from the universalism found in Zechariah that centers on Jerusalem, Jesus invites anyone who is thirsty to come to him who is the light of the world.

The narrator quotes Zechariah 9:9; 12:10; and Psalm 21:19 to interpret Jesus' triumphal entrance into Jerusalem and his passion (John 12 and 19).[17] The larger context of these texts is also concerned with the universal significance of the God of Israel. The prophet predicts that God's reign will extend over the waters as far as the sea, that the house of Judah will be a blessing among the nations, and that many peoples and nations will come to Jerusalem seeking the face of the Lord (8:13, 22, 23; 9:10). For John, Jesus is the one who reveals God and the king who reigns supreme even above political powers. Jesus' crucifixion is also interpreted using a quotation from Zechariah. The narrator clarifies that the piercing of Jesus' side was intended to fulfill Scripture (19:37; Zech 12:10). The larger context of Zechariah 12:10 portrays the universal authority of the Lord. Zechariah says that the Lord is the Creator (12:1) and the shepherd of the flock (11:7). John portrays Jesus as both taking an active role in creation (1:3, 10) and as the shepherd who has other sheep (10:16). John also quotes Isaiah 53:1 to explain people's unbelief. Again, the larger context of this Old Testament text comprises important instances of universal language. According to Isaiah, the offspring of the suffering servant will inherit the nations (54:3), and the Lord will reveal his power before all the nations (52:10). They in turn will be astonished at him and will see the salvation that comes from God (52:10, 15). The humiliation Jesus suffered under the soldiers who took his garments is interpreted by using Psalm 21:19. Since this psalm resonates with Johannine themes such as kingship and the mocking of Jesus (Ps 21:8, 29), the reader is encouraged to look at the larger context of this psalm, which concludes

---

[17] In light of available early copies of Psalms, it is likely that scribes usually copied long sections of specific Old Testament books: PSI Congr. XX 1 (probably containing originally at least the whole of Ps 1); P.Lond.Lit. 204 (originally containing a number of psalms); P.Mich. III 133 (probably originally containing the whole book of Psalms); LDAB 3083 (possibly containing substantial portions of the book of Psalms).

with a straightforward hope that nations will worship the Lord (21:27-28, 30) and the portrayal of the Lord as the master over the nations (21:29).

The Isaianic servant is evoked in the episode of Greeks who want to see Jesus in Jerusalem. The use of the cluster "exaltation," "glorification," "seeing," and "hearing" in John 12 and Isaiah suggests that the evangelist used the larger context of Isaiah 53:1 (quoted in John 12:38) to interpret Jesus' death, the unbelief of his opponents, and the hope for the nations to behold the Lamb of God who takes away the sin of the world.

The observation that attention to the larger context of the Old Testament quotations helps explain Johannine universalism is enhanced by way of contrast with those quotations used by characters in the narrative that oppose Jesus.[18] His dialogue partners in a synagogue in Capernaum use Psalm 78:24 as part of their arguments against Jesus. The larger context of this text lacks instances of universal language and abounds in references to judgment for those who disobey the Lord. Another example is the use of Psalm 118:25-26 by the crowds to hail Jesus in his entrance to Jerusalem. Conspicuously, the larger context of this Old Testament text lacks instances of universal language.[19]

---

[18] Several scholars have noticed John's use of the larger context of his Old Testament quotations. For example, C. K. Barrett, *The Gospel according to St. John: An Introduction with Commentary and Notes on the Greek Text* (Philadelphia: Westminster, 1978), 27–30; Johannes Beutler, "Psalm 42/43," in *Habt keine Angst: Die erste johanneische Abschiedsrede (Joh 14)*, Stuttgarter Bibelstudien 116 (Stuttgart: Katholisches Bibelwerk, 1984); idem, "Der alttestamentlich-jüdische Hintergrund der Hirtenrede in Joh 10," in *The Shepherd Discourse of John 10 and Its Context: Studies by Members of the Johannine Writings Seminar*, ed. Johannes Beutler and Robert T. Fortna, SNTSMS 67 (Cambridge: Cambridge University Press, 1991), 18–32.

[19] There are seventeen references to Scripture that quote specific sections from the Old Testament (1:23; 2:17; 6:31, 45; 7:38, 42; 8:17; 10:34; 12:15, 34, 38, 40; 13:18; 15:25; 19:24, 36, 37), according to Maarten J. J. Menken, *Old Testament Quotations in the Fourth Gospel: Studies in Textual Form*, CBET 15 (Kampen: Kok Pharos, 1996), 11. Seven of those quotations are taken from contexts where the universal significance of the God of Israel is prominent. These seven citations are found in Isaiah (40:3; 53:1; 54:13), Zechariah (9:9; 12:10; 14:8), and Psalms (21:19). The universal outlook of Isaiah, for example, is very prominent. Isaiah begins his account of his vision with a universal calling: "hear, O heaven, and give ear, O earth" (1:2). His vision recorded in Isa 6:1-13 has also universal overtones. The seraphim above the enthroned Lord called to one another and said, "The whole earth (πᾶσα ἡ γῆ) is full of his glory (δόξης)" (6:3). Isaiah sees the glory of God extending throughout the whole earth.

John's use of the Old Testament to shape his presentation of the universal significance of Jesus is also allusive and shows his commitment to Israel's Scriptures and Jewish traditions. A good number of his instances of universal language stem from Jewish tradition either implicitly or explicitly. For example, Jesus refers to Moses lifting up the serpent in the desert to explain that everyone who believes in Jesus has eternal life, he uses the Jewish tradition of Jacob's well as a background to his offer of living water to a woman in Samaria, and he reinterprets the story of the provision of mana in the desert claiming that he is the bread from heaven that gives life to the world.

There are fewer direct uses of Jewish tradition (e.g., temple, Sabbath, creation, festivals) to support the universal significance of Jesus. His challenge to the temple and the cleansing of the court of the gentiles indicates that he is the place where a proper encounter between God and humanity takes place. The two healings during the Sabbath make all the more striking Jesus' claim that he received two divine prerogatives, that is, the execution of judgment upon humanity and the giving of life to the world. The Feast of Tabernacles, with its emphasis on light, frames Jesus' claims that he is the light of the world that testifies against the evil works of the world and who came into the world for judgment. The Passover festival shapes the portrayal of Greeks wanting to see Jesus and Jesus' prediction that he will attract all people to himself through his glorification. After the resurrection, Jesus performs an act that resembles that of the Creator God as a reminder of his authority over creation. Jesus breathing on his disciples symbolizes that they receive from Jesus the Spirit and universal authority to forgive sins. Even more allusive is imagery such as sheep and vine that might be connected to Jewish traditions. The Old Testament imagery of sheep lurks in the background of Jesus' claim that he has other sheep that he must bring into his fold and in his request to Peter to take care

---

Although Isaiah's prophecy mainly concerns judgment for Israel, he predicts that "in the last days (ἐσχάταις ἡμέραις) . . . all the nations (πάντα τὰ ἔθνη) shall come" to the house of God (2:2). Isaiah prophesizes that "many nations (ἔθνη πολλά)" will say, "Come, let us go up to the mountain of the Lord and to the house of the God of Jacob" (2:3). These many nations, however, will not come to Jerusalem to destroy it. They will be there to be instructed by God and to obey him: "He will announce to us his way, and we will walk in it" (2:3).

of his sheep. The imagery of a vine with much fruit that Jesus uses to explain the worldwide scope of the disciples' mission resonates with Old Testament traditions of God's people as a vine.

However, John lacks important instances of Jewish tradition that are prominent in the Synoptic Gospels. Two examples are telling. The first is the absence of the title "son of David" in reference to Jesus. It might be the case that "John may represent a 'universalizing' of the traditions of Jesus' Davidic descent: Jesus now exercises his messianic office . . . as the King of Israel who has authority over all flesh."[20] John also played down some debates over Jewish ritual and practice that are prominent in the Synoptic Gospels perhaps "in the interest of presenting Jesus to those beyond the confines of Jesus' own time and place."[21] Since it seems this Gospel addresses "questions that many religious traditions have pondered and continue to ponder," it is fair to conclude that this "is a universal Gospel."[22]

Universalistic emphases in Jewish tradition are not exclusively found in the Old Testament. Second Temple Jewish texts include a number of instances that deal with the religious status of gentiles. Between the harsh exclusion of Jubilees 15:25-26 and the quasi-pluralism of Letter of Aristeas 16, one finds several patterns of universalism.[23] One of them has been called "sympathization." Texts such as Josephus, *Jewish War* 2.560; 2 Maccabees 3:12; Philo, *Moses* 2.21 demonstrate that some gentiles were sympathetic with Judaism, for example, "worshipping at the Jerusalem temple; adopting some aspects of Jewish custom and belief; associating with the Jewish community."[24] Some other texts portray gentiles "who fully adopt a Jewish way of life and are incorporated into the Jewish community."[25] These gentiles embrace circumcision and are called pros-

---

[20] Marianne Meye Thompson, *John: A Commentary*, NTL (Louisville: Westminster John Knox, 2015), 7.

[21] Thompson, *John*, 7–8. Cf. Robert Kysar, *John the Maverick Gospel*, 3rd ed. (Louisville: Westminster John Knox, 2007), 149: "beneath the basic concerns of the Gospel . . . lie some universal religious questions."

[22] Kysar, *John*, 149.

[23] T. L. Donaldson, *Judaism and the Gentiles: Jewish Patterns of Universalism (to 135 CE)* (Waco, Tex.: Baylor University Press, 2007), 4.

[24] Donaldson, *Universalism*, 10. The reference to Second Temple Jewish texts is taken from p. 471nn4–9.

[25] Donaldson, *Universalism*, 10.

elytes (e.g., Theodotus, *Fragment* 4; Jos. Asen. 12:3-5; 15:2-7).[26] A third pattern of universalism in ancient Jewish sources is "ethical monotheism."[27] It is expressed in texts that "consider it possible for gentiles to acquire accurate and adequate knowledge of the one true God, or to relate to this God in appropriate ways, without any knowledge of Judaism or association with the Jewish community."[28] A clear example of this pattern is found in Josephus, *Against Apion* 2.281, "Our earliest imitators were the Greek philosophers, who . . . were Moses's disciples."[29] Finally, a number of ancient Jewish texts also reflect an eschatological universalism. 1 Enoch 10:21–11:2, for example, envisions the righteousness of humanity and the universal worship of the God of Israel: "All the sons of men will become righteous; and all the peoples will worship (me); and all will bless me and prostrate themselves. And all the earth will be cleansed from all defilement and from all uncleanness."[30]

Cosmography

Although the Gospel of John has numerous references to ὁ κόσμος (the world, or cosmos), the only components of the universe that are mentioned in the text are the places where Jesus taught during his earthly ministry. Therefore, the use of cosmography here is limited.[31] The attention that John gives to space in the Gospel coheres with his larger presentation of Jesus as the owner of creation who was sent into his world to engage it with life and light. This engagement is a divine attack against the illegitimate ruler who enslaves humanity with lies subjecting the world to darkness and death. After Jesus' resurrection, the Spirit is sent to this world as a witness to a different world. More precisely, the Spirit witnesses the divine vision of the world, that is,

---

[26] Donaldson, *Universalism*, 481. The references to Second Temple Jewish texts are taken from pp. 100, 141.

[27] Donaldson, *Universalism*, 11.

[28] Donaldson, *Universalism*, 493.

[29] Quoted in Donaldson, *Universalism*, 494.

[30] Quoted in Donaldson, *Universalism*, 78.

[31] The importance of space in the Gospel of John is remarked on by D. Mollat, "Remarques sur le vocabulaire spatial du quatrième évangile," *Studia Evangelica* 1 (1957): 321–28; and Jerome H. Neyrey, "Spaced Out: 'Territoriality' in the Fourth Gospel," *HTS Teologiese Studies / Theological Studies* 58 (2002): 632–63.

unity of humanity linked through love. The disciples are the prime example of such a different world because they are to live in unity showing sacrificial love among themselves.

Jesus' earthly ministry is grounded in specific spaces that are highly significant. His progressive confident move from Jerusalem and Judea, to Samaria, and to Galilee signals that he is the owner of creation who has authority to interact with people from diverse ethnic, religious, and even political backgrounds. His offer of eternal life is open to all those who want to believe in him. Jesus is even found in pagan territory interacting with the representative of the Roman Empire. His discussions with Pilate in the praetorium where he is identified as a king demonstrates that his authority has no geographical limitations. He is a witness to the truth even in those places regarded as impure by traditional Jewish belief. It is highly significant that Jesus is found more than once in the temple. Although there is no single explicit reference to the court of the gentiles in the Gospel of John, the clues provided by the narrator are too obvious to be missed. The cleansing of the temple likely took place in that court where the business conducted would have disrupted appropriate worship from the gentiles. Pilate's judgment of Jesus likely took place in the court of the gentiles, where visitors from different parts of the world might have been exposed to the ironic presentation of Jesus as king.

The scenario of Jesus' activity is cosmic. The Father is portrayed as the one greater than all things (10:29) who sent his Son into the world (10:36) because he loves his creation (3:16). The mission of the Spirit is cosmic since he will convict the world concerning sin, righteousness, and judgment (16:8). The Spirit will achieve this worldwide mission through the disciples who are sent into the world (17:11) with authority to forgive sins (4:38; 20:21-22). They engage a world that cannot receive the Spirit (14:17), hates Jesus and his disciples (15:18; 17:14), and does not know the Father (17:25). This is the dramatic condition of the world. Although it was created through the Word and it is the recipient of God's love, it rejects Jesus and his disciples. This negative portrayal of the world as a whole does not allow a strong characterization of the Gospel of John as anti-Jewish. The narrator provides several examples of Jews embracing (e.g., the disciples) or rejecting Jesus (5:18). However, the impression the readers get is that the Johannine "world" is anti-Jesus. The Gospel depicts not the progressive incorporation of gentiles into Judaism but the incorporation of Judaism into the world that opposes God's revelation. "The bottom line is that in the literary universe of John the primary and essential difference is located with great care between Jesus and the entirety of humankind."[32] Jesus, however, engages Jews, Samaritans, and pagans with his light and his offer of life, and there is an example of a ruler associated with the political powers who believed in Jesus along with his family (4:53-54) as there are some Roman soldiers who mock Jesus as an emperor (19:2-3).

From the point of view of the narrator, therefore, the Johannine Jesus cannot appropriately be characterized as a "stranger from heaven." He is the legitimate owner of creation that became flesh in order to claim his authority over all flesh. Only Jesus has received from the Father an unlimited endowment of revelation and power to engage the world that he loves with light and life. It is the world that perceives Jesus as stranger because they are under the authority of the "ruler of this world" who enslaved them with darkness, falsehood, and death. What humanity calls reality is, from the perspective of the narrator, a dangerous illusion.

Irony

Irony is a distinctive Johannine feature. It is used, among other things, to enhance the reader's appreciation of Jesus' universal significance.[33] The narrator employs it initially to highlight the dramatic condition of the world. Although everything was created through the Word, the world actively rejected Jesus. This portrayal in turn warrants the universal

---

[32] Trond Skard Dokka, "Irony and Sectarianism in the Gospel of John," in *New Readings in John*, ed. Johannes Nissen and Sigfred Pedersen, JSNTSS 182 (Sheffield: Sheffield Academic Press, 1999), 82–107, here 102.

[33] Irony has three important features, according to D. C. Muecke, *Irony*, The Critical Idiom 13 (London: Methuen 1970), 35: "(i) a contrast of appearance and reality, (ii) a confident unawareness . . . that the appearance is only an appearance, and (iii) the comic effect of this unawareness of a contrasting appearance and reality" (quoted in Culpepper, *Anatomy*, 166–67). See also Dokka, "Irony," in Nissen and Pederson, *New Readings in John*, 91; Wead, *Literary Devices*, 47–68; Paul D. Duke, *Irony in the Fourth Gospel* (Atlanta: John Knox, 1983); Culpepper, *Anatomy*, 165–80; and H. Clavier, "L'ironie dans le quatrième Évangile," in *Studia Evangelica*, ed. K. Aland, F. L. Cross, J. Daniélou, H. Riesenfeld, and W. C. van Unnik, TU 73 (Berlin: Akademie-Verlag, 1959), 261–76.

mission of Jesus. The highest concentration of irony to express Jesus' universal significance is found in the passion narratives. Jesus' Jewish people side with the world because they acknowledge the authority of Caesar but reject Jesus' kingship. Jesus was consecrated by the Father and sent into the world, but he is found in defiled territory giving testimony in front of Pilate. He sits in the seat of judgment to judge the one who has all judgment in his hands. Pilate claims that he has authority over the one through whom the world was created. Although the Roman soldiers mock Jesus as an emperor, his authority is actually above any earthly ruler. The exaltation of Jesus that draws all people to himself is his humiliation.

John has used two secondary characters who employ instances of universal language without realizing the full import of their words. Jesus' brothers encourage him to show himself to *the world*, without believing that Jesus was sent into the world by the Father to make a public display of his all-encompassing authority from the cross, and some religious leaders ask whether Jesus will go to the dispersion of the Greeks and to teach the Greeks. Since the religious leaders' question expects a negative answer, they do not believe that the significance of Jesus and the message about him should extend to Greeks. John portrays some religious leaders as fearing that everyone will believe in him. Their fears are, ironically, the goal of Jesus' mission on earth to enable all his creation to embrace him as the revelation of the Father.

Some scholars of Johannine language agree that "the phenomenon of irony plays a prominent role" in shaping a sectarian community behind the text.[34] It is supposed that only members of a putative sectarian community were able to catch the irony of the "anti-language" of the Gospel of John. This, however, is not the only possible conclusion. I have attempted to read this text in a sequential fashion, illuminating current units in light of previous dialogues, discourses, and stories.[35] Several

---

[34] See Dokka, "Irony," in Nissen and Pederson, *New Readings in John*, 91, 95. At the time of the writing of his article, Dokka noticed in scholarship an "increasing emphasis on aspects of the Gospel which seem to indicate an alienated or hostile relation to the world" (85). Several scholars characterized Johannine language as a *Sondersprache*, i.e., "a sub-language, understood by insiders alone" (88).

[35] I have paid attention to universal language mainly in the order in which these instances occur in the Gospel so as to allow any plan of development that may have been implicit in the final form of the text to stand out. Therefore, I have dealt with the

times I have observed how earlier parts of the Gospel clarify the meaning of later sections. For example, implications which were suggested by the gathering of broken fragments in John 6 are later stated explicitly by Jesus' straightforward teaching about him gathering his people. This sequential disclosure, I suggest, does not depend exclusively on a privileged reader who was a member of the putative sectarian Johannine community. Any reader who reads this text is educated by the narrator and influenced by the narrative to reject some interpretations as incorrect and embrace others as correct, from the point of view of the narrator.[36] That does not mean that the reader needs to agree with the narrator. Even if a reader is not sympathetic to Johannine thought, such a reader is able to disambiguate instances of symbolism and irony in the text in light of what the Gospel itself offers as truth. For example, I have not detected irony in John's use of Old Testament quotations to shape the universal significance of Jesus. Potentially, any reader familiar with the Old Testament (either sympathetic or not with the message of the Gospel of John) may see the connections between Jewish tradition and Johannine thought. The goal of the Gospel is that the reader will eventually believe his narrative and, therefore, may experience eternal life.

---

flow of the narrative beginning with the prologue and concluding with the epilogue in a linear fashion. See Peter M. Phillips, *The Prologue of the Fourth Gospel: A Sequential Reading*, LNTS 294 (London: T&T Clark, 2006), 26. The goal has been to follow the progressive development of the narrative, looking at the text as a functioning whole. See J. Frey, "Wege und Perspektiven der Interpretation des Johannesevangeliums: Überlegungen auf dem Weg zu einem Kommentar," in *Die Herrlichkeit des Gekreuzigten: Studien zu den Johanneischen Texten I*, WUNT 307 (Tübingen: Mohr Siebeck, 2013), 3–41, here 37.

[36] Wayne A. Meeks ("The Man from Heaven in Johannine Sectarianism," *JBL* 91 [1972]: 44–72, here 55) notes, "One of the most striking characteristics of the evangelist's literary procedure [is] the elucidation of themes by progressive repetition." The Johannine themes "become clear only as their progressive development is traced through the Gospel" (57) (see also Edwyn Clement Hoskyns, *The Fourth Gospel*, ed. Francis Noel Davey [London: Faber and Faber, 1967], 67).

CONCLUSION

This study has provided an enhanced description of the widely perceived universalism of the Gospel of John by following its narrative sequence, by focusing on prominent literary elements in the text and by controlling the reading process through the privileged information that the narrator shares with the reader in the prologue, the statement of purpose, the parentheses, and Jesus' prayer.[37] John does

---

[37] For example, see D. Moody Smith, "Johannine Christianity: Some Reflections on its Character and Delineation," *NTS* 21 (1975): 222–48, here 248; R. Alan Culpepper, "Inclusivism and Exclusivism in the Fourth Gospel," in *Word, Theology, and Community in John*, ed. John Painter, R. Alan Culpepper, and Fernando Segovia (St. Louis: Chalice, 2002), 85–108; Paul N. Anderson, *The Riddles of the Fourth Gospel: An Introduction to John* (Minneapolis: Fortress, 2011), 34–35; and Craig R. Koester, *Symbolism in the Fourth Gospel: Meaning, Mystery, Community,* 2nd ed. (Minneapolis: Fortress, 2003), 42–44. Also, Donatien Mollat, *Études Johanniques*, Parole de Dieu (Paris: Du Seuil, 1979), 24: "C'est ce nouvel aspect de la personnalité du Christ [i.e., his universal significance], dans le IVᵉ évangile, qu'il faut examiner." Although the idea that the Gospel of John is a universal Gospel is widely perceived in scholarship, there is no satisfactory full-scale study of this topic. Chester Warren Quimby (*John, the Universal Gospel* [New York: Macmillan, 1947]) argued that John's gospel is completely universalized in light of Hellenistic traditions (54, 65). This seems to be the same judgment found in Adolf Harnack, *The Mission and Expansion of Christianity in the First Three Centuries*, trans. James Moffatt (New York: Harper & Brothers, 1962), 42: "as a whole, the [Fourth] gospel is saturated with statements of a directly universalistic character."

not defend the universal authority of the Father; he presupposes it. However, this Gospel does present Jesus as a figure of universal significance because he is portrayed as the owner of creation who actively engages humanity with eternal life.[38] Since the universality of the God of Israel is exclusively found in Jesus, the "Fourth Gospel presents a particular message with a universal scope."[39] Jesus' universal mission is continued by the Spirit, who is a witness to a different world and who acts through the disciples.[40] They are to love each other and live in unity in the middle of a world dominated by darkness, dispersion, and hate.[41] Although the disciples will face opposition from the world,

---

Bart Reker ("Perspective universelle du salut selon le quatrième Évangile" [Diss., Pontificia Universitas Gergoriana, 1964]) relates the Gospel of John to Jewish tradition, but his study is limited to soteriological universalism.

[38] "Universality is itself an expression of the unlimited claim that God makes on his whole creation" (Ferdinand Hahn, *Mission in the New Testament*, trans. Frank Clarke, SBT 47 [Naperville, Ill.: Alec R. Allenson, 1965], 156). See also Paul N. Anderson, "Anti-Semitism and Religious Violence as Flawed Interpretations of the Gospel of John," in *John and Judaism: A Contested Relationship in Context*, ed. R. Alan Culpepper and Paul N. Anderson, SBLRBS 87 (Atlanta: SBL, 2017), 265–311, here 267: "The Forth Gospel represents . . . a universalist appeal to all seekers of truth."

[39] Craig R. Koester, "Jesus as the Way to the Father in Johannine Theology (John 14,6)," in *Theology and Christology in the Fourth Gospel: Essays by the Members of the SNTS Johannine Writings Seminar*, ed Gilbert van Belle, J. G. Van der Watt, and P. J. Maritz, BETL 184 (Leuven: Leuven University Press, 2005), 117–33, here 214.

[40] "The gift of God, of salvation, which he brings is realized in . . . [the community of disciples], not in a cosmic vacuum" (Teresa Okure, *The Johannine Approach to Mission: A Contextual Study of John 4:1–42*, WUNT 2/31 [Tübingen: Mohr, 1988], 131). Cf. Normand Provencher, "Singularité de Jésus et universalité du Christ," in *Jésus: Christ universel? Interprétations anciennes et appropriations contemporaines de la figure de Jésus*, ed. Jean-Claude Petit and Jean-Claude Breton, Héritage et Projet 44 (Montreal: Fides, 1990), 9–24, here 21: "la Résurrection peut être considérée comme le passage de la singularité historique que dénomme le nom 'Jésus' à la fonction universelle que désigne le prédicat 'Christ.'"

[41] The distinctive character of the disciples' lives is illustrated by Jesus' own message during his earthly ministry: love as opposed to hate; truth as opposed to lie; peace and joy as opposed to fear, restlessness and grief. See Sjef van Tilborg, "Cosmological Implications of Johannine Christology," in *Theology and Christology in the Fourth Gospel: Essays by the Members of the SNTS Johannine Writings Seminar*, ed. G. van Belle, J. G. van der Watt, and P. Maritz, BETL 184 (Leuven: Leuven University Press, 2005), 483–502, here 492–95.

they fulfill their mission with the assurance that Jesus has already conquered the world and that he will judge the living and the dead in the future. The final cosmic judgment remains in Jesus' hands.

This reading implies, first, that the ruler of this world is an illegitimate monarch that dominates humanity with darkness, steals the light that God gave to his creation, and brings death to the world. Second, it also suggests that the current reality dominated by division and dispersion is not God's purpose for his creation. Third, this reading shows that the seeming victory of the world over Jesus through his crucifixion and over his disciples through persecution is, at best, not final, and, at worst, a faulty perception of reality.[42]

The universal perspective that has been running through the entire Gospel was intentionally crafted by a careful artificer who used Jewish tradition, particularly the Old Testament, in his depiction of Jesus vis-à-vis the world.[43] The Gospel of John, with all its wide openness to the world, remains Jewish to the core.[44] John intentionally deepened the Jewish element of the all-encompassing significance of Jesus and the message about him.[45] It is not necessary to posit that John radically

[42] Cf. the dramatic words of Albert Schweitzer, *The Quest of the Historical Jesus: A Critical Study of Its Progress from Reimarus to Wrede*, 3rd ed. (London: Adam & Charles Black, 1954), 2: "[Jesus] destroyed the world into which He was born."

[43] The universal significance of the God of Israel is found in the Old Testament (e.g., 2 Sam 7:19) and other Jewish texts. However, there is no unified tradition in this respect. There are texts that offer very negative assessments of the history, present, and future of the nations (e.g., 1QS, 1QM, Jub.) and documents that reflect a positive attitude towards those outside Judaism (e.g., 1 En., 4 Ezra, Wis, Let. Aris.). See Miguel Pérez Fernández, "La apertura a los gentiles en el judaísmo intertestamentario," *EstBíb* 41 (1983): 83–106.

[44] Some previous research associated the Gospel of John with gnostic thought. This had an impact in the way scholars interpreted instances of universal language in this text. For example, Á. P. Orban (*Les dénominations du monde chez les premiers auteurs chrétiens*, Graecitas Christianorum Primaeva 4 [Nijmegen: Dekker & van der Vegt, 1970]) indicated that the noun κόσμος has the sense "world estranged from God" in gnostic texts but it lacks pejorative overtones in the sense "inhabited earth" in Judeo-Hellenistic contexts. Orban suggested that gnostic thought influenced John's use of this noun.

[45] Cf. Arthur Darby Nock, *Early Gentile Christianity and Its Hellenistic Background* (New York: Harper & Row, 1964), 41, "In a measure, developing Christianity deepened its Jewish element."

transformed or even betrayed his Jewish traditions through a process of high Hellenization in order to better appreciate the comprehensive scope of Jesus' significance.[46] It is neither compulsory to suppose that John's thoroughly Jewish background prevented him from portraying Jesus and the message about him as universal in scope.[47] On the

---

[46] A clear example of the view that the Gospel of John should be set in a Hellenistic context is Rudolf Bultmann's interpretation of Jesus asking the beloved disciple to take his mother as his own (19:27). Since this scene is lacking in the Synoptic Gospels, Bultmann thought that there is no historicity behind it and that it should have symbolic meaning. Specifically, Bultmann argued that Mary represents those Jews who have embraced the theological meaning of Jesus' crucifixion and should feel at home among the gentiles, and the beloved disciple represents gentile disciples who are to honor Judaism as a mother who gave birth to Christianity (*The Gospel of John: A Commentary*, trans. G. R. Beasley-Murray, R. W. N. Hoare, and J. K. Riches, The Johannine Monograph Series 1 [Eugene: Wipf and Stock, 2014], 673). Decades earlier, Wilhelm Bousset (*Kyrios Christos: Geschichte des Christusglaubens von den Anfängen des Christentums bis Irenaeus*, FRLANT 4 [Göttingen: Vandenhoeck & Ruprecht, 1913]) attempted to show that Hellenistic ideas found their way into the Christology and worship of Christianity beginning with Paul. Albert Schweitzer (*Die Mystik des Apostels Paulus* [Tübingen: Mohr, 1930], 338–40), however, argued that Paul's eschatology is continuous with that of Jesus and that those responsible for Hellenizing Christianity were early church fathers and, above all, the Gospel of John. Also, Benjamin W. Bacon (*The Gospel of the Hellenists* [New York: Henry Holt, 1933]) maintained that John was written for the Hellenistic world because its author, John the Elder, was a representative of Hellenistic Christianity writing from Ephesus. Wilbert Francis Howard (*The Fourth Gospel in Recent Criticism and Interpretation* [London: Epworth, 1931], 176) suggested that "the general outlook of the Gospel of John is determined by religious forces which belong to a period much later than the lifetime of Jesus, and to a *milieu* remote from Palestinian Judaism." Cf. Wilhelm Heitmüller, 'Das Johannes-Evangelium', in *Die Schriften des Neuen Testaments neu übersetzt und für die Gegenwart erklärt*, 3rd ed., vol. 4 (Göttingen: Vandenhoeck & Ruprecht, 1918), 16–18.

[47] W. C. van Unnik ("The Purpose of St. John's Gospel," in Aland et al., *Studia Evangelica*, 382–411, here 410), for example, concluded that "the purpose of the Fourth Gospel was to bring the visitors of a synagogue in the Diaspora (Jews and Godfearers) to belief in Jesus as the Messiah of Israel." A similar conclusion was reached by K. Bornhäuser (*Das Johannesevangelium: Eine Missionsschrift für Israel*, BFCT 2/15 [Gütersloh: C. Bertelsmann, 1928]), but, at that time, did not command much attention. See also K. G. Kuhn, "Problem der Mission," *Evangelische Missionszeitschrift* 11 (1954): 161–68, here 167; Hahn, *Mission*, 152; and J. Louis Martyn, *History and Theology in the Fourth Gospel*, 3rd ed. (Nashville: Abingdon, 2003). Subsequent research has arrived at similar conclusions. Wayne Meeks claimed that there is "hardly a hint of a specifically gentile mission" in the Gospel of John ("Breaking Away: Three New

contrary, the full import of several instances of universal language in this Gospel is better appreciated when its Old Testament quotations are taken within their own literary contexts. The Gospel of John is a universal Gospel not *despite* its commitment to Jewish tradition but precisely *because* its author is deeply rooted in such a tradition. This rhetorical move (i.e., John's use of the Old Testament) would give legitimacy to a narrative based otherwise on dubious witnesses. Those who support the image of Jesus as the rightful owner of creation who rules above all humanity are a prisoner (3:24), Samaritans (4:9), a woman (11:2), and a Jew accused of blasphemy (10:33). Conversely, those who held religious and political power during Jesus' earthly ministry ridiculed the one who is above all things. Religious leaders embraced the authority of Caesar and rejected the kingship of Jesus. Pilate, the representative of Roman political power in Judea, and his soldiers mocked Jesus as king and emperor. Paradoxically, in the Gospel of John glorification is found in humiliation, power belongs to the powerless, true authority is dissociated from the Roman Empire, victory is achieved through service and sacrifice.

The reading of the Gospel of John offered here has the potential to help us further ponder several debated issues in the interpretation of this text. I list them here as areas suggestive for further exploration. They are related to Johannine Christology, the use of this Gospel in early Christianity, and the possible political dimensions of this text.

Stranger from Heaven?

More than a decade ago R. Alan Culpepper judged that the growing influence of narrative criticism in the interpretation of this text "is changing our understanding of the Fourth Gospel's core themes."[48] If our analysis of the literary deployment and rhetoric force of instances

---

Testament Pictures of Christianity's Separation from the Jewish Communities," in *"To See Ourselves as Others See Us": Christians, Jews, "Others" in Late Antiquity,* ed. Jacob Neusner and Ernest S. Frerichs, Scholars Press Studies in the Humanities [Chico, Calif.: Scholars Press, 1985], 93–115, here 97) and the text itself "could hardly be regarded as a missionary tract" ("The Man from Heaven in Johannine Sectarianism," *JBL* 91 [1972]: 44–72, here 70).

[48] R. Alan Culpepper, "Symbolism and History in John's Account of Jesus' Death," in *Anatomies of Narrative Criticism: The Past, Present, and Futures of the Fourth*

of universal language proves convincing, the still influential suggestion that the Johannine Jesus is *primarily* a stranger from heaven should be reconsidered. This dominant notion is rooted in the correct observation that the "special patterns of language" reflected in this Gospel are the hallmark of John's text in early Christian literature.[49] Wayne Meeks, for example, famously focused on the descent and ascent motif in order to explore the symbolic universe found in the text and concluded that Jesus is "the Stranger *par excellence*."[50] He stated his major finding as follows: "In every instance the [descent/ascent] motif points to contrast, foreignness, division, judgment."[51] In turn, Meeks used his conclusions to draw some deductions about the community behind the Gospel. Such deductions were prefaced by due cautionary words: "Unfortunately we have no independent information about the organization of the Johannine group, and even the Johannine literature gives little description of the community and hardly any statements that are directly 'ecclesiological.'"[52] This, however, did not deter him from providing a description of the social status of the putative community behind the Gospel and even an explanation about the original function of the Gospel of John as a text. Specifically, Meeks asserted that the community behind the Gospel saw itself as "unique, alien

---

Gospel as Literature, ed. Tom Thatcher and Stephen D. Moore, SBLRBS 55 (Leiden: Brill, 2008), 39–54, here 54.

[49] Meeks, "Man from Heaven," 44. Cf. Catrin H. Williams, "Another Look at 'Lifting Up' in the Gospel of John," in *Conception, Reception, and the Spirit: Essays in Honor of Andrew T. Lincoln*, ed. J. Gordon McConville and Lloyd K. Pietersen (Eugene, Ore.: Cascade, 2015), 58: "a profoundly enigmatic mode of speech." In this recent article (2015), Williams refers to Jesus as "stranger from heaven" (58). See also M. de Jonge, *Jesus, Stranger from Heaven and Son of God: Jesus Christ and the Christians in Johannine Perspective*, ed. and trans. John E. Steely, Sources for Biblical Study 11 (Missoula: Scholars, 1977).

[50] Meeks, "Man from Heaven," 50, 68 (emphasis in original). "The pattern, descent and ascent, becomes the cipher for Jesus' unique self-knowledge as well as for his foreignness to the men of this world" (60); "the alien from all men of the world" (69); "the Stranger from the world above" (71).

[51] Meeks, "Man from Heaven," 67.

[52] Meeks, "Man from Heaven," 69.

from its world, under attack, misunderstood" and the Gospel of John was intended to reinforce the community's social isolation.[53]

The real author and his historical situation cannot be fully reconstructed with a high degree of certainty or without much speculation. Although it is not the task of narrative criticism to answer historical questions, "it may nevertheless cast new light on them."[54] Interpreters at least need to take full account of *all* Johannine motifs in their historical reconstructions.[55] The present study shows the need to take into consideration the several instances of universal language in our understanding of the Johannine presentation of Jesus. Once the various and seemingly contradictory trends of Johannine thought are brought together, a more complex and sophisticated understanding of the Johannine Jesus and the group or groups who first received this text should emerge. As an analogy, take the specific issue of Christology. If interpreters focus exclusively on those patterns of language which seem to portray Jesus as uniquely related to God, the Gospel of John can be accused of "naïve docetism."[56] However, if those texts that clearly indicate that Jesus was fully identified with humanity are also allowed to contribute to our understanding of Jesus, a more nuanced opinion about Johannine Christology can be reached.[57]

I have argued here that an important component of John's presentation of Jesus is the depiction of Jesus as the rightful owner of creation who casts out the illegitimate ruler who dominates this world through

---

[53] Meeks, "Man from Heaven," 70, 71. Meeks refers to the Gospel of John as "an etiology of the Johannine group" (69) and to the Johannine community as a "small group of believers isolated over against 'the World'" (68).

[54] Culpepper, "Symbolism," in Thatcher and Moore, *Anatomies of Narrative Criticism*, 54.

[55] Furthermore, it is risky to limit the interpretation of Johannine instances of universal language through a reconstruction of the putative historical situation of the Johannine community that is based on the reading of selected Johannine motifs. See Lars Kierspel, *The Jews and the World in the Fourth Gospel: Parallelism, Function, and Context*, WUNT 2/220 (Tübingen: Mohr Siebeck, 2006), 182.

[56] Ernst Käsemann, *The Testament of Jesus: A Study of the Gospel of John in the Light of Chapter 17*, trans. Gerhard Krodel (London: SCM, 1968), 25–26.

[57] Larry W. Hurtado, *Lord Jesus Christ: Devotion to Jesus in Earliest Christianity* (Grand Rapids: Eerdmans, 2003), 353–96.

falsehood.[58] It is difficult to imagine that people associated with the Gospel of John in the first century saw in this Gospel a motivation for social isolation. This text even claims that the sanctification of Jesus' followers, that is, their separation from the world, should fuel their engagement with humanity in this world. Although further research will be needed in order to gain clarity about the mind-set of the supposed Johannine community or communities behind the Gospel, the results of this research may support a current trend that challenges the influential view that those who first received the Gospel of John were a conventicle of people isolated from their environment and even from other early Christian groups.[59]

Further research that pursues a reconstruction of the historical situation of those who first received this Gospel should deal with the lack of direct evidence. In lieu of independent historical data, our scholarly guesses may be sharpened through comparing the Gospel of John with contemporary texts and by assessing its early reception. The Qumran texts offer us evidence of a truly sectarian Jewish group, socially isolated. Pauline letters are a rich source of information about early groups of followers of the risen Christ who had a multiethnic vision of God's community. Josephus' works may provide a window into the

---

[58] As Andrew T. Lincoln (*Truth on Trial: The Lawsuit Motif in the Fourth Gospel* [Peabody, Mass.: Hendrickson, 2000], 258) puts it, "In the trial's verdict, 'the ruler of this world' is driven out (12:31), has no power over Jesus (14:30), and has been condemned (16:11) . . . the world rightly belongs to the one who has come into it from above to bring salvific judgment."

[59] Martin Hengel, *The Johannine Question* (London: SCM Press, 1989); Richard Bauckham, *The Testimony of the Beloved Disciple: Narrative, History, and Theology in the Gospel of John* (Grand Rapids: Eerdmans, 2007); Edward W. Klink III, *The Sheep of the Fold: The Audience and Origin of the Gospel of John*, SNTSMS 141 (Cambridge: Cambridge University Press, 2007); Jonathan Bernier, *Aposynagōgos and the Historical Jesus in John: Rethinking the Historicity of the Johannine Expulsion Passages*, BibInt 122 (Leiden: Brill, 2013). For a review of trends in the interpretation of the putative Johannine community, see Wally V. Cirafesi, "The Johannine Community Hypothesis (1868–Present): Past and Present Approaches and a New Way Forward," *CurBR* 12 (2014): 173–93; idem, "The 'Johannine Community' in (More) Current Research: A Critical Appraisal of Recent Methods and Models," *Neot* 48 (2014): 341–64; and Johannes Beutler, "Von der johanneischen Gemeinde zum Relecture-Modell," *TP* 90 (2015): 1–18.

mentality of a first-century Jew highly involved in the larger Roman Empire. How are instances of universal language used in texts of such diverse genres as the Community Rule, the letter to the Romans, and *Against Apion*? How distinctive is John in relation to those texts in its use of universal language?[60]

A Sectarian Text?

This study has shown that the Johannine reader does not necessarily need to be a member of a putative sectarian Johannine community to understand an important component of the message of the text. Although the use of irony, symbolism, and Jewish imagery makes the interpretative process challenging, the text itself provides enough clues for any reader (sympathetic or not with the message of the story) to appreciate the perspective of the narrator about the universal significance of Jesus.[61] This, in turn, might imply that the Gospel of John does not necessarily need to be construed as intended to have a limited circulation for the benefit of a socially and religiously isolated community.[62] Jesus forecasts for his church "a universality which the evangelist can hardly have supposed to be fully realized in his time."[63] The

---

[60] For example, Kåre Sigvald Fuglseth, *Johannine Sectarianism in Perspective: A Sociological, Historical, and Comparative Analysis of Temple and Social Relationships in the Gospel of John, Philo, and Qumran*, NovTSup 119 (Leiden: Brill, 2005).

[61] Cf. Friederike Kunath, *Die Präexistenz Jesu im Johannesevangelium: Struktur und Theologie eines johanneischen Motivs*, BZNW 212 (Berlin: de Gruyter, 2016), 368: "Gegen das Unverständnis der Jünger und der Juden geht der ideale Leser bis zum Ende des Motivs und dem Ende der Erzählung mit und versteht—angeleitet durch den Geist—die hinter die Schöpfung zurückreichende Tiefe des Weges Jesu."

[62] Bauckham, *Testimony*, 12: "As the author's lifework, the permanent embodiment of his personal calling to testify to Jesus, the Gospel of John was not occasioned by fluctuating local circumstances but by the author's convictions about the universal significance of Jesus and his story." He also indicates that "it begins to look as though the Fourth Gospel envisages a wider readership than perhaps any other New Testament text does" (123). Cf. Anderson, "Anti-Semitism," in Culpepper and Anderson, *John and Judaism*, 309: "John's Gospel . . . is also the greatest source of Christian universalism (John 1:9; 6:45)"; and p. 310, "The greatest Johannine scandal is not its exclusivism but its universal inclusivism, which defies religious, political, and societal bounds."

[63] C. H. Dodd, *The Interpretation of the Fourth Gospel* (Cambridge: Cambridge University Press, 1953), 7.

universality of God's salvation already given in Jesus' exaltation on the cross, "in itself suggests that the evangelist has in view a non-Christian public to which he wishes to appeal."[64]

J. Louis Martyn famously suggested that the "Gospel of John originated in a local church—or group of churches—markedly distinct from the types of Christianity that were developing during the same period into the Great Church."[65] Martyn's form-critical method means that he excludes from consideration parts he considers later additions, most notably John 21.[66] Famously, he also focused his attention on John 9:22.[67] Martyn contended that the Johannine community developed in a time when most Christian evangelism took place in the synagogues of Ephesus.[68] This group of Christians continued a mission to Jews, but they later suffered a painful expulsion from the synagogue (so 9:22). In response, these Jewish Christians became a "discrete community."[69]

Martyn proposed that particular Johannine ideas that are interpreted as reflecting a concern for gentiles should be read within his larger proposed framework of an alienated group of Jewish Christians. Locutions such as "the Passover, the festival of the Jews" (6:4) are taken as reflective of a group made up of former Jews.[70] The translation of terms into Greek, such as the use of "teacher" for "rabbi" in 1:38, were taken by Martyn as post-Johannine additions that offer no evidence of missionary concerns of the original community.[71] The references

---

[64] Dodd, *Interpretation*, 8.

[65] J. Louis Martyn, "A Gentile Mission That Replaced an Earlier Jewish Mission?" in *Exploring the Gospel of John: In Honor of D. Moody Smith*, ed. C. Clifton Black and R. Alan Culpepper (Louisville: Westminster John Knox, 1996), 124–44, here 124.

[66] Martyn, "Mission," in Culpepper and Black, *Exploring the Gospel of John*, 136n1.

[67] Martyn, *History and Theology*. It is difficult to exaggerate the influence of this work on later Johannine scholarship.

[68] Martyn, "Mission," in Culpepper and Black, *Exploring the Gospel of John*, 125.

[69] Martyn, "Mission," in Culpepper and Black, *Exploring the Gospel of John*, 125.

[70] Martyn ("Mission," in Culpepper and Black, *Exploring the Gospel of John*, 126) suggests a periphrasis here: "Passover, the feast of the Jews who celebrate it, in distinction from the members of our community, who do not do so, being no longer 'Jews' in the sense in which we ourselves use that term."

[71] Martyn, "Mission," in Culpepper and Black, *Exploring the Gospel of John*, 127, follows here John Painter, *The Quest for the Messiah*, 2nd ed. (Nashville: Abingdon,

to Greeks (Ἕλλην) in 7:35 and 12:20 point not to gentiles who have nothing to do with Judaism, but to those God-fearers associated with the synagogues,[72] and furthermore the Johannine community itself.[73] The "other sheep" in 10:16 refers to other Jewish Christian communities who also suffered in their original synagogue settings.[74] Caiaphas' prophecy in 11:49-52 promises the unification of those who are already "children of God," i.e., other "Jewish-Christian conventicles."[75] His proposal also demands that if John intended to portray his community as a missionary group directed to the gentiles, he would have given some straightforward description of their journey.[76] His overall conclusion is that "the community's sense of mission—at the time of the Gospel—was significantly different from the sense of mission characteristic of the Great Church."[77]

Other considerations apart, Martyn seems to set every reference that might point to the comprehensive scope of Jesus' significance within his larger reconstruction of a sectarian community expelled from the synagogue. He also disregards John 21 and other sections of the Gospel as later additions. These decisions have a direct impact on his conclusions. Since Martyn's proposal does not work with the final form of the Gospel, it serves as an explanation of the putative outlook of a suggested community behind a text whose form is different from the reconstructed text we possess today. At one level, one can only imagine the situations behind the texts based on the evidence provided by the texts themselves. Furthermore, a consideration of other early Christian texts should help us picture the historical situation behind the Gospel of John. An example from Paul's encounter with synagogue leaders after his acceptance of Christ as Messiah should suffice for now. This encounter was painful (as portrayed by Luke in Acts 17:10-15).

1993), 131. Martyn suggested that the same redactor that included John 21 was responsible for such a parenthesis.

[72] Martyn, "Mission," in Culpepper and Black, *Exploring the Gospel of John*, 128, 131–33.

[73] Martyn, "Mission," in Culpepper and Black, *Exploring the Gospel of John*, 128.

[74] Martyn, "Mission," in Culpepper and Black, *Exploring the Gospel of John*, 130.

[75] Martyn, "Mission," in Culpepper and Black, *Exploring the Gospel of John*, 131.

[76] Martyn, "Mission," in Culpepper and Black, *Exploring the Gospel of John*, 133.

[77] Martyn, "Mission," in Culpepper and Black, *Exploring the Gospel of John*, 135.

However, far from Paul becoming the leader of a discrete community with no regard for gentiles, this experience with synagogue leaders actually boosted his mission among gentiles. It is possible that similar painful encounters with synagogue leaders led the author of the final form of the Gospel of John in another direction, i.e., a focus on mission to the Jews in the diaspora. We cannot know for sure what he did, but the antecedent we find in Paul makes the former option more plausible. At another level, Martyn briefly mentioned Jesus' interaction with Pontius Pilate (John 18–19), a gentile,[78] but minimized Pilate's significance by asserting that his presence in the narrative is merely the result of a pressure exerted by the passion tradition.[79] However, most scholars recognize the thoroughly Johannine portrayal of Jesus' encounter with Pilate.[80] If he included Pilate solely in order not to betray tradition, why did he take care to produce a long and detailed description of his encounter and dialogues with Jesus?

The original audience of the final form of the Gospel of John is elusive. This study shows the need of further research about the reception of this text in the earliest available evidence.[81] Previous research

[78] Martyn, "Mission," in Culpepper and Black, *Exploring the Gospel of John*, 133.

[79] Martyn, "Mission," in Culpepper and Black, *Exploring the Gospel of John*, 133.

[80] Helen K. Bond, *Pontius Pilate in History and Interpretation*, SNTSMS 100 (Cambridge: Cambridge University Press, 1998), 163–93.

[81] Some intriguing pieces are (1) the identification in the "epitaph of Abercius" (216 CE) of a follower of Jesus as a "disciple of the holy shepherd" (μαθητὴς ποιμένος ἁγνοῦ, line 3); (2) a marble inscription from Attica (300–450 CE) with the words φ(ῶς) Χ(ριστοῦ) φ(αίνει) π(ᾶσι); (3) a graffiti type inscription with an allusion to John 1:1 found in Wadi Haggag (perhaps late forth century); (4) the use of the incipit of the Gospel of John in ancient amulets (e.g., *BGU* III 954; P.Cair.Cat. 10696; P.Heid. inv. L 5; PSI VI 719; P.Vindob. G 348). W. Lüdtke and T. Nissen, *Die Grabschrift des Aberkios: Ihre überlieferung und Ihr text* (Leipzig: G. B. Teubner, 1910), II, 37; R. Merkelbach, "Grabepigramm und Vita des Bischofs Aberkios von Hierapolis," *Epigraphia Anatolica* 28 (1995): 125–39; C. Breytenbach et al., eds., *Inscriptiones Christianae Graecae: A Digital Collection of Greek Early Christian Inscriptions from Asia Minor and Greece* (Berlin: Edition Topoi, 2016), Inscription ICG 2222; E. Sironen, *The Late Roman and Early Byzantine Inscriptions of Athens and Attica* (Helsinki: Hakapaino Oy, 1997), 338; E. Popescu, ed., *Inscripţiile greceşti şi latine din secolele IV-XII descoperite în România*, Academia Scientiarum Socialium et Politicarum Dacoromana (Bucharest: Editura Academiei Republicii Socialiste Române, 1976), 136; A. Negev, *The Inscriptions of Wadi Haggag: Sinai*, Qedem 6 (Jerusalem: Hebrew University of Jerusalem, 1977), 73; T. de

has shown that the Gospel of John was one of the most-copied texts (at least in Egypt) in the second century[82] and that its ideas were appropriated by early Christians associated with an emergent orthodox tradition,[83] but these ideas also influenced other texts that are now known as heterodox.[84] However, the specific question about whether the universal language of this Gospel had a lasting influence on the memory of early Christians is still waiting for a sophisticated formulation.[85] Specifically, one should ask whether there is any evidence that imagery associated with the all-encompassing authority of the

---

Bruyn, "Papyri, Parchments, Ostraca, and Tablets Written with Biblical Texts in Greek and Used as Amulets: A Preliminary List," in *Early Christian Manuscripts: Examples of Applied Method and Approach*, ed. T. J. Kraus and T. Nicklas, TENTS 5 (Leiden: Brill, 2010), 145–89, here 166–69; B. C. Jones, *New Testament Texts on Greek Amulets from Late Antiquity*, LNTS 554 (London: Bloomsbury T&T Clark, 2016), 147–51.

[82] Consider the several extant papyri from the second and third centuries with sections of this Gospe: 𝔓45, 𝔓52, 𝔓66, 𝔓75, 𝔓90, 𝔓95, 𝔓106, 𝔓107, 𝔓108, 𝔓109, 𝔓119, 𝔓121. See also J. R. Royse, *Scribal Habits in Early Greek New Testament Papyri*, NTTS 36 (Leiden: Brill, 2008), 17–31; J. Chapa, "The Early Text of John," in *The Early Text of the New Testament*, ed. C. H. Hill and M. J. Kruger (Oxford: Oxford University Press, 2012), 140–56; and A. Mugridge, *Copying Early Christian Texts: A Study of Scribal Practice*, WUNT 362 (Tübingen: Mohr Siebeck, 2016), 9, 244, 250–51.

[83] J. Allenbach et al., *Des origines à Clément d'Alexandrie et Tertullien*, vol. 1 of *Biblia Patristica: Index des citations et allusions bibliques dans la littérature patristique*, CADP (Paris: Centre National de la Recherche Scientifique, 1975); J. Reuss, *Johannes-Kommentare aus der Griechischen Kirche*, TUGAL 89 (Berlin: Akademie-Verlag, 1966); T. Rasimus, ed., *The Legacy of John: Second-Century Reception of the Fourth Gospel*, NovTSup 132 (Leiden: Brill, 2010); C. E. Hill, *The Johannine Corpus in the Early Church* (Oxford: Oxford University Press, 2004; repr. 2007); R. A. Culpepper, *John, the Son of Zebedee: The Life of a Legend* (Edinburgh: T&T Clark, 2000), 114–119; F. M. Braun, *Jean le théologien et son Évangile dans l'Église Ancienne*, EBib (Paris: Gabalda, 1959), 156–60.

[84] E. Pagels, *The Johannine Gospel in Gnostic Exegesis: Heracleon's Commentary on John*, SBLMS 17 (Nashville: Abingdon, 1973); C. Barth, *Die Interpretation des Neuen Testaments in der valentinianischen Gnosis* (Leipzig: J. C. Hinrichs, 1911); J. D. Kaestli, J. M. Poffet, and J. Zumstein, eds., *La communauté johannique et son histoire: La trajectoire de l'évangile de Jean aux deux premiers siècles* (Geneva: Labor et Fides, 1990).

[85] Cf. J. A. T. Robinson, *Twelve New Testament Studies* (London: SCM, 1962), 112: "There are no more universalistic sayings in the New Testament than in the fourth Gospel" (see also Hahn, *Mission*, 154). Cf. Trond Skard Dokka, "Irony and Sectarianism in the Gospel of John," in *New Readings in John*, ed. Johannes Nissen and Sigfred Pedersen, JSNTSS 182 (Sheffield: Sheffield Academic Press, 1999), 82–107, here 102: "An analysis of the Johannine language (*langue*) with a view to the question of

Johannine Jesus was known, used, and preserved in early artifacts that can be linked to what scholars call "proto-orthodox" Christianity.[86] Here I can only offer a couple of general examples. The first example is taken from P.Egerton 3 (P.Lond.Chris. 2) which includes three Johannine quotations that are expressive of Jesus' universal significance, 1:9, 14, 29.[87] Why did the hand behind this third-century text found in Oxyrhynchus select these Johannine ideas that refer to the Word as the true light who enters the world (1:9), to Jesus as showing solidarity with humanity (1:14), and to the Lamb of God who takes away the sin of the world (1:29)?[88] The second example is less direct.[89] Terra-cotta lamps from central Italy show that Christians around 175–225 CE might have used pagan shepherd lamps in their daily life.[90]

---

sectarianism has to be supplemented by an analysis both of linguistic *usage* (*parole*) and of the reception of the Gospel."

[86] For a brief discussion of "proto-orthodox" Christianity, see Larry W. Hurtado, *Destroyer of the gods: Early Christian Distinctiveness in the Roman World* (Waco, Tex.: Baylor University Press, 2016), 10–12.

[87] H. I. Bell and T. C. Skeat, *Fragments of an Unknown Gospel and Other Early Christian Papyri* (London: British Museum, 1935), 45–49.

[88] Epiphanius combines John 1:14 and 1:29 in *Pan.* 2.2.252. See R. Yuen-Collingridge, "Hunting for Origen in Unidentified Papyri: The Case of P.Egerton 2 (= *inv.* 3)," in *Early Christian Manuscripts: Examples of Applied Method and Approach*, ed. T. J. Kraus and T. Nicklas, TENTS 5 (Leiden: Brill, 2010), 39–57, here 57n76.

[89] There are several examples of disputed references to the Gospel of John in ancient artifacts. For example, M. Naldini (*Il Cristianesimo in Egitto: Lettere private nei papiri dei secoli II–IV*, Studi e testi di papirologia 3 [Firenze: Edizioni Dehoniane Bologna, 1968], 66) finds a parallel between a letter dated August 23, 133, and John 16:27. The letter (P.Mich 8.482) has [ὡ]ς φειλῶ σοι ὁ θεὸς ἐμὲ φειλήσι, while John 16:27 has ὁ πατὴρ φιλεῖ ὑμᾶς, ὅτι ὑμεῖς ἐμὲ πεφιλήκατε. Another example is a marble tablet found in Rome (279 CE) with an allusion to the idea that Jesus' disciples are not from this world (8:23; 13:1; 15:19; 17:6, 15). See A. E. Gordon and J. S. Gordon, *Album of Dated Latin Inscriptions* (Berkeley: University of California Press, 1965), 3:96–97, no. 302.

[90] Paul Corby Finney, *The Invisible God: The Earliest Christians on Art* (Oxford: Oxford University Press, 1994), 126: "it is reasonable to suppose that at least an occasional Christian customer in central Italy will have been prompted to purchase" shepherd lamps instead of lamps portraying more overly pagan symbols. Hill (*Johannine Corpus*, 161), however, is more confident: "Surely some did." For pictures of these lamps, see D. M. Bailey, *A Catalogue of the Lamps in the British Museum. Roman Lamps Made in Italy* (London: British Museum, 1980), plates 1–104, esp. 72–86.

Specifically, they used lamps with the image of a man carrying a ram or a sheep on his shoulders. Although sheep imagery is found in several Old Testament and New Testament texts, the combination of light and shepherd imagery is peculiarly Johannine. A case in point is the good shepherd discourse in John 10:1-18, which is framed by a miraculous story that illustrates the idea that Jesus is light (9:5; 10:21).[91] Both images are expressive of Jesus' universal significance. He is the light of the world (1:4; 8:12; 11:9; 12:46) who enlightens humanity (1:9; 3:19). The shepherd has other sheep who do not belong yet to his fold (10:16).[92] How influential was Johannine universalism in allowing early Christians to appropriate artifacts regarded as pagan?[93]

A Spiritual Gospel?

The Gospel of John has been traditionally identified as the "spiritual" Gospel.[94] This designation, however, can lead to misunderstandings about important dimensions of the text. A "spiritual" reading might imply that the Gospel of John simply looks inward, to the individual spiritual experience of members of a putative Johannine community.[95]

---

[91] There is no clear break between the two stories in the earliest manuscripts. See Victor Martin and Rodolphe Kasser, *Papyrus Bodmer XV: Evangile de Jean chap. 1–15* (Colony: Bibliotheca Bodmeriana, 1961), 60, 88.

[92] Tertullian, for example took the lost sheep as non-Christians because the "Good Shepherd" (*pastor bonus*) is "Lord" of the "universal nations" (*uniuersarum gentium, Pud.* 7.6). C. Munier, *La pudicité*, SC 394 (Paris: Cerf, 1993), 176–77.

[93] Cf. Clement of Alexandria's use of the shepherd imagery in a string of phrases that are taken from the Gospel of John. Jesus is the "heavenly Word, the Savior," the light that shines forth from the darkness, and the good shepherd sent to the world because his constant purpose has been to "save the flock of men" (*Protr.* 11).

[94] This is the judgment of Clement of Alexandria as preserved in Eusebius, *Hist. eccl.* 6.14.7: "John, perceiving that the external (τὰ σωματικά) facts had been made plain in the Gospel . . . inspired by the Spirit (πνεύματι), composed a spiritual (πνευματικόν) Gospel." Eusèbe de Césarée, *Histoire Ecclésiastique*, SC 41 (Paris: Cerf, 1955), 107; Philip Schaff and Henry Wace, eds., *A Select Library of Nicene and Post-Nicene Fathers of the Christian Church* (Grand Rapids: Eerdmans, 1971), 1:261.

[95] The portrayal of this popular perception of the Gospel of John is found in Lincoln, *Truth*, 262. He finds this notion in Rudolf Bultmann, *Theology of the New Testament*, trans. Kendrick Grobel (Waco, Tex.: Baylor University Press, 2007), 2:11–14.

Although there is "individualism" in the Gospel of John,[96] the overall concern of the Johannine Jesus is with the whole world. Take, for example, Jesus' individual dialogue with Nicodemus in John 3. This personal encounter that initially is concerned with a "spiritual" birth concludes with a discourse about God's love for the world expressed in Jesus bringing life and light to humanity. Jesus' universal mission includes him bringing light where there is darkness and denouncing the evil works of the world. Take, as another example, Jesus' personal encounter with the Samaritan woman. Although Jesus offers her living water for eternal life, the story ends with Samaritan people identifying Jesus with an acclamation that was reserved for Roman rulers: "Savior of the world." At least implicitly, this designation carries a challenge to political authorities of the time who were recognized as bringing "salvation" to people from the Roman Empire. These examples provide "a rather different picture of the stance of the Christian community toward the world from that painted by those who suggest the Fourth Gospel has a dualistic attitude that . . . simply looks inward and treats salvation as an experience of the individual in some spiritual sphere."[97]

Without diminishing the "spiritual," "inward," and "individual" dimensions found in the text, the Gospel of John is also concerned with the world as a whole. Jesus encourages his disciples to engage a world that he has already conquered in order to bring glory to the Father. The way they should relate to creation, however, is very different from the way those who hold religious and political power engage the world. They take advantage of humanity using lies and hate in order to obtain self-glorification. Jesus, instead, offers his life in sacrifice as a service to God's creation in order to bring light, life, and freedom to humanity, so that the Father may be glorified. Since the current status of the world does not resemble the divine vision of the cosmos, Jesus became flesh to shape the future of God's creation.

---

[96] C. F. D. Moule, "The Individualism of the Fourth Gospel," *NovT* 5 (1962): 171–90; Richard Bauckham, *Gospel of Glory: Major Themes in Johannine Theology* (Grand Rapids: Baker Academic, 2015), 1–20.

[97] Lincoln, *Truth*, 262.

Future further reflections about these findings should be properly set in the Gospel's larger first-century Roman imperialistic context.[98] The explicit mention of the Roman emperor in the passion narratives and the several instances of Johannine language that might find resonances in such a political context (e.g., authority, peace, kingdom) should encourage further questions. One should ask, for instance, how John's universalism was heard in its larger first-century Mediterranean milieu. Some contemporary pagan sources use instances of universal language as part of a larger political agenda. Flavius Arrianus (95–175 CE) depicts Alexander declaring Persians to be his kinsmen (συγγενεῖς) and praying "that the Macedonians and the Persians should enjoy harmony as partners in the government" (*Anabasis* 7.11.8–9).[99] This Greek historian attributes to Alexander a "fusion of races" and a "brotherhood of mankind."[100] Another example is the account of Augustus's stewardship found at Ancyra in Asia Minor, a region

---

[98] Valuable explorations of this topic include David Rensberger, "The Politics of John: The Trial of Jesus in the Fourth Gospel," *JBL* 103 (1984): 394–411; Warren Carter, *John and Empire: Initial Explorations* (London: T&T Clark, 2008); Jean K. Kim, *Woman and Nation: An Intercontextual Reading of the Gospel of John from a Postcolonial Feminist Perspective* (Leiden: Brill, 2004); Michael Labahn, "Heiland der Welt," in *Zwischen den Reichen: Neues Testament und Römische Herrschaft*, ed. Michael Labahn and Jürgen Zangenberg, Texte und Arbeiten zum neutestamentlichen Zeitalter 36 (Tübingen: Francke Verlag, 2002), 147–73; William Loader, *Jesus in John's Gospel: Structure and Issues in Johannine Christology* (Grand Rapids: Eerdmans, 2017), 466; Kierspel, *Jews*, 192–200; and Tom Thatcher, *Greater Than Caesar: Christology and Empire in the Fourth Gospel* (Minneapolis: Fortress, 2009).

[99] P. A. Brunt, *Arrian: Anabasis Alexandri*, LCL 269 (Cambridge, Mass.: Harvard University Press, 1983), 2:241.

[100] Ian Worthington, *Alexander the Great: A Reader*, 2nd ed. (London: Routledge, 2012), 276. On the one hand, Alexander's army comprised foreigners, he married women from cultures different from his own, and he even shared the table with foreigners in a banquet of reconciliation. On the other hand, Macedonians and Greeks controlled the highest ranks in his administration, foreign noblewomen were given to Alexander's men in order to weaken the political power of other cultures, and Macedonians sat next to him in the banquet of reconciliation possibly "in order to emphasize their racial superiority" (277). See also E. Badian, "Alexander the Great and the Unity of Mankind," *Historia* 7 (1958): 425–44; W. W. Tarn, "Alexander the Great and the Unity of Mankind," *Proceedings of the Cambridge Philological Society* 19 (1933): 123–66; and C. G. Thomas, "Alexander the Great and the Unity of Mankind," *Classical Journal* 63 (1968): 258–60.

deemed to be the place where this Gospel was produced. This account, known as *Res Gestae divi Augusti* or *Monumentum Ancyranum*, is written in both Latin and Greek. Since Augustus made Ephesus the capital of proconsular Asia, it became the seat of the governor, and it was second in importance only to Rome. It is not impossible to imagine that a copy of the *Res Gestae* was also preserved in Ephesus.[101] *Res Gestae* portrays Augustus as bringing forgiveness and freedom to foreign nations, and extending friendship to foreign kings: "The foreign nations which could with safety be pardoned I preferred to save rather than to destroy," "I freed the entire people, at my own expense, from the fear and danger in which they were," and "a large number of other nations experienced the good faith of the Roman people during my principate who never before had had . . . friendship with the Roman people."[102] Therefore, the "whole habitable world voted him no less than celestial honors" (Philo, *Legat.* 145–154). How did this larger political context affect the way early Christians heard the message about the universal significance of Jesus found in the Gospel of John?

[101] Paul Trebilco, *The Early Christians in Ephesus from Paul to Ignatius*, WUNT 166 (Tübingen: Mohr Siebeck, 2004), 14.

[102] Velleius Paterculus, *Compendium of Roman History*, trans. Frederick W. Shipley, LCL 152 (Cambridge, Mass.: Harvard University Press, 1992), 349, 353, 395, 397.

BIBLIOGRAPHY

Aalen, Sverre. *Die Begriffe "Licht" und "Finsternis" im Alten Testament, im Spätjudentum und im Rabbinismus.* Oslo: J. Dybward, 1951.

Akagi, Kai. "The Light from Galilee: The Narrative Function of Isaiah 8:23–9:6 in John 8:12." *NovT* 58 (2016): 380–93.

Aland, Barbara, et al. *Novum Testamentum Graece: Nestle-Aland.* 28th rev. ed. Stuttgart: Deutsche Bibelgesellschaft, 2012.

Alday, Salvador Carrillo. *El Evangelio según san Juan: El Evangelio del Camino, de la Verdad y de la Vida.* Estella: Verbo Divino, 2010.

Allenbach, J., et al. *Des origines à Clément d'Alexandrie et Tertullien.* Vol. 1. *Biblia Patristica: Index des citations et allusions bibliques dans la littérature patristique.* CADP. Paris: Centre National de la Recherche Scientifique, 1975.

Ameling, Walter. "Neues Testament und Epigraphik aus der Perspektive der epigraphischen Forschung." In *Epigraphik und Neues Testament,* edited by Thomas Corsten, Markus Öhler, and Joseph Verheyden, 5–26. Tübingen: Mohr Siebeck, 2016.

Anderson, Paul N. "Anti-Semitism and Religious Violence as Flawed Interpretations of the Gospel of John." In *John and Judaism: A Contested Relationship in Context,* edited by R. Alan Culpepper and Paul N. Anderson, 265–311. SBLRBS 87. Atlanta: SBL, 2017.

———. *The Riddles of the Fourth Gospel: An Introduction to John.* Minneapolis: Fortress, 2011.

———. "The *Sitz im Leben* of the Johannine Bread of Life Discourse and Its Evolving Context." In *Critical Readings of John 6,* 1–59. BibInt 22. Leiden: Brill, 1997.

Bacon, Benjamin W. *The Gospel of the Hellenists.* New York: Henry Holt, 1933.

Badian, E. "Alexander the Great and the Unity of Mankind." *Historia* 7 (1958): 425–44.

Bailey, D. M. *A Catalogue of the Lamps in the British Museum: Roman Lamps Made in Italy*. London: British Museum, 1980.

Barrett, C. K. *The Gospel according to St. John: An Introduction with Commentary and Notes on the Greek Text*. Philadelphia: Westminster, 1978.

Barth, C. *Die Interpretation des Neuen Testaments in der valentinianischen Gnosis*. Leipzig: J. C. Hinrichs, 1911.

Bauckham, Richard. *God Crucified: Monotheism and Christology in the New Testament*. Grand Rapids: Eerdmans, 1998.

_____. *Gospel of Glory: Major Themes in Johannine Theology*. Grand Rapids: Baker Academic, 2015.

_____. *The Testimony of the Beloved Disciple: Narrative, History, and Theology in the Gospel of John*. Grand Rapids: Baker Academic, 2007.

Bauer, W., F. W. Danker, W. F. Arndt, and F. W. Gingrich, eds. *A Greek-English Lexicon of the New Testament and Other Early Christian Literature*. Chicago: University of Chicago Press, 2000.

Bauer, Walter. *Das Johannesevangelium*. HNT 6. Tübingen: Mohr Siebeck, 1933.

Beck, David R. *The Discipleship Paradigm: Readers and Anonymous Characters in the Fourth Gospel*. BibInt 27. Leiden: Brill, 1997.

Becker, J. "Aufbau, Schichtung und theologiegeschichtliche Stellung des Gebetes in Joh 17." *ZNW* 60 (1969): 56–83.

Beirne, Margaret M. *Women and Men in the Fourth Gospel: A Genuine Discipleship of Equals*. JSNTSup 242. London: Sheffield Academic, 2003.

Bekken, Jarle. *The Lawsuit Motif in John's Gospel from New Perspectives: Jesus Christ, Crucified Criminal and Emperor of the World*. NovTSup 158. Leiden: Brill, 2015.

Bell, H. I., and T. C. Skeat. *Fragments of an Unknown Gospel and Other Early Christian Papyri*. London: British Museum, 1935.

Bernier, Jonathan. *Aposynagōgos and the Historical Jesus in John: Rethinking the Historicity of the Johannine Expulsion Passages*. BibInt 122. Leiden: Brill, 2013.

Beutler, Johannes. *Das Johannesevangelium: Kommentar*. Freiburg: Herder, 2013.

_____. "Der alttestamentlich-jüdische Hintergrund der Hirtenrede in Joh 10." In *The Shepherd Discourse of John 10 and Its Context: Studies by Members of the Johannine Writings Seminar*, edited by Johannes Beutler and Robert T. Fortna. 18–32. SNTSMS 67. Cambridge: Cambridge University Press, 1991.

_____. "Greeks Come to See Jesus (John 12,20f)." *Bib* 71 (1990): 333–47.

_____. "Jesus in Judea." *In die Skriflig* 49 (2015): 1–6.

_____. "Psalm 42/43." In *Habt keine Angst: Die erste johanneische Abschiedsrede (Joh 14)*. Stuttgarter Bibelstudien 116. Stuttgart: Katholisches Bibelwerk, 1984.

_____. "Von der johanneischen Gemeinde zum Relecture-Modell." *TP* 90 (2015): 1–18.

Blass, F., A. Debrunner, and W. Funk. *A Greek Grammar of the New Testmaent and Other Early Christian Literature*. Chicago: University of Chicago Press, 1961.

Blumell, Lincoln H., and Thomas A. Wayment, eds. *Christian Oxyrhynchus: Texts, Documents, and Sources*. Waco, Tex.: Baylor University Press, 2015.

Bond, Helen K. *Pontius Pilate in History and Interpretation*. SNTSMS 100. Cambridge: Cambridge University Press, 1998.

Borgen, Peder. *Bread from Heaven: An Exegetical Study of the Concept of Manna in the Gospel of John and the Writings of Philo*. Leiden: Brill, 1965.

_____. "Logos Was the True Light: Contributions to the Interpretation of the Prologue of John." *NovT* 14 (1972): 115–30.

Bornhäuser, K. *Das Johannesevangelium: eine Missionsschrift für Israel*. Vol. 15. BFCT 2. Gütersloh: C. Bertelsmann, 1928.

Bourgel, J. "Brethren or Strangers? Samaritans in the Eyes of Second-Century BCE Jews." *Bib* 98 (2017): 382–408.

Bousset, Wilhelm. *Kyrios Christos: Geschichte des Christusglaubens von den Anfängen des Christentums bis Irenaeus*. FRLANT 4. Göttingen: Vandenhoeck & Ruprecht, 1913.

Boyle, J. L. "The Last Discourse (Jn 13, 31-16, 33) and Prayer (Jn 17): Some Observations on Their Unity and Development." *Bib* 56 (1975): 210–22.

Braun, F. M. *Jean le théologien et son Évangile dans l'Église Ancienne*. EBib. Paris: Gabalda, 1959.

Brendsel, Daniel J. *"Isaiah Saw His Glory": The Use of Isaiah 52–53 in John 12*. BZNW 208. Berlin: de Gruyter, 2014.

Breytenbach, C., K. Hallof, U. Huttner, J. Krumm, S. Mitchell, J. M. Ogereau, E. Sironen, M. Veksina, and C. Zimmermann, eds. *Inscriptiones Christianae Graecae: A Digital Collection of Greek Early Christian Inscriptions from Asia Minor and Greece*. Berlin: Edition Topoi, 2016.

Brouwer, Wayne. *The Literary Development of John 13–17: A Chiastic Reading*. SBLDS 182. Atlanta: SBL, 2000.

Brown, Raymond Edward, ed. *The Gospel according to John*. 2 vols. The Anchor Bible 29. Garden City, N.Y.: Doubleday, 2000.

Bruneau, P. "Les Israélites de Délos et la juiverie délienne." *BCH* 106 (1982): 465–504.

Brunt, P. A. *Arrian: Anabasis Alexandri*. Vol. 2. LCL 269. Cambridge, Mass.: Harvard University Press, 1983.

Bultmann, Rudolf. *The Gospel of John: A Commentary*. Translated by G. R. Beasley-Murray, R. W. N. Hoare, and J. K. Riches. The Johannine Monograph Series 1. Eugene, Ore.: Wipf & Stock, 2014.

_____. *Theology of the New Testament*. Translated by Kendrick Grobel. Waco, Tex.: Baylor University Press, 2007.

Burney, C. F. *The Aramaic Origin of the Fourth Gospel*. Oxford: Clarendon, 1922.

Busse, Ulrich. "Die 'Hellenen' Joh 12, 20ff. und der sogenannte 'Anhang' Joh 21." In *The Four Gospels 1992: Festschrift Frans Neirynck*, edited by F. van Sagbroeck, C. M. Tuckett, G. van Belle, and J. Verheyden, 2083–100. BETL 3. Leuven: Leuven University Press, 1992.

_____. "Theologie oder Christologie im Johannesprolog?" In *Studies in the Gospel of John and Its Christology: Festschrift Gilbert van Belle*, edited by Joseph Verheyden,

Geert van Oyen, Michael Labahn, and Reimund Bieringer, 1–36. BETL 265. Leuven: Peeters, 2014.

Bynum, Wm. Randolph. *The Fourth Gospel and the Scriptures: Illuminating the Form and Meaning of Scriptural Citation in John 19:37.* NovTSup 144. Leiden: Brill, 2012.

Carson, D. A. *The Gospel according to John.* Grand Rapids: Eerdmans, 1991.

Carter, Warren. *John and Empire: Initial Explorations.* London: T&T Clark, 2008.

Cassen, N. H. "A Grammatical and Contextual Inventory of the Use of κόσμος in the Johannine Corpus with Some Implications for a Johannine Cosmic Theology." *NTS* 19 (1972): 81–91.

Chanikuzhy, Jacob. *Jesus, the Eschatological Temple: An Exegetical Study of Jn 2,13-22 in the Light of the Pre-70 CE Eschatological Temple Hopes and the Synoptic Temple Action.* CBET 58. Leuven: Peeters, 2012.

Chapa, J. "The Early Text of John." In *The Early Text of the New Testament*, edited by C. H. Hill and M. J. Kruger, 140–56. Oxford: Oxford University Press, 2012.

Cirafesi, Wally W. "The Johannine Community Hypothesis (1868–Present): Past and Present Approaches and a New Way Forward." *CurBR* 12 (2014): 173–93.

———. "The 'Johannine Community' in (More) Current Research: A Critical Appraisal of Recent Methods and Models." *Neot* 48 (2014): 341–64.

Clavier, H. "L'ironie dans le quatrième Évangile." In *Studia Evangelica*, edited by K. Aland, F. L. Cross, J. Daniélou, H. Riesenfeld, and W. C. van Unnik. TU 73. Berlin: Akademie-Verlag, 1959.

Collins, Raymond F. "'You Call Me Teacher and Lord—and You Are Right. For That Is What I Am' (John 13,13)." In *Studies in the Gospel of John and Its Christology: Festschrift Gilbert van Belle*, edited by Joseph Verheyden, Geert van Oyen, Michael Labahn, and Reimund Bieringer, 327–48. BETL 265. Leuven: Peeters, 2014.

Coloe, Mary L. "Gentiles in the Gospel of John: Narrative Possibilities—12.12-43." In *Attitudes to Gentiles in Ancient Judaism and Early Christianity*, edited by David C. Sim and James S. McLaren, 209–213. LNTS 499. London: Bloomsbury T&T Clark, 2013.

Conway, Colleen M. *Men and Women in the Fourth Gospel: Gender and Johannine Characterization.* SBLDS 167. Atlanta: SBL, 1999.

Croy, N. Clayton. "Translating for Jesus: Philip and Andrew in John 12:20-22." *Neot* 49 (2015): 145–74.

Culpepper, R. Alan. *Anatomy of the Fourth Gospel: A Study in Literary Design.* Philadelphia: Fortress, 1983.

———. "C. H. Dodd as a Precursor to Narrative Criticism." In *Engaging with C. H. Dodd on the Gospel of John: Sixty Years of Tradition and Interpretation*, edited by T. Thatcher and C. Williams. Cambridge: Cambridge University Press.

———. "'Children of God': Evolution, Cosmology, and Johannine Thought." In *Creation Stories in Dialogue: The Bible, Science, and Folk Traditions*, 3–31. BibInt 139. Leiden: Brill, 2015.

———. "Designs for the Church in the Imagery of John 21:1-14." In *Studies in the Gospel of John and Its Christology: Festschrift Gilbert van Belle*, edited by Joseph

Verheyden, Geert van Oyen, Michael Labahn, and Reimund Bieringer, 501–18. BETL 265. Leuven: Peeters, 2014.

_____. "Inclusivism and Exclusivism in the Fourth Gospel." In *Word, Theology, and Community in John*, edited by John Painter, R. Alan Culpepper, and Fernando F. Segovia, 85–108. St. Louis: Chalice, 2002.

_____. *John, the Son of Zebedee: The Life of a Legend.* Edinburgh: T&T Clark, 2000.

_____. "The Prologue as Theological Prolegomenon to the Gospel of John." In *The Prologue of the Gospel of John: Its Literary, Theological, and Philosophical Contexts. Papers Read at the Colloquium Ioanneum 2013*, edited by Jan G. van der Watt, R. Alan Culpepper, and Udo Schnelle, 3–26. WUNT 359. Tübingen: Mohr Siebeck, 2016.

_____. "Reading Johannine Irony." In *Exploring the Gospel of John: In Honor of D. Moody Smith*, edited by C. Clifton Black and R. Alan Culpepper, 193–207. Louisville: Westminster John Knox, 1996.

_____. "Symbolism and History in John's Account of Jesus' Death." In *Anatomies of Narrative Criticism: The Past, Present, and Futures of the Fourth Gospel as Literature*, edited by Tom Thatcher and Stephen D. Moore, 39–54. SBLRBS 55. Leiden: Brill, 2008.

_____. "The Theology of the Johannine Passion Narrative: John 19:16-20." *Neot* 31 (1997): 21–37.

Daly-Denton, Margaret. *David in the Fourth Gospel: The Johannine Reception of the Psalms.* AGJU 47. Leiden: Brill, 2000.

Davies, Margaret. *Rhetoric and Reference in the Fourth Gospel.* JSNTSup 69. Sheffield: Sheffield Academic, 1992.

Davies, W. D. "Reflections on Aspects of the Jewish Background of the Gospel of John." In *Exploring the Gospel of John: In Honor of D. Moody Smith*, edited by R. Alan Culpepper and C. Clifton Black, 43–64. Louisville: Westminster John Knox, 1996.

Day, Janeth Norfleete. *The Woman at the Well: Interpretation of John 4:1-42 in Retrospect and Prospect.* BIS 61. Leiden: Brill, 2002.

De Boer, Martinus C. "The Original Prologue to the Gospel of John." *NTS* 61 (2015): 448–67.

de Bruyn, T. "Papyri, Parchments, Ostraca, and Tablets Written with Biblical Texts in Greek and Used as Amulets: A Preliminary List." In *Early Christian Manuscripts: Examples of Applied Method and Approach*, edited by T. J. Kraus and T. Nicklas, 145–89. TENTS 5. Leiden: Brill, 2010.

Denaux, Adelbert. "The Twofold Purpose of the Fourth Gospel: A Reading of the Conclusion to John's Gospel (20,30-31)." In *Studies in the Gospel of John and Its Christology: Festschrift Gilbert Van Belle*, edited by Joseph Verheyden, Geert van Oyen, Michael Labahn, and Reimund Bieringer, 519–36. BETL 265. Leuven: Peeters, 2014.

Dennis, John A. *Jesus' Death and the Gathering of True Israel.* WUNT 2/217. Tübingen: Mohr Siebeck, 2006.

Derrett, J. Duncan M. "Christ, King and Witness (John 18,37)." *Bibbia e Oriente* 162 (1989): 189–98.

Dettwiler, Andreas. *Die Gegenwart des Erhöhten: Eine exegetische Studie zu den johanneischen Abschiedsreden (Joh 13,31–16,33) unter besonderer Berücksichtigung ihres Relecture-Charakters.* FRLANT 169. Göttingen: Vandenhoeck & Ruprecht, 1995.

Devillers, Luc. "Jean 9, ou la christologie interactive de Jean." In *Studies in the Gospel of John and Its Christology: Festschrift Gilbert Van Belle*, edited by Joseph Verheyden, Geert van Oyen, Michael Labahn, and Reimund Bieringer, 227–38. BETL 265. Leuven: Peeters, 2014.

Dodd, C. H. *According to the Scriptures: The Sub-structure of New Testament Theology.* London: Nisbet, 1952.

_____. *The Interpretation of the Fourth Gospel.* Cambridge: Cambridge University Press, 1953.

Dokka, Trond Skard. "Irony and Sectarianism in the Gospel of John." In *New Readings in John*, edited by Johannes Nissen and Sigfred Pederson, 82–107. JSNTSup 182. Sheffield: Sheffield Academic, 1999.

Donaldson, Terence L. *Judaism and the Gentiles: Jewish Patterns of Universalism (to 135 CE).* Waco, Tex.: Baylor University Press, 2007.

Duke, Paul D. *Irony in the Fourth Gospel.* Atlanta: John Knox, 1985.

Engberg-Pedersen, Troels. *John and Philosophy: A New Reading of the Fourth Gospel.* Oxford: Oxford University Press, 2017.

Ensor, P. W. *Jesus and His "Works": The Johannine Sayings in Historical Perspective.* WUNT 2/85. Tübingen: J. C. B. Mohr, 1996.

Estes, Douglas. "Time." In *How John Works: Storytelling in the Fourth Gospel*, edited by Douglas Estes and Ruth Sheridan, 41–57. SBLRBS 86. Atlanta: SBL, 2016.

Eusèbe de Césarée. *Histoire Ecclésiastique.* SC 41. Paris: Cerf, 1955.

Fenton, J. C. *The Gospel according to John.* New Clarendon Bible. Oxford: Clarendon, 1970.

Fernández, Miguel Pérez. "La apertura a los gentiles en el judaísmo intertestamentario." *EstBíb* 41 (1983): 83–106.

Fernández Marcos, Natalio, and María Spottorno Díaz-Caro. *La Biblia griega: Septuaginta.* Vol. 4. Biblioteca de Estudios Bíblicos 128. Salamanca: Sígueme, 2015.

Finney, Paul Corby. *The Invisible God: The Earliest Christians on Art.* Oxford: Oxford University Press, 1994.

Förster, Hans. "Die Begegnung am Brunnen (Joh 4.4-42) im Licht der 'Schrift': Überlegungen zu den Samaritanern im Johannesevangelium." *NTS* 61 (2015): 201–18.

_____. "Überlegungen zur Übersetzung von Joh 20,19 und 20,29." *Glotta* 92 (2016): 86–105.

Fortin, Anne. "Jésus et les gens de Samarie." *SémiotBib* 157 (2015): 15–33.

Frey, Jean Baptiste. *Corpus Inscriptionum Judaicarum: Recueil des inscriptions juives qui vont du IIIᵉ siècle avant Jésus-Christ au VIIᵉ siècle de notre ère.* Rome: Pontificio Istituto di Archaeologia Cristiana, 1936.

Frey, Jörg. "Between Torah and Stoa: How Could Readers Have Understood the Johannine Logos?" In *The Prologue of the Gospel of John: Its Literary, Theological, and Philosophical Contexts*. *Papers Read at the Colloquium Ioanneum 2013*, edited by Jan G. van der Watt, R. Alan Culpepper, and Udo Schnelle, 189–234. WUNT 359. Tübingen: Mohr Siebeck, 2016.

―――. "Jesus und Pilatus: Der wahre König und der Repräsentant des Kaisers im Johannesevangelium." In *Christ and the Emperor: The Gospel Evidence*, edited by Gilbert Van Belle and Joseph Verheyden, 337–93. BTS 20. Leuven: Peeters, 2014.

―――. "Love-Relations in the Fourth Gospel: Establishing a Semantic Network." In *Love-Relations in the Fourth Gospel: Establishing a Semantic Network*, edited by Gilbert Van Belle and P. J. Maritz, 171–98. BETL 223. Leuven: Peeters, 2009.

―――. "Wege und Perspektiven der Interpretation des Johannesevangeliums: Überlegungen auf dem Weg zu einem Kommentar." In *Die Herrlichkeit des Gekreuzigten: Studien zu den Johanneischen Texten I*, 3–41. WUNT 307. Tübingen: Mohr Siebeck, 2013.

Frey, J., and U. Poplutz, eds. *Narrativität und Theologie im Johannesevangelium*. Biblisch-Theologische Studien 130. Göttingen: Vandenhoeck & Ruprecht, 2012.

Fridrichsen, Anton. "La pensée missionnaire dans le Quatrième Évangile." *Arbeiten und Mitteilungen aus dem neutestamentlichen Seminar zu Uppsala* 4 (1937): 39–45.

Fuglseth, Kåre Sigvald. *Johannine Sectarianism in Perspective: A Sociological, Historical, and Comparative Analysis of Temple and Social Relationships in the Gospel of John, Philo, and Qumran*. NovTSup 119. Leiden: Brill, 2005.

Gordon, A. E., and J. S. Gordon. *Album of Dated Latin Inscriptions*. Berkeley: University of California Press, 1965.

Gourgues, Michel. "Les échos du discours d'adieu dans les récits johanniques de christophanie pascale (Jean 20)." In *Studies in the Gospel of John and Its Christology: Festschrift Gilbert van Belle*, edited by Joseph Verheyden, Geert van Oyen, Michael Labahn, and Reimund Bieringer, 485–99. BETL 265. Leuven: Peeters, 2014.

Grappe, Christian. "Le debut du quatrième évangile (Jean 2 à 5), témoin d'un dialogue avec d'autres traditions religieuses?" *RHPR* 96 (2016): 113–25.

Grelot, Pierre. *Los targumes: Textos escogidos*. Navarra: Verbo Divino, 1987.

Grob, F. *Faire l'oeuvre de Dieu: Christologie et éthique dans L'Evangile de Jean*. Paris: Presses Universitaires de France, 1986.

Haenchen, Ernst. *John 1: A Commentary on the Gospel of John, Chapters 1-6*. Edited by Robert W. Funk with Ulrich Busse. Translated by Robert W. Funk. Hermeneia. Philadelphia: Fortress, 1984.

―――. *John 2: A Commentary on the Gospel of John, Chapters 7-21*. Edited by Robert W. Funk with Ulrich Busse. Translated by Robert W. Funk. Hermeneia. Philadelphia: Fortress, 1984.

Hagelia, Hallvard. "A Crescendo of Universalism: An Exegesis of Isa 19:16-25." In *Nomen et Nomina: Festskrift till Stig Norin*, 73–88. SEÅ 70. Uppsala: Uppsala Exegetiska Sällskap, 2005.

Hahn, Ferdinand. *Mission in the New Testament.* Translated by Franke Clarke. SBT 47. Naperville, Ill.: Alec R. Allenson, 1965.

Hallyn, Fernand, and Georges Jacques. "Aspects du Paratexte." In *Introduction aux Études Littéraires: Méthode du Texte,* edited by Maurice Delcroix and Fernand F. Hallyn, 202–15. Paris: Duculot, 1987.

Harnack, Adolf. *The Mission and Expansion of Christianity in the First Three Centuries.* Translated by James Moffatt. New York: Harper & Brothers, 1962.

Harris, Rendel. *Testimonies.* 2 vols. Cambridge: Cambridge University Press, 1916.

Hasitschka, M. "Die beiden 'Zeichen' am See von Tiberias: Interpretation von Joh 6 in Verbindung mit Joh 21,1–14." *SNTSU* 24 (1999): 85–102.

Heitmüller, Wilhelm. "Das Johannes-Evangelium." In *Die Schriften des Neuen Testaments neu übersetzt und für die Gegenwart erklärt,* vol. 4. 3rd ed. Göttingen: Vandenhoeck & Ruprecht, 1918.

Hengel, Martin. *The "Hellenization" of Judaea in the First Century after Christ.* London: SCM; Philadelphia: Trinity Press International, 1989.

———. *The Johannine Question.* London: SCM, 1989.

Hengstenberg, E. W. *Das Evangelium des heiligen Johannes.* 3 vols. Berlin: G. Schlawitz, 1863.

Hera, Marianus Pale. *Christology and Discipleship in John 17.* WUNT 2/324. Tübingen: Mohr Siebeck, 2013.

Hill, J. C. E. *The Johannine Corpus in the Early Church.* Oxford: Oxford University Press, 2004.

Hoskyns, Edwyn Clement. *The Fourth Gospel.* Edited by Francis Noel Davey. London: Faber and Faber, 1967.

Howard, Wilbert Francis. *The Fourth Gospel in Recent Criticism and Interpretation.* London: Epworth, 1931.

Hübenthal, Sandra. *Transformation und Aktualisierung: Zur Rezeption von Sach 9–14 im Neuen Testament.* Stuttgarter Biblische Beiträge 57. Stuttgart: Katholisches Bibelwerk, 2006.

Hurtado, Larry W. *Destroyer of the gods: Early Christian Distinctiveness in the Roman World.* Waco, Tex.: Baylor University Press, 2016.

———. *Lord Jesus Christ: Devotion to Jesus in Earliest Christianity.* Grand Rapids: Eerdmans, 2003.

Hylen, Susan. *Allusion and Meaning in John 6.* BZNW 137. Berlin: de Gruyter, 2005.

Janzen, Gerald J. "The Scope of Jesus' High Priestly Prayer in John 17." *Encounter* 67 (2006): 1–26.

Jones, B. C. *New Testament Texts on Greek Amulets from Late Antiquity.* LNTS 554. London: Bloomsbury T&T Clark, 2016.

Jones, Larry Paul. *The Symbol of Water in the Gospel of John.* JSNTSup 145. Sheffield: Sheffield Academic, 1997.

Jonge, M. de. *Jesus: Stranger from Heaven and Son of God; Jesus Christ and the Christians in Johannine Perspective.* Sources for Biblical Study 11. Missoula, Mo.: Scholars, 1977.

Judge, Peter J. "Come and See: The First Disciples and Christology in the Fourth Gospel." In *Studies in the Gospel of John and Its Christology: Festschrift Gilbert Van Belle*, edited by Joseph Verheyden, Geert van Oyen, Michael Labahn, and Reimund Bieringer, 61–69. BETL 265. Leuven: Peeters, 2014.

Kaestli, J. D., J. M. Poffet, and J. Zumstein, eds. *La communauté johannique et son histoire: La trajectoire de l'évangile de Jean aux deux premiers siècles.* Geneva: Labor et Fides, 1990.

Kanagaraj, Jey J. *John: A New Covenant Commentary.* New Covenant Commentary Series. Cambridge: Lutterworth, 2013.

Karakolis, Christos. "The Logos-Concept and Dramatic Irony in the Johannine Prologue and Narrative." In *The Prologue of the Gospel of John: Its Literary, Theological, and Philosophical Contexts; Papers Read at the Colloquium Ioanneum 2013*, edited by Jan G. van der Watt, R. Alan Culpepper, and Udo Schnelle, 139–56. WUNT 359. Tübingen: Mohr Siebeck, 2016.

Karrer, M. "Jesus, der Retter (Sōtēr): Zur Aufnahme eines hellenistischen Prädikats in Neuen Testament." *ZNW* 93 (2002): 153–76.

Käsemann, Ernst. *The Testament of Jesus: A Study of the Gospel of John in the Light of Chapter 17.* Translated by Gerhard Krodel. London: SCM, 1968.

Kearsley, Rosalinde A., ed. *Greeks and Romans in Imperial Asia: Mixed Language Inscriptions and Linguistic Evidence for Cultural Interaction until the End of AD III.* Inschriften Griechischer Städte aus Kleinasien 59. Bonn: Habelt, 2001.

Keener, Craig S. *The Gospel of John: A Commentary.* Peabody, Mass.: Hendrickson, 2003.

Kellum, L. Scott. *The Unity of the Farewell Discourse: The Literary Integrity of John 13.31–16.33.* JSNTSup 256. London: T&T Clark, 2004.

Kieffer, René. "The Implied Reader in John's Gospel." In *New Readings in John*, edited by Johannes Nissen and Sigfred Pederson, 47–65. Edinburgh: T&T Clark, 2004.

Kierspel, Lars. *The Jews and the World in the Fourth Gospel: Parallelism, Function, and Context.* WUNT 2/220. Tübingen: Mohr Siebeck, 2006.

Kim, Jean K. *Woman and Nation: An Intercontextual Reading of the Gospel of John from a Postcolonial Feminist Perspective.* Leiden: Brill, 2004.

King, N. Q. "The 'Universalism' of the Third Gospel." In *Studia Evangelica*, edited by Kurt Aland et al., 199–205. TUGAL 73. Berlin: Akademie-Verlag, 1959.

Klink, Edward W., III. *Sheep of the Fold: The Audience and Origin of the Gospel of John.* SNTSMS 141. Cambridge: Cambridge University Press, 2007.

Kobel, Esther. *Dining with John: Communal Meals and Identity Formation in the Fourth Gospel and Its Historical and Cultural Context.* BibInt 109. Leiden: Brill, 2011.

Koester, Craig R. "Jesus as the Way to the Father in Johannine Theology (John 14,6)." In *Theology and Christology in the Fourth Gospel: Essays by the Members of the SNTS Johannine Writings Seminar*, edited by Gilbert van Belle, J. G. Van der Watt, and P. J. Maritz, 117–133. BETL 184. Leuven: Leuven University Press, 2005.

———. "'The Savior of the World' (John 4:42)." *JBL* 109 (1990): 665–80.

———. *Symbolism in the Fourth Gospel: Meaning, Mystery, Community.* 2nd ed. Minneapolis: Fortress, 2003.

Kok, Jacobus (Kobus). "The Plenipotentiary Idea as Leitmotiv in John's Gospel." *In die Skriflig* 49 (2015): 1–9.

Kossen, H. B. "Who Were the Greeks of John xii 20?" In *Studies in John*, 97–110. NovTSup 24. Leiden: Brill, 1970.

Kraabel, A. T. "New Evidence of the Samaritan Diaspora Has Been Found on Delos." *BA* 47 (1984): 44–46.

Kruse, Colin G. *The Gospel according to John: An Introduction and Commentary*. TNTC 4. Downers Grove, Ill.: InterVarsity, 2008.

Kuhn, K. G. "Problem der Mission." *Evangelische Missionszeitschrift* 11 (1954): 161–68.

Kunath, Friederike. *Die Präexistenz Jesu im Johannesevangelium: Struktur und Theologie eines johanneischen Motivs*. BZNW 212. Berlin: de Gruyter, 2016.

Kysar, Robert. *John the Maverick Gospel*. 3rd ed. Louisville: Westminster John Knox, 2007.

Labahn, Michael. "Heiland der Welt." In *Zwischen den Reichen: Neues Testament und Romische Herrschaft*, edited by Michael Labahn and Jürgen Zangenberg, 147–73. Texte und Arbeiten zum neutestamentlichen Zeitalter 36. Tübingen: Francke Verlag, 2002.

LaCocque, André. "'*Et aspicient ad me quem confixerunt*.'" In *Pensar la Biblia: Estudios exegéticos y hermenéuticos*, edited by André LaCocque and Paul Ricoeur, translated by Antonio Martínez Riu. Barcelona: Herder, 2001.

Lagrange, M. J. *Évangile selon saint Jean*. 5th ed. EBib. Paris: Gabalda, 1936.

Larsen, Kasper Bro. "Plot." In *How John Works: Storytelling in the Fourth Gospel*, edited by Douglas Estes and Ruth Sheridan, 97–113. SBLRBS 86. Atlanta: SBL, 2016.

Lattey, Cuthbert. "The Praetorium of Pilate." *JTS* 31 (1930): 180–82.

Léon-Dufour, Xavier. "Situation de Jean 13." In *Die Mitte des Neuen Testaments: Einheit und Vielfalt neutestamentlicher Theologie*, edited by Ulrich Luz and Hans Weder, 131–41. Göttingen: Vandenhoeck & Ruprecht, 1983.

Lett, Jonathan. "The Divine Identity of Jesus as the Reason for Israel's Unbelief in John 12:36-43." *JBL* 135 (2016): 159–73.

Lincoln, Andrew T. *The Gospel according to Saint John*. BNTC 4. New York: Hendrickson, 2005.

———. *Truth on Trial: The Lawsuit Motif in the Fourth Gospel*. Peabody, Mass.: Hendrickson, 2000.

Lindars, Barnabas. *The Gospel of John: Based on the Revised Standard Version*. NCB. Grand Rapids: Eerdmans, 1981.

———. *New Testament Apologetic: The Doctrinal Significance of the Old Testament Quotations*. London: SCM, 1961.

Lindemann, Andreas. "*Orbis Romanus* und OIKOYMENH: Römischer und urchristlicher Universalismus." In *Christ and the Emperor: The Gospel Evidence*, edited by Gilbert van Belle and Joseph Verheyden, 51–100. BTS 20. Leuven: Peeters, 2014.

Llewelyn, S. R., ed. *A Review of the Greek Inscriptions and Papyri Published 1984-85*. NewDocs 8. Grand Rapids: Eerdmans, 1998.

_____, ed. *New Documents Illustrating Early Christianity: A Review of the Greek Inscriptions and Papyri Published in 1986–87.* NewDocs 9. Grand Rapids: Eerdmans, 2002.

Loader, William. *Jesus in John's Gospel: Structure and Issues in Johannine Christology.* Grand Rapids: Eerdmans, 2017.

Loisy, Alfred. *Le quatrième Évangile.* 1st ed. Paris: Alphonse Picard et Fils, 1903.

_____. *Le quatrième Évangile.* 2nd ed. Paris: Émile Nourry, 1921.

Long, George. *The Discourses of Epictetus with the Encheiridion and Fragments.* New York: A. L. Burt, 1900.

Louw, Johannes P., and Eugene A. Nida. *Greek-English Lexicon of the New Testament Based on Semantic Domains.* 2nd ed. Vols. 1 and 2. New York: United Bible Societies, 1989.

Lüdtke, W., and T. Nissen. *Die Grabschrift des Aberkios: Ihre überlieferung und Ihr text.* Leipzig: G. B. Teubner, 1910.

Maritz, Petrus, and Gilbert Van Belle. "The Imagery of Eating and Drinking in John 6:35." In *Imagery in the Gospel of John: Terms, Themes, and Theology of Johannine Figurative Language,* edited by Jörg Frey, Jan G. van der Watt, and Ruben Zimmermann, 333–52. WUNT 200. Tübingen: Mohr Siebeck, 2006.

Marrow, Stanley B. "Κόσμος in John." *CBQ* 64 (2002): 90–102.

Martin, Victor, and J. W. B. Barns. *Papyrus Bodmer II. Supplément.* Cologny: Bibliotheca Bodmeriana, 1962.

Martin, Victor, and Rodolphe Kasser. *Papyrus Bodmer XV: Evangile de Jean chap. 1–15.* Cologny: Bibliotheca Bodmeriana, 1961.

Martyn, J. Louis. "A Gentile Mission That Replaced an Earlier Jewish Mission?" In *Exploring the Gospel of John: In Honor of D. Moody Smith,* edited by R. Alan Culpepper and C. Clifton Black, 124–44. Louisville: Westminster John Knox, 1996.

_____. "Glimpses Into the History of the Johannine Community." In *L'Évangile de Jean: Sources, redaction, théologie,* edited by M. de Jonge, 149–75. BETL 44. Leuven: Leuven University Press, 1977.

Mead, A. H. "The βασιλικός in John 4.46-53." *JSNT* 23 (1985): 69–72.

Meeks, Wayne A. "Breaking Away: Three New Testament Pictures of Christianity's Separation from the Jewish Communities." In *"To See Ourselves as Others See Us": Christians, Jews, "Others" in Late Antiquity,* edited by Jacob Neusner and Ernest S. Frerichs, 93–115. Scholars Press Studies in the Humanities. Chico, Calif.: Scholars Press, 1985.

_____. "The Man from Heaven in Johannine Sectarianism." *JBL* 91 (1972): 44–72.

_____. *The Prophet-King: Moses Traditions and the Johannine Christology.* NovTSup 14. Leiden: Brill, 1967.

Menken, Maarten J. J. *Old Testament Quotations in the Fourth Gospel: Studies in Textual Form.* CBET 15. Kampen: Kok Pharos, 1996.

Merkelbach, R. "Grabepigramm und Vita des Bischofs Aberkios von Hierapolis." *Epigraphia Anatolica* 28 (1995): 125–39.

Merlier, O. ""Ονομα et ἐν ὀνόματι dans le IVᵉ Évangile." *Revue des Études Grecques* 47 (1934): 180–204.

Metzger, Bruce M. *A Textual Commentary on the Greek New Testament.* 2nd ed. Stuttgart: German Bible Society, 2007.

Michaels, J. Ramsey. *The Gospel of John.* NICNT. Grand Rapids: Eerdmans, 2010.

Minear, S. "Diversity and Unity: A Johannine Case-Study." In *Die Mitte des Neuen Testaments: Einheit und Vielfalt neutestamentlicher Theologie,* edited by Ulrich Luz and Hans Weder, 162–75. Göttingen: Vandenhoeck & Ruprecht, 1983.

Mollat, Donatien. *Études Johanniques.* Parole de Dieu. Paris: Éditions du Seuil, 1979.

———. "Remarques sur le vocabulaire spatial du quatrième évangile." *Studia Evangelica* 1 (1957): 321–28.

Moloney, Francis J. "The Function of Prolepsis in the Interpretation of John 6." In *Critical Readings of John 6,* 129–48. BibInt 22. Leiden: Brill, 1997.

———. *Johannine Studies, 1975–2017.* WUNT 372. Tübingen: Mohr Siebeck, 2017.

———. "The Literary Unity of John 13:1-38." In *Johannine Studies 1975–2017,* 405–26. WUNT 372. Tübingen: Mohr Siebeck, 2017.

———. "Narrative and Discourse at the Feast of Tabernacles: John 7:1–8:59." In *Word, Theology, and Community in John,* edited by John Painter, R. Alan Culpepper, and Fernando Segovia, 155–72. St. Louis: Chalice, 2002.

———. "Who Is 'the Reader' in/of the Fourth Gospel?" In *The Interpretation of John,* edited by John Ashton, 2nd ed., 997. Edinburgh: T&T Clark.

Morrison, C. D. "Mission and Ethic: An Interpretation of Jn 17." *Int* 19 (1965): 259–73.

Moser, Marion. *Schriftdiskurse im Johannesevangelium: Eine narrative-intertextuelle Analyse am Paradigma von Joh 4 und Joh 7.* WUNT 2/380. Tübingen: Mohr Siebeck, 2014.

Moule, C. F. D. "The Individualism of the Fourth Gospel." *NovT* 5 (1962): 71–190.

———. "The Individualism of the Fourth Gospel." In *Essays in New Testament Interpretation,* 91–109. Cambridge: Cambridge University Press, 1982.

Moxnes, Halvor. "The Mission of Jesus to 'the Totality of the Jewish Land' in Schleiermacher's Life of Jesus." In *The Mission of Jesus,* edited by Samuel Byrskog and Tobias Hägerland, 25–39. WUNT 391. Tübingen: Mohr Siebeck, 2005.

Muecke, D. C. *Irony.* The Critical Idiom 13. London: Methuen, 1970.

Mugridge, Alan. *Copying Early Christian Texts: A Study of Scribal Practice.* WUNT 362. Tübingen: Mohr Siebeck, 2016.

Munier, C. *La pudicité.* SC 394. Paris: Cerf, 1993.

Naldini, M. *Il Cristianesimo in Egitto: Lettere private nei papiri dei secoli II–IV.* Studi e testi di papirologia 3. Florence: Edizioni Dehoniane Bologna, 1968.

Negev, A. *The Inscriptions of Wadi Haggag: Sinai.* Qedem 6. Jerusalem: Hebrew University of Jerusalem, 1977.

Neyrey, Jerome H. "Space Out: 'Territoriality' in the Fourth Gospel." *HTS Teologiese Studies / Theological Studies* 58 (2002): 632–63.

Nielsen, Jesper Tang. "The Lamb of God: The Cognitive Structure of a Johannine Metaphor." In *Imagery in the Gospel of John: Terms, Forms, Themes, and Theology of Johannine Figurative Language*, edited by Jörg Frey, Jan G. van der Watt, and Ruben Zimmermann, 217–56. WUNT 200. Tübingen: Mohr Siebeck, 2006.

Nock, Arthur Darby. *Early Gentile Christianity and Its Hellenistic Background*. New York: Harper & Row, 1964.

Obielosi, Dominic. "Καὶ καθὼς Μωϋσῆς ὕψωσεν τὸν ὄφιν . . . (John 3,14-15) and the Influence of Isaiah 52,13 LXX." *EstBíb* 72 (2014): 217–35.

Odeberg, Hugo. *The Fourth Gospel: Interpreted in Its Relation to Contemporaneous Religious Currents in Palestine and the Hellenistic-Oriental World*. Uppsala: Almqvist & Wiksell, 1929.

Oehler, Wilhelm. *Zum Missionscharakter des Johannesevangeliums*. Vol. 42. BFCT 4. Gütersloh: C. Bertelsmann, 1941.

Okure, Teresa. *The Johannine Approach to Mission: A Contextual Study of John 4:1-42*. WUNT 2/31. Tübingen: Mohr, 1988.

Olson, Birger. "The Meanings of John 13,10: A Question of Genre?" In *Studies in the Gospel of John and Its Christology: Festschrift Gilbert van Belle*, edited by Joseph Verheyden, Geert van Oyen, Michael Labahn, and Reimund Bieringer, 317–25. BETL 265. Leuven: Peeters, 2014.

Orban, Á. P. *Les dénominations du monde chez les premiers auteurs chrétiens*. Graecitas Christianorum Primaeva 4. Nijmegen: Dekker & van der Vegt, 1970.

O'Rourke, John J. "Asides in the Gospel of John." *NovT* 21 (1979): 210–19.

Pagels, E. *The Johannine Gospel in Gnostic Exegesis: Heracleon's Commentary on John*. SBLMS 17. Nashville: Abingdon, 1973.

Paterculus, Vellerius. *Compendium of Roman History*. Translated by Fredrerick W. Shipley. Loeb 152. Cambridge, Mass.: Harvard University Press, 1992.

Phillips, Peter M. *The Prologue of the Fourth Gospel: A Sequential Reading*. LNTS 294. London: T&T Clark, 2006.

Pixner, Bargil. "Praetorium." *ABD* 5:447–49.

Pollard, T. E. "The Father-Son and God-Believer Relationship according to St John: A Brief Study of John's Use of Prepositions." In *L'Évangile de Jean: Sources, rédaction, théologie*, edited by Martinus de Jonge et al., 363–69. BETL 44. Gembloux: J. Duculot, 1977.

Popescu, E., ed. *Inscripțiile grecești și latine din secolele IV–XII descoperite în România*. Academia Scientiarum Socialium et Politicarum Dacoromana. Bucharest: Editura Academiei Republicii Socialiste Române, 1976.

Poplutz, Uta. "'. . . und hat unter uns gezeltet' (Joh 1,14b): Die Fleischwerdung des Logos im Licht der *Schechina*-Theologie." *SacScript* 13 (2015): 101–14.

Prosinger, Franz. "Vorschlag einer dynamisch-Konzentrischen Struktur des Johannesprologs." *Bib* 97 (2016): 244–63.

Provencher, Normand. "Singularité de Jésus et universalité du Christ." In *Jésus: Christ universel? Interprétations anciennes et appropriations contemporaines de la figure de Jésus*, edited by Jean-Claude Petit and Jean-Claude Breton, 9–24. Héritage et Projet 44. Montreal: Fides, 1990.

Quimby, Chester Warren. *John, the Universal Gospel*. New York: Macmillan, 1947.

Rae, M. "The Testimony of Works in the Christology of John's Gospel." In *The Gospel of John and Christian Theology*, edited by R. Bauckham and C. Mosser, 295–310. Grand Rapids: Eerdmans, 2008.

Randall, J. F. "The Theme of Unity in Jn 17,20-23." *ETL* 41 (1965): 373–94.

Randolph, C. B. "The Sign of Interrogation in Greek Minuscule Manuscripts." *Classical Philology* 5 (1910): 309–19.

Rasimus, T., ed. *The Legacy of John: Second-Century Reception of the Fourth Gospel.* NovTSup 132. Leiden: Brill, 2010.

Reim, G. *Studien zum alttestamentlichen Hintergrund des Johannesevangeliums.* SNTSMS 22. Cambridge: Cambridge University Press, 1974.

Reinhartz, Adele. *The Word in the World: The Cosmological Tale in the Fourth Gospel.* SBLMS 45. Atlanta: Scholars Press, 1992.

Reker, Bart. "Perspective universelle du salut selon le quatrième Évangile." Rome: Pontificia Universitas Gregoriana, 1964.

Rensberger, David. "The Politics of John: The Trial of Jesus in the Fourth Gospel." *JBL* 103 (1984): 394–411.

Resseguie, James L. "Point of View." In *How John Works: Storytelling in the Fourth Gospel*, edited by Douglas Estes and Ruth Sheridan, 79–96. SBLRBS 86. Atlanta: SBL, 2016.

———. *The Strange Gospel: Narrative Design and Point of View in John.* BibInt 56. Leiden: Brill, 2001.

Reuss, J. *Johannes-Kommentare aus der Griechischen Kirche.* TUGAL 89. Berlin: Akademie-Verlag, 1966.

Rissi, M. "'Voll grosser Fische, hundertdreiundfünfzig': Joh. 21,1–14." *TZ* 35 (1979): 73–89.

Robinson, John A. T. "The Destination and Purpose of St. John's Gospel." *NTS* 6 (1959–1960): 117–31.

———. "The 'Others' of John 4, 38: A Test of Exegetical Method." *Studia Evangelica* 1 (1959): 510–15.

———. *Twelve New Testament Studies.* Eugene: Wipf & Stock, 2009.

Romero, J. A. "Gematria and John 21, 11—the Children of God." *JBL* 97 (1978): 263–64.

Royse, J. R. *Scribal Habits in Early Greek New Testament Papyri.* NTTS 36. Leiden: Brill, 2008.

Rusam, Dietrich. "Die Samen- und Vererbungslehre der Stoa als religionsgeschichtlicher Hintergrund für die Bezeichnung der Glaubenden im Johanneischen Schrifltum." *BZ* 59 (2015): 279–87.

Sanders, J. N. *A Commentary on the Gospel according to St John.* Edited by B. A. Mastin. BNTC. London: Adam & Charles Black, 1968.

Schaff, Philip, and Henry Wace, eds. *A Select Library of Nicene and Post-Nicene Fathers of the Christian Church.* Vol. 1. Grand Rapids: Eerdmans, 1971.

Schleiermacher, Friedrich. *The Life of Jesus.* Translated by S. Maclean Gilmour. Philadelphia: Fortress, 1975.

Schnackenburg, Rudolf. *The Gospel according to St. John.* 3 vols. New York: Seabury, 1968–1982.

Schnelle, Udo. "Aus der Literatur zum Johannesevangelium 1994–2010. Erster Teil: Die Kommentare als Seismographen der Forschung." *TRu* 75 (2010): 265–303.

_____. "Die Reihenfolge der johanneischen Schriften." *NTS* 57 (2011): 91–113.

_____. *Das Evangelium nach Johannes.* THKNT 4. Leipzig: Evangelische Verlagsanstalt, 2016.

Schweitzer, Albert. *Die Mystik des Apostels Paulus.* Tübingen: Mohr, 1930.

_____. *The Quest of the Historical Jesus: A Critical Study of Its Progress from Reimarus to Wrede.* 3rd ed. London: Adam & Charles Black, 1954.

Segalla, G. *La preghiera di Gesù al Padre (Giov 17): Un addio missionario.* Studi biblici 63. Brescia: Paideia, 1983.

Sheridan, Ruth. "John's Prologue as Exegetical Narrative." In *The Gospel of John and Genre Mosaic,* edited by Kasper Bro Larsen, 171–90. Studia Aarhusiana Neotestamentica 3. Göttingen: Vandenhoeck & Ruprecht, 2015.

_____. "They Shall Look upon the One They Have Pierced: Intertextuality, Intratextuality and Anti-Judaism in John 19:37." In *Searching the Scriptures: Studies in Context and Intertextuality,* edited by Craig A. Evans and Jeremiah J. Johnson, 191–209. LNTS 543. London: Bloomsbury T&T Clark, 2015.

Sherwood, Aaron. *Paul and the Restoration of Humanity in Light of Ancient Jewish Traditions.* Ancient Judaism and Early Christianity 82. Leiden: Brill, 2013.

Simoens, Yves. *La gloire d'aimer: Structures stylistiques et interprétatives dans le Discours de la Cène (Jn 13–17).* AnBib 90. Rome: Biblical Institute, 1981.

Sironen, E. *The Late Roman and Early Byzantine Inscriptions of Athens and Attica.* Helsinki: Hakapaino Oy, 1997.

Smith, D. Moody. "Johannine Christianity: Some Reflections on its Character and Delineation." *NTS* 21 (1975): 22–48.

_____. *John.* ANTC. Nashville: Abingdon, 1999.

Sosa Siliezar, Carlos Raúl. *Creation Imagery in the Gospel of John.* LNTS 546. London: Bloomsbury T&T Clark, 2018.

_____. "A Threefold Testimony to Jesus' Universal Significance in the Gospel of John." In *El Evangelio de Juan: Origen, contenido y perspectivas,* edited by Bernardo Estrada and Luis Guillermo Sarasa. Teología Hoy 80. Bogotá, Colombia: Pontificia Universidad Javeriana, 2018.

_____. "La influencia de Isaías II en Zacarías II." *Kairós* 37 (2005): 39–57.

_____. "Tres rostros de Dios en el Cuarto Evangelio." *Greg* 94 (2013): 727–37.

Stibbe, Mark W. G. *John as Storyteller: Narrative Criticism and the Fourth Gospel.* SNTSMS 73. Cambridge: Cambridge University Press, 1992.

Stube, John C. *A Greco-Roman Rhetorical Reading of the Farewell Discourse.* LNTS 309. London: T&T Clark, 2006.

Stuckenbruck, Loren T. "Evil in Johannine and Apocalyptic Perspective: Petition for Protection in John 17." In *John's Gospel and Intimations of Apocalyptic,* edited by Catrin H. Williams and Christopher Rowland, 200–32. London: Bloomsbury T&T Clark, 2013.

Sundkler, B., and A. Fridrichsen. *Contributions à l'étude de la pensée missionnaire dans le Nouveau Testament*. Arbeiten und Mitteilungen aus dem Neutestamentlichen Seminar zu Uppsala 6. Uppsala: A. B. Lundequistska Bokhandeln, 1937.

Swoboda, Ulrike. "Zur Bestimmung des Interrogativpartikels μή en Joh 7:35." *NovT* 58 (2016): 135–54.

Tarn, W. W. "Alexander the Great and the Unity of Mankind." *Proceedings of the Cambridge Philological Society* 19 (1933): 123–66.

Thatcher, Tom. *Greater Than Caesar: Christology and Empire in the Fourth Gospel*. Minneapolis: Fortress, 2009.

Thettayil, Benny. *In Spirit and Truth: An Exegetical Study of John 4:19-26 and a Theological Investigation of the Replacement Theme in the Fourth Gospel*. CBET 46. Leuven: Peeters, 2007.

Thomas, C. G. "Alexander the Great and the Unity of Mankind." *Classical Journal* 63 (1968): 258–60.

Thompson, Marianne Meye. *The God of the Gospel of John*. Grand Rapids: Eerdmans, 2001.

———. *The Humanity of Jesus in the Fourth Gospel*. Philadelphia: Fortress, 2001.

———. *John: A Commentary*. NTL. Louisville: Westminster John Knox, 2015.

Tilborg, Sjef van. "Cosmological Implications of Johannine Christology." In *Theology and Christology in the Fourth Gospel: Essays by the Members of the SNTS Johannine Writings Seminar*, edited by Gilbert Van Belle, J. G. Van der Watt, and P. J. Maritz, 483–502. BETL 184. Leuven: Leuven University Press, 2005.

———. *Reading John in Ephesus*. NovTSup 83. Leiden: E. J. Brill, 1996.

Tolmie, D. François. "The (Not So) Good Shepherd: The Use of Shepherd Imagery in the Characterization of Peter in the Fourth Gospel." In *Imagery in the Gospel of John: Terms, Forms, Themes, and Theology of Johannine Figurative Language*, edited by Jörg Frey, Jan G. van der Watt, and Ruben Zimmermann, 353–67. WUNT 200. Tübingen: Mohr Siebeck, 2006.

Traets, C. *Voir Jésus et le Père en lui, selon l'évangile de saint Jean*. Analecta Gregoriana 159. Rome: Università Gregoriana, 1967.

Trebilco, Paul. *The Early Christians in Ephesus from Paul to Ignatius*. WUNT 166. Tübingen: Mohr Siebeck, 2004.

Tukasi, E. O. *Determinism and Petitionary Prayer in John and the Dead Sea Scrolls: Ideological Reading of John and the Rule of Community (1QS)*. LSTS 66. London: T&T Clark, 2008.

Ulrichsen, J. H. "Jesus—der neue Tempel? Ein kritischer Blick auf die Auslegung von Joh 2,13-22." In *Neotestamentica et Philonica*, edited by D. E. Aune, T. Seland, and J. H. Ulrichsen, 202–14. NovTSup 106. Leiden: Brill, 2003.

van Belle, Gilbert. *Les parenthèses dans l'évangile de Jean*. Leuven: Leuven University Press, 1985.

Van den Bussche, Henri. *Jean: Commentaire de l'évangile spirituel*. Bible et vie chrétienne. Bruges: Desclée De Brouwer, 1967.

Vanhoye, A. "L'oeuvre du Christ, don du Père (Jn 5,36 et 17,4)." *RSR* 48 (1960): 377–419.

van Unnik, W. C. "The Purpose of St. John's Gospel." In *Studia Evangelica*, 382–411. TUGAL 73. Berlin: Akademie-Verlag, 1959.

Vignolo, Roberto. "Quando il libro diventa archivio–e quando deconstruire glorifica: Il cartello della croce (Gv 19,16b-22) come vettore cristologico e scritturistico della testimonianza giovannea." *RivB* 63 (2015): 465–512.

Vollmer, Cornelius. "Zu den Toponymen Lithostroton und Gabbatha in Joh 19,13: Mit einem Lokalisierungsversuch des Prätoriums des Pilatus." *ZNW* 106 (2015): 184–200.

von Herder, Johann Gottfried. *Von Gottes Sohn, der Welt Heiland: Nach Johannes Evangelium; Nebst einer Regel der Zusammenstimmung unsrer Evangelien aus ihrer Entstehung und Ordnung*. Riga: Hartknoch, 1797.

Von Wahlde, Urban C. *Commentary on the Gospel of John*. Vol. 2 of *The Gospel and Letters of John*. Grand Rapids: Eerdmans, 2010.

Walker, W. O. "The Lord's Prayer in Matthew and in John." *NTS* 28 (1982): 235–56.

Wead, David W. *The Literary Devices in John's Gospel*. Theologische Dissertationen 4. Basel: Friedrich Reinhardt Kommissionsverlag, 1970.

Wheaton, Gerry. *The Role of Jewish Feasts in John's Gospel*. SNTSMS 162. Cambridge: Cambridge University Press, 2015.

Whitenton, Michael R. "The Dissembler of John 3: A Cognitive and Rhetorical Approach to the Characterization of Nicodemus." *JBL* 135 (2016): 141–58.

Wieser, Thomas. "Community—Its Unity, Diversity and Universality." *Semeia* 33 (1985): 83–95.

Wiles, Maurice F. *The Spiritual Gospel: The Interpretation of the Fourth Gospel in the Early Church*. Cambridge: Cambridge University Press, 1960.

Williams, C. H. "Another Look at 'Lifting Up' in the Gospel of John." In *Conception, Reception, and the Spirit: Essays in Honor of Andrew T. Lincoln*, edited by J. Gordon McConville and Lloyd K. Pietersen, 58–77. Eugene, Ore.: Cascade, 2015.

———. "'He Saw His Glory and Spoke about Him': The Testimony of Isaiah in Johannine Christology." In *Honouring the Past and Shaping the Future: Religious and Biblical Studies in Wales; Essays in Honour of Gareth Lloyd Jones*, edited by Robert Pope, 53–80. Leominster, UK: Gracewing, 2003.

———. "Judas (Not Iscariot): What's in a Name?" In *Character Studies in the Fourth Gospel: Narrative Approaches to Seventy Figures in John*, edited by Steven A. Hunt, D. François Tolmie, and Ruben Zimmermann, 550–53. WUNT 314. Tübingen: Mohr Siebeck, 2013.

———. "(Not) Seeing God in the Prologue and Body of John's Gospel." In *The Prologue of the Gospel of John: Its Literary, Theological, and Philosophical Contexts; Papers Read at the Colloquium Ioanneum 2013*, edited by Jan G. van der Watt, R. Alan Culpepper, and Udo Schnelle, 79–98. WUNT 359. Tübingen: Mohr Siebeck, 2016.

Williams, P. J. "Not the Prologue of John." *JSNT* 33 (2011): 375–86.

Witmer, Stephen E. *Divine Instruction in Early Christianity*. WUNT 2/246. Tübingen: Mohr Siebeck, 2008.

Worthington, Ian. *Alexander the Great: A Reader*. 2nd ed. London: Routledge, 2012.

Yuen-Collingridge, R. "Hunting for Origen in Unidentified Papyri: The Case of *P.Egerton 2* (= *inv.* 3)." In *Early Christian Manuscripts: Examples of Applied Method and Approach*, edited by T. J. Kraus and T. Nicklas, 39–57. TENTS 5. Leiden: Brill, 2010.

Zimmermann, Ruben. "From a Jewish Man to the Savior of the World: Narrative and Symbols Forming a Step by Step Christology in John 4,1-42." In *Studies in the Gospel of John and Its Christology: Festschrift Gilbert Van Belle*, edited by Joseph Verheyden, Geert van Oyen, Michael Labahn, and Reimund Bieringer, 99–118. BETL 264. Leuven: Peeters, 2014.

_____. *Puzzling the Parables of Jesus: Methods and Interpretation.* Minneapolis: Fortress, 2015.

Zingg, E. *Das Reden von Gott als "Vater" im Johannesevangelium.* Herders biblische Studien 48. Freiburg: Herder, 2006.

Zumstein, Jean. "Au Seuil de la passion (Jean 12)." In *Studies in the Gospel of John ad Its Christology: Festschrift Gilbert Van Belle*, edited by Joseph Verheyden, Geert van Oyen, Michael Labahn, and Reimund Bieringer, 257–288. BETL 264. Leuven: Peeters, 2014.

_____. *Das Johannesevangelium.* Edited by Dietrich-Alex Koch. KEKNT. Göttingen: Vandenhoeck & Ruprecht, 2016.

_____. "Intratextuality and Intertextuality in the Gospel of John." In *Anatomies of Narrative Criticism: The Past, Present, and Futures of the Fourth Gospel as Literature*, edited by Tom Thatcher and Stephen D. Moore, translated by Mike Gray, 121–35. SBLRBS 55. Leiden: Brill, 2008.

_____. *Kreative Erinnerung: Relecture und Auslegung im Johannesevangelium.* Abhandlungen zur Theologie des Alten und Neuen Testaments 84. Zürich: Theologischer, 2004.

INDEX OF ANCIENT SOURCES